CW01108690

The Reception of Jane Austen
and Walter Scott

Continuum Reception Studies

The Reception of Blake in the Orient
Edited by Steve Clark and Masashi Suzuki

The International Reception of T. S. Eliot
Edited by Shyamal Bagchee and Elisabeth Däumer

Forthcoming volumes include:

The International Reception of Emily Dickinson
Edited by Domhnall Mitchell and Maria Stuart

The International Reception of Samuel Beckett
Edited by Matthew Feldman and Mark Nixon

Laurence Sterne and French Literary Culture
by Lana Asfour

The Reception of Wordsworth in Nineteenth Century Germany
by John Williams

Writers Reading Shakespeare
by William Baker

The Reception of Jane Austen and Walter Scott

A Comparative Longitudinal Study

Annika Bautz

continuum

Continuum
The Tower Building
11 York Road
London SE1 7NX

80 Maiden Lane, Suite 704
New York
NY 10038

www.continuumbooks.com

Copyright © Annika Bautz 2007

All rights reserved. No part of this publication may be reproduced or transmitted in any form or by any means, electronic or mechanical, including photocopying, recording, or any information storage or retrieval system, without prior permission in writing from the publishers.

Annika Bautz has asserted her right under the Copyright, Designs and Patents Act, 1988, to be identified as Author of this work.

British Library Cataloguing-in-Publication Data
A catalogue record for this book is available from the British Library.

ISBN: 0-8264-9546X
      978-08264-95464

Library of Congress Cataloging-in-Publication Data
A catalog record of this book is available from the Library of Congress.

Typeset by YHT Ltd, London
Printed and bound in Great Britain by Biddles Ltd, King's Lynn, Norfolk

Contents

Acknowledgements	vii
Abbreviations	ix
Introduction	1
Part 1: *The Contemporary Response, 1811–1818*	
1 Reviewing in the Romantic Period	7
2 Austen and Scott Reviewed, 1812–1818	15
3 Private Readers' Responses in Letters and Diaries, 1811–1818	47
Part 2: *The Victorian Response*	
4 Editions, 1832–1912	77
5 Library Catalogues, 1832–1912	89
6 Victorian Reviews and Criticism, 1865–1880	93
Part 3: *The Later-twentieth-century Response*	
7 Editions, 1913–2003	117
8 Media Reception and Cultural Status, 1990–2003	119
9 Critical Reception, 1960–2003	135
Retrospect	167
Notes	171
Bibliography	183
Index	195

Acknowledgements

My most extended thanks go to Claire Lamont, whose wisdom, care and unremitting support have made it a pleasure and a privilege to work with her. Her generosity will always be remembered. I am immensely grateful to William St Clair for his enthusiasm and encouragement, as well as for inspiring comments. Among the many other people without whom this book would not have been possible, I am particularly indebted to Thomas Rischbeck, Richard Temperley, Matthew Rubery, David Hewitt, Michael Rossington, Julian Dawson and Wolfgang Wendt. To my parents, Eva-Gabriele Bautz and Thomas Wendt, I am deeply thankful for their unwavering love and support. To Meriol and John Penn I am profoundly grateful for helping me in more ways than I can express. To my grandmother Annemarie Bautz I am greatly indebted for her enthusiasm about the project, *joie de vivre* and care.

Among the many libraries whose resources I have used, I wish to thank especially the Literary and Philosophical Society of Newcastle upon Tyne, the Robinson Library at Newcastle University and the National Library of Scotland.

My thanks also go to colleagues at Continuum: Colleen Coalter, Sophie Cox, Joanna Kramer, Anna Sandeman and Anya Wilson.

Abbreviations

Academy	The Academy
AJR	The Antijacobin Review
Ant	The Antiquary
AugR	The Augustan Review
BC	The British Critic
BEM	Blackwood's Edinburgh Magazine
BLM	The British Lady's Magazine
BOL	The Bride of Lammermoor
BR	The British Review
Cal Merc	Caledonian Mercury
CH	The Critical Heritage
Chambers's	Chambers's Journal
Champ	The Champion
ContR	The Contemporary Review
Cornhill	Cornhill Magazine
CR	The Critical Review
DBF	Database of British Fiction 1800–1829
E	Emma
EclR	The Eclectic Review
EdM	The Edinburgh Magazine and Literary Miscellany
EdRefl	The Edinburgh Reflector
EEWN	Edinburgh Edition of the Waverley Novels
EM	European Magazine and London Review
ER	The Edinburgh Review
EWDM	The Englishwomen's Domestic Magazine
FR	Fortnightly Review
G	The Guardian
GM	The Gentleman's Magazine
GMann	Guy Mannering
HOM	The Heart of Mid-Lothian
I	Ivanhoe
Ind	The Independent
InS	Independent on Sunday
LLG	The London Literary Gazette
London Soc	London Society

LQR	London Quarterly Review
Macmillan's	Macmillan's Magazine
MM	Monthly Museum
MP	Mansfield Park
MR	The Monthly Review
NA	Northanger Abbey
NA&P	Northanger Abbey and Persuasion
NAR	New Annual Register
NBR	North British Review
NC	The Nineteenth Century
NMM	The New Monthly Magazine
N & Q	Notes and Queries
NR	The New Review
OM	Old Mortality
P	Persuasion
PP	Pride and Prejudice
QR	The Quarterly Review
R	Redgauntlet
RR	Rob Roy
SS	Sense and Sensibility
SM	The Scots Magazine
Spect	The Spectator
St Paul's	St Paul's Magazine
ST	Sunday Times
T	The Times
TOM	The Tale of Old Mortality
W	Waverley

Introduction

> Walter Scott has no business to write novels, especially good ones. It is not fair. He has fame and profit enough as a poet, and should not be taking the bread out of other people's mouths. I do not like him, and do not mean to like Waverley if I can help it – but fear I must.
> Jane Austen, letter to Anna Austen (28 September 1814)[1]

> Also read again and for the third time at least Miss Austen's very finely written novel of *Pride and Prejudice*. That young lady had a talent for describing the involvements and feelings and characters of ordinary life which is to me the most wonderful I ever met with.
> Walter Scott, journal entry (14 March 1826)[2]

Although Jane Austen and Sir Walter Scott were contemporaries who knew each other's works, they never met. The clergyman's daughter, who seldom ventured outside her circle of family and friends in her small southern English village, lived in a different world from the Edinburgh lawyer whose immense international fame brought him a fortune, a title, a grand baronial house and the friendship of the King. Their styles of writing too could hardly be more different, the carefully observed descriptions of the manners of rural life among the English middling classes and the grand romantic tales of many nations and many epochs. In one respect, however, Austen and Scott have turned out not only to be similar but unique among novelists of the Romantic period. From the moment their novels were first published until the present day, they have been continuously kept in print, continuously admired, analysed and read.

What is also striking is how disparate have been the reasons offered for justifying that admiration and eagerness to read Austen's and Scott's works. A reviewer writing in 1813 commends *Pride and Prejudice* because an 'excellent lesson may be learned from the elopement of Lydia: – the work also shows the folly of letting young girls have their own way, and the dangers which they incur in associating with the officers who may be quartered in or near their residence'.[3] In 1990, a critic sees Austen as engaging in an argument about female sexuality, since Marianne's marriage to Colonel Brandon asserts 'women's right to find a second love'.[4] Early nineteenth-century readers of Scott were particularly struck by his bold characterizations, his wide social and geographical scope and his combining realism with romance. Later he was admired for his masculine morality – a Victorian reviewer commends 'the pleasure of that healthy open-air life, with that manly companion'.[5] A late-twentieth-century editor praises Scott's awareness of the unreliability of any version of history, so that in *Ivanhoe* 'Jews and women inhabit a different history from the official, imperial one of expansion and synthesis'.[6]

This study compares the literary reputations of Austen and Scott over two centuries. While Austen's works rise from relative obscurity to extraordinary popularity, Scott's novels fall from being the first best-sellers in history to being hardly read at all. In view of these opposing developments, the project considers when, and conditioned by what, changes in the reception of the two authors' works take place. Which factors determine a work's reception at a particular point in history, and to what extent does reading depend on the text itself as opposed to the reader's literary and cultural context? What was it about the texts of the feminine, English Jane Austen and the masculine, Scottish Walter Scott that appealed to readers at different times and in different cultures?

My starting point is neither the presumption that the text itself has a true meaning that it is the task of the reader to reveal, nor that, in the absence of fixity, every reader makes his or her own meaning. Wolfgang Iser sees the reader as 'co-creator' of the text: each reader actively fills in the 'gaps' or 'blanks' (*Leerstellen*) that a text leaves, yet in doing so is dependent on the structure of the text.[7] This study adopts Iser's notion of a text's reception being determined by the interaction between text and reader. However, in contrast to Iser, it focuses on groups of readers rather than individuals, and on the impact of historical, literary and cultural context on these actual readers.

Hans Robert Jauss draws attention to the cumulative expectations of historical readers with which they approach a text, and on the dependence of interpretation on this 'horizon of expectation'. The horizon changes over time, so that 'a literary work is not an object that stands by itself and that offers the same view to each reader in each period'.[8] However, while Jauss sees these expectations as determined by readers' literary-historical context, my study takes into account the larger cultural-historical context, and the effects that social, gender and other differences between readers may have had on their readings. My study also distinguishes between different readers reading in the same historical period.

Readers belong to an 'interpretive community',[9] since they read as part of their social, cultural or literary group. This project therefore distinguishes between kinds of readers by dividing critical from public responses throughout. All preceding studies on Austen's and Scott's receptions focus on critical reputation.[10] That focus excludes the majority of readers, however, so that this book adds the public dimension to the incomplete picture drawn by previous works. Both Austen and Scott are exceptional in having achieved at a period over the course of their reception history high critical acclaim simultaneously with an immense public popularity.

Reputation can only be assessed in relative rather than absolute terms. Previous studies have been concerned with aspects of the receptions of either Austen or Scott and treat the authors' receptions as isolated entities.[11] This book has as its factual basis the publication history of both authors over the whole 200-year span. For assessing relative popularity, reception and the changing interests of critics and readers, I have divided the study into specific time intervals, chosen for their representative quality. This enables the effects of gradual changes to be more clearly perceived. Relating the reputations of the two authors to one another in a comparative longitudinal study allows the long-run trends in the reception of each author to be traced. It also illuminates the broader culture of the successive reading audiences who gave both authors their loyalty across six generations.

Part 1

The Contemporary Response, 1811–1818

Chapter 1

Reviewing in the Romantic Period

The early nineteenth century was the heyday of periodical criticism. Walter Scott writes in 1809 that Reviews 'have at present an interest and importance altogether unknown in any former part of our literary history'[1] and William Hazlitt sees reviewing as specific to his age, which is 'nothing, if not critical'.[2]

More than 60 periodicals carried reviews,[3] since they were not confined to those periodicals that were exclusively devoted to reviewing, such as *The Monthly Review* or *The British Critic*. Magazines such as *The Gentleman's Magazine* or *The British Lady's Magazine* would include reviews alongside accounts of the proceedings of parliament, abstracts on foreign affairs, miscellaneous correspondence and articles, stock reports, a register of eminent births and marriages, and selected poetry.

Reviewing periodicals had already been popular in the eighteenth century. *The Monthly Review* (1749–1845), *The Critical Review* (1756–1817) and *The British Critic* (1793–1826) are among those that had been launched before 1800. Their initial ambition had been to include summaries of all new publications, without necessarily giving judgements. This policy became self-defeating as the number of publications increased, and resulted in a series of short notices while still leaving out the majority of publications. The output of novels was especially prodigious so that, as Peter Garside points out, by 1806 *The Critical Review* only covered about a quarter of new novels and *The Monthly Review* even fewer.[4] From the first decade of the nineteenth century onwards it was thus increasingly an achievement for a novel to be reviewed at all.

The format of early nineteenth-century Reviews was inherited from the eighteenth century. The majority of reviewing periodicals appeared monthly. They consisted of a main part of between 80 and 100 pages containing 9–15 long articles (3–20 pages each), and an end-section called the catalogue, which was between 10 and 24 pages long and contained between 9 and 28 short reviews (between 1 sentence and 3 pages long). New publications that were regarded as less important but still worthy of inclusion were placed in the catalogue. The fact that a work was reviewed at all was an indication that it was considered to have some merit, and this was qualified by the length and location of the review. *The Critical Review* discusses *Sense and Sensibility*, an anonymous female author's first publication, in the main part, whereas *The British Critic* notices it in the catalogue, a difference reflected in the tenor of the overall verdicts on the novel in these two reviews.

The first periodical that substantially differed from this eighteenth-century mode of reviewing was *The Edinburgh Review*, which was founded in 1802. Instead of including articles on as many publications as possible, it discussed a limited number of new publications in greater detail, usually still including lengthy plot summaries and quotations, but with the emphasis on comment. It appeared quarterly rather than monthly, leaving time for more careful selection and criticism.

The stir it occasioned was immense. Walter Bagehot describes the founding of *The Edinburgh Review* as 'a grave constitutional event',[5] and Scott sees it as causing a 'universal consternation of the book-writing and book-selling world'.[6] Like 'great revolutionists'[7] the *Edinburgh* reviewers changed the nature of reviewing, and adopted a new, more severe critical tone – Lord Byron refers to them as 'northern wolves'[8] who prey upon authors without mercy. *The Edinburgh Review* became the model for all Reviews of the nineteenth century, as well as gradually changing many of the existing ones: they began to include fewer works, became more severe in their critical tone, and some Reviews, such as *The British Critic*, eventually dispensed with the catalogue-section.

Though the *Edinburgh* had been founded by Whigs, both Whigs and Tories wrote for it, until political differences led to the founding of a rival Tory quarterly in 1809: *The Quarterly Review*. Its success was immediate, and it became as influential as the *Edinburgh* itself. The *Edinburgh* and the *Quarterly* presented themselves as books made to last, were bound up, and kept as series in libraries. Their price of 5 or 6 shillings[9] was prohibitive for anyone below the middle classes – though they were not as expensive as books – and circulation numbers were high: in the 1810s, the *Edinburgh* and the *Quarterly* achieved print runs each of between 12,000 and 14,000,[10] which testifies to their immense influence. There were several readers for each copy. Kathryn Sutherland quotes an estimated 3 or 4 readers per copy of the *ER* in 1814,[11] John Gross opts for the possibility of as many as 100,000 readers per issue (7–8 readers per copy).[12] By comparison, periodicals such as *The Critical Review* or *The British Critic* achieved monthly print runs of 2,000 in 1813.[13]

Though Reviews were as powerful as never before, the cultural status of reviewers remained dubious throughout the period. While Byron in 1813 refers to Francis Jeffrey and William Gifford, the editors of the *Edinburgh* and *Quarterly* respectively, as 'monarch makers in poetry and prose',[14] even Jeffrey did not regard reviewing as a job for a gentleman.[15] He welcomed the £300 a year that editing brought him, yet would rather have earned the money at the bar – and did in fact give up editing in favour of the law when the Whigs came to power in 1830.[16]

Reviewers wrote anonymously, using a corporate 'we', and the editor was responsible for everything published in his Review. While this was supposed to make criticism more easily possible, distinguished reviewers were often known to the public anyway. With very few exceptions, usually in the more radical periodicals – such as Mary Wollstonecraft writing for *The Analytical Review* – reviewers were male.[17] Most reviewers had other professions as well as being reviewers, and were thus non-specialists discussing all kinds of publications. One of the innovations the *Edinburgh* had brought in, however, was to oblige all its contributors to receive handsome pay. Since the main Reviews were owned by book publishers – *The Quarterly* by Murray, *The Edinburgh* jointly by Constable and Longman – remunerating contributors was a way of taking control, of introducing a market mechanism that enabled editors or owners to influence content.

Reviews were thus a genre that was hugely popular and prominent, yet undefined as regards literary status. Reviewers were therefore especially wary of bestowing praise onto the other genre that had a dubious literary status in the early nineteenth century: the novel. Ina Ferris points out that 'each was a borderline discourse, neither fully literary nor fully commercial', and that it is because of their similar positions that reviewers wished to condemn the novel as a 'commercial outsider'.[18] Nonetheless, while the Reviews' literary status was unclear, reading them was, as Marilyn Butler argues, 'a sign of cultivation, a ticket of entry into polite society',[19] which novel-reading decidedly was not (though ironically it was precisely in polite society that novels were primarily read). Perhaps most importantly, however, by reading Reviews contemporaries could keep up with modern knowledge.

The status of the novel was low in the early nineteenth century, in spite of the genre's general popularity. With the exception of the novels of Henry Fielding, Samuel Richardson and Laurence Sterne, the editors of Reviews regarded the genre with some disdain and the reviewing of novels therefore formed a small and insignificant part of any reviewing periodical. From its foundation in 1802 to the late 1820s *The Edinburgh Review* included just over 30 novels, while about 60–80 novels appeared each year in the first two decades of the nineteenth century and more than 80 in most years in the 1820s.[20] Where novels are reviewed, they are often not included in the main part of a periodical but considered in a short notice in the catalogue at the end of an issue. Articles frequently start off with a justification for reviewing novels at all, insisting on the discussion of a novel being an exception and their 'not in general attend[ing] to works of this description'.[21] A novel's inclusion in a reviewing periodical is therefore already a sign of unusual esteem.

In the early 1810s, *The British Critic* with its conservative political bias makes a greater distinction between novels and other genres of literature than the liberal *Critical Review*. In the first six months of 1812, *The British Critic* reviews fourteen novels, only two of which it includes in the main part. By contrast *The Critical Review*, though noticing only eight novels in the same period, discusses five of them in the main part. However, it is not possible to generalize these differences and conclude that all conservative journals were more critical towards novels than liberal Reviews, as there are opposite examples, such as the *Quarterly* reviewing more novels than the *Edinburgh* between 1810 and 1830.[22] Within a general unflattering attitude to novels, different degrees of suspicion exist in individual periodicals, independent of politics.

Almost all periodicals in the early nineteenth century had a political bias, partly because post-revolutionary Britain was more politically sensitive than it had been in the eighteenth century. Of the three political factions, Whig, Tory and Radical, the first two opposed each other's views while at the same time accepting them as valid points of view within their own social and political framework, sharing the fundamental belief in rule by an elite. Nevertheless, Scott accuses the Whig *Edinburgh Review* of incorporating politics in its assessments, which he regards 'so unjust and mischievous a criterion of judgement',[23] and Hazlitt similarly accuses Tory critics of being politically biased:

> You are a Whig, a reformer – does not that itself imply all other crimes and misdemeanours? ... You are an enthusiast in the cause of liberty: does it not follow that you are a bad poet?[24]

However, Whig and Tory reviewers usually discuss the works of authors of the opposite faction using the prevailing literary criteria, not basing their judgements on political prejudice, so that neither Austen nor Scott suffers attacks on political grounds. (There are a few exceptions in some articles on Scott's works, but they do not determine overall judgements.) While Whig and Tory adhere to the same basic principles, both vehemently oppose radical ideas. Authors such as Leigh Hunt, whose political persuasion was perceived to be outside the political mainstream acceptable to both Whig and Tory reviewers, were therefore the ones whose works were subject to judgements based on political convictions.

What added to the novel's low literary status was its being regarded as a female-dominated genre, as regards readers as well as writers. The – predominantly male – reviewers saw themselves as protecting a female readership by selecting suitable novels for them. A reviewer in *The British Critic* writes in April 1815:

> There are, we believe, few readers who are quite aware of the severity of the labour which we reviewers undergo in their service; and fewer still who feel a proper degree of gratitude for the beneficial consequences which result to them from that labour.... In the present instance, we expect that the novel-reading ladies will give us abundance of thanks, for saving them from the disappointment which they would, perhaps, have experienced had we not undertaken the serious task of reviewing Mrs Hanway's "Christabelle". To Miss Caroline, or Miss Fanny, confined at home without company on a rainy afternoon, and who has consoled herself with the hope of a rich treat from the last novel, which John has been dispatched to procure, it must assuredly be a shocking thing to find, that the anxiously-expected novel is so "abominably stupid" that she cannot get through it; and that she has no other resource than to strum over her favourite airs, draw half a rose, or a bit of a tree, or add a score of meshes to a piece of netting, which is now taken up for the hundred and fiftieth time. It is to avert from the fair such a

serious evil as this that we encounter Christabelle. Forewarned, forearmed, says the old adage.[25]

This passage reveals a number of common contemporary assumptions about the novel. First, that its readers are young women available to condescension due to their weak intellectual faculties. Second, that novel-reading is an activity to fill in time and prevent boredom, a more or less mindless pastime like drawing or needlework (as these things are presented here), rather than a useful study. Third, that novels have to be amusing, easy reading, else they cannot be got 'through' by their (female) readers. Fourth, that novel-readers belong to those classes that have servants that can be despatched on errands. The reviewer's emphasis on the young lady's being occupied with fragments of things shows her not to have the necessary patience and intellectual stamina to read anything of a higher literary value. Novels are trifles that are not to be taken seriously, just as the evils that come to the 'fair one' should she lack a novel.

Authors of novels, too, were believed to be predominantly female and, as Peter Garside has shown, novel-authorship was indeed dominated by women in the 1810s.[26] This view of a female-dominated genre already determined an individual novel's status: even a good novel could not reach great literary significance because it belonged to an entertaining, but intellectually and morally limited genre. Henry Austen, in the memoir of his sister prefaced to the 1833 'Standard Novels' edition of *Sense and Sensibility*, confirms early nineteenth-century expectations:

When 'Pride and Prejudice' made its appearance, a gentleman, celebrated for his literary attainments, advised a friend of the authoress to read it, adding, with more point than gallantry, 'I should like to know who is the author, for it is much too clever to have been written by a woman'.[27]

Quality in a novel was a surprise and led to the work's being taken out of the female domain.

Walter Scott in his anonymous review of Austen's *Emma* defends novel-reading, emphasizes the variety of quality in novels, and believes the genre to appeal to both sexes:

A novel, therefore, is frequently 'bread eaten in secret'. ... We have been pleading our own cause while stating the universal practice, and preparing [the reader] for a display of more general acquaintance with this fascinating department of literature, than at first sight may seem consistent with the graver studies to which we are compelled by duty: but in truth ... we cannot austerely condemn the source from which is drawn the alleviation of such a portion of human misery, or consider the regulation of this department as beneath the sober consideration of the critic.[28]

By this time Scott had published his first three novels (also anonymously), so that he is keen to point out the diversity of the genre, not all of which is low quality, since 'the composition of these works admits of being exalted by the higher exertions of genius'. Even as light reading, however, novels can be regarded as having some utility. Scott sees men and women as readers of novels, though they may not admit to it because of the genre's cultural stigma. While a bad novel is far beneath other genres, anyone, including the male members of the republic of letters, is justified in reading a good novel.

However, though novels were not exclusive to one sex, they were socially exclusive. While working-class men were earning between 9 and, very exceptionally, 40 shillings a week throughout the period,[29] *Sense and Sensibility* cost 15 shillings in 1811, and Walter Scott's *Waverley* cost 1 guinea (21 shillings) in 1814. Technological inventions such as the Earl of Stanhope's iron printing press (1800) were slow to affect the book trade at large, and printing remained largely a handcraft. The Napoleonic Wars caused general inflation, so that members of the working classes were even less likely to spend their wages on fiction. War features such as the blockade of Britain from 1806 led to material restrictions, especially paper-shortage. In spite of these factors, however, prices were not primarily a function of manufacturing costs. William St Clair has shown that publishers were able to drive up prices of new novels although the price of out of copyright novels continued to fall: between 1801 and 1821, the price for newly published novels went up by 300 per cent.[30] This rising price is in itself an indication of the rising status of the genre.

High prices meant, as Jane Austen lamented, that 'people are more ready to borrow & praise, than to buy',[31] but even through libraries novels are unlikely to have reached far below middle class: the most successful circulating library, William Lane's Minerva library, had a subscription fee of between two and five guineas in 1814,[32] high above a working man's means. The libraries open to working-class readers were those funded by benevolent donors, and generally did not include fiction. Novels therefore remained luxury items throughout the 1810s.

Lane was one of many circulating-library owners who was also a publisher. The novels he brought out were designed to be rented out and rapidly replaced. Minerva Press novels denoted a 'particular type of light society romance or thriller, much condemned in conduct literature'.[33] The Minerva press and library were hugely popular, which made its productions all the more suspicious to reviewers, who at the beginning of the period upheld a rigid division between quality and popularity, holding that a literary work of high quality could not appeal to undiscriminating readers. As Fiona Robertson indicates, however, this 'division between critical reputation and readerly demand was to change dramatically in the course of the period, due largely to the impact of the highly regarded and spectacularly popular novels of Scott'.[34] These were of better physical quality than Minerva publications, and they cost more. The price for Scott's novels kept increasing, with *Kenilworth* retailing at an unheard of one guinea and a half (£1.11.6) in 1821.[35] Scott introduced the 'new phenomenon of the up-market best-selling novel'.[36] By comparison, Minerva publications retailed at about 5s a volume in the 1810s, at 15s per 3-volume-set, which had by then become the dominant novel-format. Minerva novels were thus still socially exclusive, but not up-market, publications. Physical differences between novels were taken to imply qualitative differences, and it is from novels such as Minerva's that Scott wishes to set his own productions apart.

William Godwin asserts that the 'first enquiry' he poses when faced with a non-factual work is 'Can I derive instruction from it?'.[37] Because of the novel's perceived femininity reviewers did not deem intellectual instruction in novels possible, hence moral instruction became the main criterion a novel had to fulfil. It was not the only criterion for the assessment of novels, however. The study of reviews of early nineteenth-century novels reveals five prevailing criteria: moral instruction, amusement, realism (probable incidents as well as depiction of characters true to nature), story line, and style, with the first three being of particular significance for the overall verdict. The more of these a novel fulfils, the more positive the overall verdict usually is. My discussion of the reputations of Austen's and Scott's works addresses such questions as whether their novels fit into reviewers' preconceptions about novels or whether they represent something new; whether fitting into reviewers' models was a condition to acceptance or whether innovation was welcomed; and whether either author influenced reviewers' perception of the genre.

The criteria are largely content based. Literary merit to reviewers does not lie in a novel's aesthetic qualities, but in its contribution to society and hence in its place in culture. To assess the cultural value which reviewers give to a particular novel, not only the content of articles on other novels needs to be related to those on Austen's and Scott's works but also external indications: were reviews of other novels included in an issue of a periodical, how long were these articles, and where in the periodical were they placed; do reviewers deem an article on a novel worthy of being inserted among articles on more serious publications, or do they include the novel-notice in the catalogue among other novel-notices?

Chapter 2

Austen and Scott Reviewed, 1812–1818

Jane Austen's six novels were published between 1811 and 1818. Those of Walter Scott's novels published within the same time scale have been included, from *Waverley* (1814) to *The Heart of Mid-Lothian* (1818). This selection allows for a roughly equal number of novels by the two authors. It also enables consideration of the initial reception and immediate development of both authors' reputations as novelists, on a wider base than that of a single book.

Only British periodicals have been taken into consideration. For Austen, and for the first three Scott novels (*W, GMann, Ant*) all contemporary reviews that appeared up to 1818 have been included. For Scott's novels after *The Antiquary*, articles are too numerous for them all to be included, so I have selected those periodicals that also review an Austen novel (*BC, BLM, EM, GM, MR, QR*), the more important periodicals, and those that review several of Scott's works.[1]

The object is not to collate individual reviews, but to use them to explore what reviewers typically brought up in their articles on Austen's and Scott's novels – though important exceptions are also noted. The focus is therefore on one to four aspects per novel, as they are discussed in the most representative, or otherwise most significant, periodicals.

Contemporary reviews of Jane Austen's novels

Sense and Sensibility

Sense and Sensibility came out in October 1811. Its publisher was Thomas Egerton of Whitehall, who was also a circulating-library owner. He brought the novel out on commission, which meant copyright remained with the author, who accepted all costs and risks but paid the publisher a commission on sales as his reward for making the arrangements. This publishing agreement was obvious from the title page, which stated that the book was 'Printed for the Author'. *Sense and Sensibility* therefore presented itself to an initial reader as a typical circulating library production, and indeed, a census of surviving copies of her novels suggests that about half of them went to circulating libraries.[2] The price, too, would have linked Austen's novel to fiction of the Minerva category, since *SS* cost 15 shillings per 3-volume set, the price that Minerva novels generally retailed at. Austen not only covered her costs but made a profit of about £140. The first edition consisted of about 750–1000 copies,[3] while the average first edition of a novel comprised 500–750 copies.[4] The first edition of *SS* had sold out by July 1813, and the work went through a second edition during Austen's lifetime which appeared in October 1813. To achieve a reprint at all was unusual for a novel.[5] As regards sales numbers then, her first publication was already more successful than an average contemporary novel.

Notices appeared in two contemporary reviewing periodicals, *The Critical Review* and *The British Critic*. Both of these periodicals came out monthly, and both had a main part for the longer reviews and a catalogue at the end for shorter notices. Each reviewed only one other novel in the same issue as *SS*,[6] which emphasizes that for a novel, it was already an achievement to be reviewed at all. However, there are differences as regards the positioning of the article on *SS* in the two periodicals: *The Critical Review* discusses Austen's novel in the main part, and the other novel it includes in the same issue in the catalogue. *The British Critic*, which generally emphasizes the difference between novels and other genres, places both novels it reviews in May 1812 in the catalogue, though the reviewer regrets not being able to insert *SS* 'among [the] principal articles'.[7] The respective position and length of the articles on Austen's novel in the two periodicals suggest a different degree of appreciation, which is confirmed in the reviews themselves.

From the start, reviewers categorize Austen's novels as female. *Sense and Sensibility* came out anonymously, as did almost half of early nineteenth-century novels when first published.[8] The anonymity of Austen's first novel was socially defined as well as gendered, since the title page stated that the work was 'By a Lady'. This author description was unusual, though there were a few novels besides Austen's with such an indication.[9] While there is evidence to suggest that Austen wanted her novels to appear anonymously,[10] it remains unclear whether the decision to include this author description was also hers.

The first of the two reviews was the notice in *The Critical Review* in February 1812, followed by a shorter commentary in *The British Critic* in May 1812. They represent the typical situation of reviews as well as the texts they discuss being anonymous.

The reviewer in the *CR* is pleased with the contrast between Elinor and Marianne, holding Elinor up as a model of female behaviour, 'possessing great good sense, with a *proper quantity of sensibility*' (149), and seeing Marianne as moving towards sense and away from her 'delirium of sensibility' (153). Also, reviewers understand a novel's morality as constituted in its attitude to love and marriage, which emphasizes the author's femininity: she writes about what women should be concerned with, and therefore stays within the field of female propriety and morality. While this field is necessarily limited, reviewers view her writing within it positively as it enhances the novel's moral message. Thus Marianne's and Willoughby's attachment will teach young ladies that such an unbounded sensibility will lead to 'misery ... inconvenience and ridicule' (153), while it will make young men see the 'folly and criminality'

(153) of playing with a young woman's feelings. The underlying assumption is that readers will be of the same social class as the characters depicted, which renders the novel's lesson directly applicable, so that the reviewer highly praises the fact that the characters are 'in genteel life' (149). Without apparently noticing it himself, the reviewer is attracted to the novel's new kind of realism in its depiction of ordinary – though 'genteel' – characters. Although he still defines the novel's realism as 'probable [incidents]' (149), his applying *SS*'s moral lesson directly to his readers shows that he perceives Austen's different kind of realism, though he does not comment on it. Horace's criteria of 'amusement and instruction' (149) are met because the novel teaches without outright didacticism, and the reviewer can praise the novel as being '[among the few that] are worthy of any particular commendation' (149). This judgement is indirectly based on the novel's realistic depiction of contemporary society, since it is this that makes its message immediately relevant to the reader. The reviewer in *The British Critic* emphasizes the gender aspect of this realism, commenting on the author's 'intimate knowledge of life and the female characters' (*BC* 1812, 527). Again, it is not analysed how the novel displays such insight into female character, so that while oblivious to technique, reviewers yet recognize that they become more intimately acquainted with Austen's heroines than with those of other authors, which again contributes to the applicability of the moral lesson.

The reviewer in the *CR* suggests that 'the story may be thought trifling by the readers of novels, who are insatiable after *something new*. But the excellent lesson which it holds up to view and the useful moral which may be derived from the perusal, are such essential requisites, that the want of *newness* may in this instance be readily overlooked' (149). For him, story signifies an exciting plot with new events, which Austen's novel does not offer.[11] Fitting in with his focus on the story's moral message, he concentrates on its plot rather than its construction. The 'want of *newness*' in a *novel* therefore in itself becomes something new, and his comments testify to his willingness to accept a new kind of fiction that does not conform to his expectations of a novel – provided he can find a moral message in it. Again, he does not appear to realize the link between his remark and the novel's kind of realism: its moral is so useful precisely because it deals with everyday life – domestic realism – rather than with exciting events.

Of the five criteria most often applied to fiction – moral instruction, amusement, realism, story line, style – the reviewer in the *CR* sees four fulfilled in *SS*, with style not explicitly mentioned.

Pride and Prejudice

Pride and Prejudice was published in January 1813, stating 'By the author of Sense and Sensibility', rather than 'By a Lady', so that readers would only know for certain that it was written by a woman if they remembered *SS*'s title page.

All her novels followed that pattern from then on of saying 'By the author of ... ', yet female authorship is hardly ever doubted. *Pride and Prejudice* was again published by Egerton, who had this time bought the copyright, for £110, obviously expecting the novel to sell well. Instead of 'Printed for the Author', the title page therefore read 'Printed for T. Egerton', which would have conveyed to contemporary readers that the publisher had enough confidence in the novel's sales potential to take on risks and profits himself, rather than leaving both with the author. The first edition, consisting of as many as 1,250–1,500 copies, must have been disposed of quickly, since Egerton issued a second edition in October 1813.[12] The price for a 3-volume set had gone up to 18s, compared to *SS*'s 15s.

Pride and Prejudice was noticed in three contemporary reviews, *The British Critic*, *The Critical Review* and *The New Review*, in February 1813, March 1813 and April 1813 respectively. In all three, *PP* was the only novel reviewed in the respective issue, in the catalogue by the *BC* and in the main part by the other two. The *NR* had only begun to appear in January 1813 (and had folded by 1814), and *PP* was the first novel it included. In contrast to the *BC* and the *CR*, the *NR* did not include commentary but merely summarized the works it noticed.

As with the *CR*'s article on *SS*, the main points are the lessons to be learned from the work, the realistic depiction of everyday life and characters, the pleasure derived from reading the novel and its being altogether superior to others. The reviewer in the *CR* not only sees Elizabeth's 'sense and conduct [as being] of a superior order to those of the common heroines of novels' (323), but also links her to Shakespeare's 'lively Beatrice' (324) in *Much Ado About Nothing*, and twice repeats this comparison. Like Beatrice, Elizabeth is unusually independent and spirited, but it is safe to admire her since she is still within the moral boundaries of female propriety, and it is through this independence and sprightliness that she can humble Mr Darcy's 'prodigious quantity of family-pride' (322). The comparison with Shakespeare not only bestows high praise but also justifies approval of Elizabeth. This comparison was to recur repeatedly in later years, especially towards the end of the nineteenth and the beginning of the twentieth century. Of the five criteria usually applied, reviewers of *PP* see four fulfilled.

Mansfield Park

Mansfield Park appeared in May 1814, and judged by its sales numbers it was no less popular than Austen's other novels. It was again published by Egerton, on commission, and the first edition consisted of 1,250 copies – double the size of an average first edition of a novel. It cost 18 shillings, was sold out by November 1814, and brought Austen a profit of at least £320.[13] Since Egerton refused to publish a second edition Austen changed publisher, so that from the second edition of *MP* onwards her novels were published by Byron's publisher John Murray, whose imprint on a book was more prestigious than that of Egerton. In spite of this success, no contemporary reviews of *MP* have been traced. (Scott, for example, was an avid reader of Austen's novels, but seems to have been unaware of *MP*'s existence.)

Emma

Emma made up for this lack of critical notice. It was published in December 1815, and was reviewed by eight British periodicals. *Emma* was dedicated by permission to the Prince Regent, which would have already singled the novel out, as would John Murray's imprint. Murray had offered Austen £450 for the copyright of *Emma*, together with those of *MP* and *SS* (that of *PP* had been sold to Egerton and was therefore no longer in Austen's possession), but she must have denied this offer, since *Emma* was again published on commission. The 3 volumes of *Emma* cost 1 guinea, which again would have separated it from novels of the Minerva kind (retailing at 15s per 3-volume set). Of the first edition of 2,000 copies 1,250 had been sold by October 1816, and brought Austen £221, but since the second edition of *MP* (February 1816) had involved a loss she only received £38 for it.[14]

The eight British periodicals that reviewed *Emma* were *The Quarterly Review, The Champion, The Augustan Review, The British Critic, The Monthly Review, The British Lady's Magazine, The Gentleman's Magazine* and *The Literary Panorama.*

These articles are generally positive, but do not add much to the points already raised about *SS* and *PP*. The most prestigious periodical to review *Emma* was the *QR*, which was, like *Emma*, published by Murray. Its article on *Emma* is especially remarkable because the *QR* noticed very few novels. In the five issues that appeared around the one that noticed *Emma*, (between April 1815 and April 1816), only one other novel is reviewed, Scott's *The Antiquary*. To be reviewed in the *QR* would in any case have been a sign of great esteem, and to be singled out and treated like a novel by 'the author of Waverley' increases this prestige. The article on *Emma* is unsigned, but is now known to have been written by Walter Scott, and, like many reviews, it does not only deal with the latest novel, but also with previous publications by the same author (except *MP*, a fact that Austen lamented in a letter to Murray).[15]

Scott sees Austen's novels within the larger development of the genre, so that the novel, from having been the 'legitimate child of the romance' (*QR* 1815, 189), which used to relate what was possible rather than what was probable, with idealized and purified characters, has developed with Austen into a striking and realistic depiction of everyday life. Since its realism is

> composed of such common occurrences as may have fallen under the observation of most folks; and her dramatis personae conduct themselves upon the motives and principles which the readers may recognize as ruling their own and that of most of their acquaintance (193),

readers are in a better position to judge this novel's characters and events than those of a romance, which increases Scott's admiration for Austen's successful execution. He emphasizes her new kind of realism as the novel's main asset – as had previous reviewers, but Scott does so consciously, whereas other Austen critics had merely perceived it in passing, while discussing the novel's moral lesson, and without directly naming it.

Scott points out that this new novel 'must make amends [for a lack of exciting events and characters] by displaying depth of knowledge and dexterity of execution' (193). He is the first reviewer to be interested in the craftsmanship, realizing that it is the author's narrative skill that keeps the reader interested, not just the novel's content. He points out that the advantage of the novel's interest lying in its characters, realism, spirit, style, originality and dialogue rather than its story line is that these are elements that the reader can enjoy a second time without getting bored. He thus argues for the validity and even superiority of a novel without an exciting plot, something previous reviewers had only accepted reluctantly, and only as an exception. Her merit 'consists much in the force of a narrative conducted with much neatness and point, and a quiet yet comic dialogue, in which the characters of the speakers evolve themselves with dramatic effect' (199). He recognizes her technique of letting characters reveal themselves through their speech, rather than having them described by the narrator.

Scott finds the novel's moral lesson particularly useful because it can be directly applied to readers' lives, but he is more positive about how this is achieved than about the lesson itself. Like other reviewers, he sees the moral message in Austen's novels primarily in their attitude to love and marriage. However, while other reviewers tend to praise Austen for encouraging a more rational attitude towards love, Scott, who like them understands the moral as being in favour of falling prudently rather than passionately in love, sees Austen's heroes and heroines as too much on the side of prudence. While prudent love may encourage selfishness, passionate love can be qualified as the 'tenderest, noblest and best' (201) feeling. One example he gives is Elizabeth's statement that she fell in love with Darcy on first seeing Pemberley, which he takes at face value.

Northanger Abbey and *Persuasion*

These trends of giving criteria other than morality more weight are intensified in the reviews that appear on *Northanger Abbey* and *Persuasion*, the two novels published in December 1817 (1818 on the title page), after Austen's death in July 1817. Again, the novels were brought out by Murray, on commission, published together in four volumes, and prefaced by a biographical notice about the author by her brother Henry. While this biographical note finally revealed the author's name, the title page referred to 'the Author of "Pride and Prejudice", "Mansfield Park", &c'. All reviewers of Austen's last two novels are therefore aware of the existence of *MP*, whereas only one of the reviewers of *E* mentions *MP* at all (*BLM*, Sept. 1816). The edition *NA&P* consisted of 1,750 copies at 24 shillings, of which more than 1,400 were sold by the end of 1818, making a profit of £450.[16]

The two novels were reviewed in four British periodicals: *The British Critic, The Edinburgh Magazine, The Gentleman's Magazine* and *The Quarterly Review*. All these articles appeared anonymously apart from the last, which was by Archbishop Richard Whately, an unusual innovation and another indication of her rising status.

The British Critic is the only periodical to review all Austen's novels (apart from *MP*), and therefore most obviously shows up developments in reviewers' treatment of Austen's works. Like Scott, this reviewer realizes that what makes the novels different is their kind of realism, since what Austen describes has most likely happened 'to half the families in the United Kingdom' (297). However, he goes on to say that her characters have no merit in themselves, and whatever interest they excite in the mind of the reader results, almost entirely, from the unaccountable pleasure which, by a peculiarity in our nature, we derive from an imitation of any object, without any reference to the abstract value or importance of the object itself (298).

He defines Austen's realism as the truthful imitation of familiar scenes. Because he focuses on content only, he finds the pleasure readers derive from reading this 'unaccountable'. In his view, interest in Austen's novels is attributable to readers' peculiarity of nature, not to Austen's skill. He introduces an issue which keeps recurring in Austen criticism throughout the nineteenth century: as well as praising her realism, he also sees it as being a necessity to her, since

> in imagination, of all kinds, she appears to have been extremely deficient; not only her stories are utterly and entirely devoid of invention, but her characters, her incidents, her sentiments, are obviously all drawn exclusively from experience. (297)

That he still praises her novels highly shows the willingness to accept her kind of novel, in spite of its not fulfilling all his criteria. Lack of imagination in the author is a wider criticism to make than shortage of exciting events in the novels, and testifies to the development of the novel up to 1818: as Scott had pointed out in his review, 'splendid scenes of an imaginary world' were replaced by Austen with 'common occurrences' (*QR* 1815, 193).

What is also new in reviews from 1818 onwards is the inclusion of the identity of the author in reviewers' discussions of Austen's novels. Hitherto, the focus of the reviews had been exclusively on the novels themselves. Now the author had a name, and since *NA&P* appeared with a 'Biographical Notice' written by Jane Austen's brother Henry, the novelist now had a personality and a life that could be included in reviews. This inclusion gives reviews the twist that would remain for most of the nineteenth century, intensified by the appearance of the next biographical account of Austen, the 1870 *Memoir* written by Austen's nephew: with the view of the author as a gentle and benevolent woman comes a view of the novels as the fitting productions of just such a character. The reviewer in *The British Critic* in his article on *NA&P* maintains that Austen

> never dips her pen in satire; the follies which she holds up are ... mere follies, ... and she treats them, as such, with good-humoured pleasantry; mimicking them so exactly that we always laugh at the ridiculous truth of the imitation, but without ever being incited to indulge in feelings, that might render us ill-natured or intolerant in society. (298)

This insistence on gentleness and the absence of satire in her novels comes in with the discussion of her biography. It is also presented in a personal way, since the reviewer emphasizes the origin of the novel's qualities in its author by repeated use of personal pronouns, which stress the femininity of the writer. Since the reviewer has discussed the Biographical Notice earlier in his article, this underlines the gentleness of author and novel.

Reviewers' definition of morality becomes more general: it is no longer necessarily a specific lesson, but a general benevolent attitude towards society that is being taught, fitting in with what Henry Austen presents as his sister's overall benevolent attitude to life. If Scott had been the only critic to discuss Austen within the larger developments of the novel-genre hitherto, reviewers' concern with her biography made them even less likely to consider her novels in an artistic way. Following Henry Austen's depiction, reviewers see Austen as a kind-hearted woman who lived in an isolated country village, and 'became an authoress entirely from inclination'[17] rather than for fame or profit or because she thought her novels fit to rank with those of other novelists; she was so modest as to have to be persuaded to give novels to the world and 'always sought, in the faults of others, something to excuse, to forgive or forget'.[18] Accordingly, reviewers do not see Austen as contributing to the techniques of novel-writing, but to the overall morality of life. While the Biographical Notice thus hinders rather than advances analysis of Austen's novels, it contributes to reviewers assigning the novels a high place within the genre because of its depiction of the author as living a benevolent and moral doctrine, as well as promoting this in her novels. Of the five conventional criteria, *NA* fulfils four, and in addition is criticized for its lack of imaginative elements.

This continuing focus on morality is further emphasized in the reviewer's verdict on *P*. Though he highly praises *NA*, he states that *P*'s '*moral* ... seems to be, that young people should always marry according to their inclinations and upon their own judgment' (301), and since he takes exception to this, he does not discuss the novel any further. Morality is still his main concern, without which no novel can be given approval. And though the definition of morality now also encompasses general attitude, it still includes specific, directly applicable, lessons, such as who should determine young girls' marriage partners.

Because *The British Critic* is the only periodical to review all Austen's novels (except *MP*), its articles show both Austen's higher status in 1818 compared to that in 1812 as well as shifts in what reviewers mention. The reviewer in the *BC* in 1818 reminds readers that they have 'already received several admired productions' (294) from this author, and sees them as displaying 'some of the best qualities of the best sort of novels, ... [and] a degree of excellence that has not been often surpassed' (296). The superior position accorded to Austen's novels compared to others from 1812 onwards, as well as the rise in her reputation, is not only obvious from reviews' content, but also from the length of the individual articles. Periodicals treat Austen's novels more positively than the other novels they review. These external changes, too, are documented by articles on her in *The British Critic*: from noticing her early novels in articles of one page, *The British Critic* goes to an eight-page review of *NA&P*. While earlier articles on Austen had appeared in the catalogue, at the end of an issue, rather than in the main part, *The British Critic* had dispensed with its catalogue by 1818. Including an article on Austen's novels therefore necessarily meant reviewing them in the main part, but could still have meant placing them at the end of the issue. Instead, the article is the fifth out of thirteen in the March 1818 issue. Only one other novel is included, Godwin's *Mandeville*, reviewed in a shorter article and more negatively. In 1818, the inclusion of a novel in a reviewing periodical at all is generally still a distinction, since Austen's reviewer takes care to point out that the periodical only reviews 'the better sort of novels' (*BC* 1818, 293). But the praise given to her by reviewers as a superior – female – novelist was not enough to create a long-lasting interest. None of her novels is reprinted after 1818 until Richard Bentley includes all of them in his series of Standard Novels in 1833.[19]

Contemporary reviews of Walter Scott's novels

Waverley was published in July 1814, during what the publishing world called the dead season, and was immediately successful. The first edition consisted of 1,000 copies, compared to 750–1,000 copies that had been published of *SS* on its first appearance, and to 500–750 copies that usually comprised the first edition of a novel. While Scott's Edinburgh publisher Archibald Constable had obviously expected *Waverley* to sell better than other fiction, he had not been confident enough to buy the copyright for the £1,000 that Scott had wanted, so that the novel was published on half profits, like many first novels by anonymous authors. The extent of *Waverley*'s success was unprecedented: the first edition sold out in less than a month, and a second edition of 2,000 copies was issued, which likewise sold out within weeks. Before the end of the year, several reissues of the second edition had appeared, as well as a third edition,[20] with title pages announcing seven separate editions in 1814 alone, (though four of these were not new editions in the bibliographical sense). *Waverley* produced unseen profits for author and publisher – the fourth 'edition' alone brought 'each party £440', according to John Gibson Lockhart, who comments: 'Well might Constable regret that he had not ventured to offer £1000 for the whole copyright of Waverley!'[21]

Thirteen reviews appeared, which was more than had previously seemed conceivable for a novel.[22] Most of these reviews appeared throughout the autumn of 1814, not immediately on the appearance of the first edition. Reviewers were therefore reacting to the work's popularity, rather than creating it. They became part of a trend of admiring the Waverley novels, which makes their opinions all the more relevant to an assessment of Scott's critical and public reputation. The order that Ina Ferris illustrates, of 'text-critic-public',[23] thus did not apply in the case of *Waverley*. Because nothing like it had previously appeared, it is especially with regard to *Waverley* that reviewers voice their sense of unfamiliarity with a work of this kind.

Genre – *Waverley*

The title page read 'WAVERLEY; | OR, | 'TIS SIXTY YEARS SINCE. | IN THREE VOLUMES.', followed by the Edinburgh and London publishers' imprints. It therefore did not give an indication of either genre or authorship – in contrast to Austen's title pages, which from the start did not leave any doubt as to generic classification, or to author's sex: 'SENSE AND SENSIBILITY: | A NOVEL. | IN THREE VOLUMES. | BY A LADY.', and then the publisher's imprint. *Waverley* does not define its genre explicitly, though ''Tis Sixty Years Since' was an unusual subtitle since it marks out the work's setting precisely.

Reviewers find it difficult to place *Waverley* generically. Setting contributed to generic classification, but was not definitive. A romance dealt with improbable incidents and was therefore likely to be set vaguely, somewhere in the distant past. Reviewers see *Waverley* as incorporating elements from the usually contrasting genres of fantastical romance, realistic novel and history. The term 'historical novel' did not appear in a Review until *The Eclectic Review* used it in 1817, and even then it took some time to become generally established,[24] which reflects reviewers' reluctance to classify Scott's works as novels while the status of novels was still low.[25] Reflecting the growing status of the novel, the reviewer in *The Edinburgh Reflector* comments in his review of *The Heart of Mid-Lothian* in August 1818 that it is not 'degrading to [this author's works] … to call them novels' (*EdRefl* 1818, 43). Although the outward appearance and price of the early editions of *Waverley* had already put it in a separate category from the Minerva and circulating-library publications, its format was still that of a work of fiction.

Anonymity – *Waverley*

Like Austen's and many other novels in the 1810s *Waverley* was published anonymously, with Scott not publicly acknowledging authorship of any of his novels until 1826. Of the thirteen contemporary reviews of *Waverley*, all apart from two (*QR, Cal Merc*) discuss its authorship, though this interest fades in articles on the subsequent novels. Since reviewers are not usually interested in who the author of an anonymous novel might be, this shows that they do not regard *Waverley* as an ordinary novel, but as necessarily the work of a higher intellect than that which critics usually associate with novel-writing. With few exceptions (*AJR, Scourge, MM*), reviewers argue from 'sufficient internal evidence' (*NMM* 1814, 156) for Scott's being the author of *Waverley* – a speculation that Scott publicly denied. Yet reviewers know of none so capable as the 'the most admired poet of the age' (*SM* 1814, 533). The merit of the work is such that 'if it be indeed the work of an author hitherto unknown, Mr. Scott would do well to look to his laurels, and to rouse himself for a sturdier competition than any he has yet had to encounter' (*ER* 1814, 243). In spite of this conviction, however, reviewers continue to refer to him as the 'author of Waverley'. Also, reviewers agree that the author of *Tales of My Landlord* is identical with the author of *Waverley*.

Even where other names are suggested, they are always those of men – female authorship of a work with so wide a social, historical and intellectual scope as *Waverley* appears to have been out of the question. As if to make entirely certain that reviewers continue to place *Waverley* in a different category from the ordinary female-authored novels, Scott writes in his preface to what was termed the third edition (in fact second edition, second issue, the only change being an additional preliminary gathering containing the preface) that 'it must remain uncertain, whether *Waverley* be the work of a poet or a critic, a lawyer or a clergyman, or whether the writer ... [be] three gentlemen at once',[26] which put male authorship definitely beyond doubt. Male authorship in a female-dominated genre would have contributed to reviewers' sense of novelty – as well as opening up the possibility for a more serious work. The reviewer in *The British Critic* writes in his article on *Waverley* which appeared in August 1814, before the third edition, that 'the loyalty and strength of the political sentiments clearly prove the author to be a man of a sound and vigorous mind' (*BC* 1814, 209), indicating that because of the work's scope of content, it could not possibly have been written by a woman.

Since it is from 'internal evidence' that reviewers arrive at the conclusion that *Waverley* is by Scott, it is the quality of the work that elevates this novel, rather than its presumed author's name.

There is one review that testifies to the opposite, and this is the most negative review of *Waverley*. The *CR* does not notice *Waverley* until March 1815 – over seven months after its first appearance. Even then, the reviewer grudgingly remarks that he only discusses the novel because it is attributed to Scott, whose 'name ... claims attention' (*CR* 1815, 288). He defines the work as a novel, which influences his verdict: why 'a poet of established fame, should dwindle into a scribbler of novels' (288) he cannot comprehend. These statements underline the very different literary status a poet and a novelist had, and further explain why the majority of reviewers are tentative about *Waverley*'s genre. It also shows, however, that while content initially led reviewers to assume Scott to be the work's author, by March 1815 that belief had spread, so that this reviewer gives *Waverley* attention he would have withheld had it not been attributed to Scott. Also by March 1815, the unprecedented success of *Waverley* would have been even more obvious, making it more difficult for a reviewing periodical to ignore the work. It is thus a combination of content, male authorship, the possibility of Scott's authorship, and immense public popularity that leads to *Waverley*'s being included in 13 Reviews.

History – *Waverley*

Reviewers' sense of *Waverley*'s newness is to a large extent due to the work's inclusion of real historical – as well as romantic and exotic – elements. The majority of reviewers are positive about this mixture of fiction and fact, though whether they approve or not depends partly on their definition of history. John Wilson Croker, in his article on *Waverley* in *The Quarterly Review* (July 1814), criticizes a work 'in which real and fictitious personages, and actual and fabulous events are mixed together to the utter confusion of the reader, and the unsettling of all accurate recollections of past transactions' (*QR* 1814, 377), showing that for Croker, history constitutes itself mainly in events that have to be recorded accurately. He therefore regards the novel as belonging to the genre of 'historical romance' (377). Romance implies a work of fiction without realistic events or characters, and Croker wishes fiction and history to be told separately because a mixture confuses the reader. As with reviews of Austen's novels, the deciding factor is whether a work of fiction produces beneficial effects on the reader, but while with Austen reviewers focus on morality, Croker complains about wrong factual information.

Not everyone shares Croker's definition of history as a chronological sequence of events. Both Francis Jeffrey in *The Edinburgh Review* and John Merivale in *The Monthly Review* interpret history as social history, concerning people and their society as well as events. A historical tale can give either, like *Waverley*, 'motives and principles of actions', which can be portrayed by both real and fictitious people and events, or 'the chronological succession of those actions themselves' (*MR* 1814, 275). For John Merivale, writing in *The Monthly Review*, the author of *Waverley* is primarily a 'historian' (280), whose realistic picture of 'character, customs, and opinions of [a] class and period of society' is more 'historically valuable' (275) than the events that took place. Francis Jeffrey in his *Edinburgh Review* article similarly praises the author of *Waverley* precisely because he brings to light what the conventional historian does not. These two therefore approve of *Waverley*'s depiction of history.

The majority of reviewers, however, share Croker's definition of history, but in contrast to him, most approve of the mixture of fiction and fact. Just as Croker is against this way of relating history because it confuses rather than instructs readers, these reviewers approve of history being told in a way that provides instruction and amusement. Placing 'feigned characters ... [into] real scenes' (*BC* 1814, 206) is permissible as long as the events are historically correct. In reviews of both Austen's and Scott's novels reviewers insist on instruction, only while with Austen's novels they insist on moral instruction, they now substitute this with historical instruction. In spite of moral instruction having been the main criterion in assessments of Austen's novels, reviewers are willing to alter that criterion for Scott's novels, though not yet to dispense with it. Reviewers' concept of morality is essentially domestic, concentrating on issues such as filial obedience and female propriety. Public morality, such as the question of civil war, or more particularly which side to support, is not taken into account.

Because reviewers understand history as a record of events rather than societies, they do not see the relevance of that past for their own culture, so that *Waverley*'s instruction hinges on its accurate account of past events. The unanimity of reviewers in their view of *Waverley* as a mixture of narrative modes, and their overall approval of this shows how similarly they react to the content of Scott's work: they approve of the inclusion of history and see this as elevating the work above other works of fiction because it instructs, and they insist on instruction as the main measure of quality.

Reviewers have the desire to place his works into a new, as yet undefined, genre. The kind of instruction Austen provides is exactly that which reviewers require superior novels to give, so that while hers are superior to most novels, they are yet definitely within the novel-genre. Since reviewers' assessments depend on instruction they focus on content, and because the novelty of Scott's novels is largely of content reviewers address it.

Scottishness – *Waverley*

Reviewers put even more stress on Scottishness than on history, so that it becomes the main issue in reviews. All apart from one review (*CR*) are positive about Scottishness. It contributes to reviewers' sense of *Waverley*'s newness, partly through adding to their perception of the work as a mixture of romantic and realistic elements. Reviewers see characters, landscape and events as realistically depicted, while the Scottish setting at the same time renders the novel's plot romantic and remote from their experience. Since Scott assures readers in the last chapter of *Waverley* that 'the most romantic parts of this narrative are precisely those which have a foundation in fact',[27] reviewers can feel justified in giving attention to this work. Several reviewers accordingly commend the novel because it takes 'its romantic character from *facts*' (*Champ* 1814, 238).

What they most emphasize is Scotland's being different from the rest of Britain. Reviewers often do not distinguish between Highlands and Lowlands but see all of Scotland as romantic; and where they do differentiate, both Highlands and Lowlands are seen as remote from anything English. Even the fact that these two distinct peoples and regions exist in the same country makes Scotland different from England, and while at least the English-speaking Lowlands could have been linked to England, the reviewers only focus on the differences.

Waverley's 'character is far too common to need a comment' *(BC* 1814, 205), and Donald Bean Lean is not analysed because 'savages of all countries are so nearly alike in their habits, that [reviewers] need waste no more time on Donald' (*QR* 1814, 367). What interests reviewers are the unfamiliar Scottish characters, foreign in their bearing and outlook, and yet so realistically depicted that reviewers see them as representing the Scottish people in general – again, mostly without distinguishing Highlanders and Lowlanders. Some reviewers, however, emphasize especially the differences between Highland culture and their own, so that the Highlanders' 'grandeur of uncultivated magnificence' (*Scourge* 1814, 293), as well as the 'rude splendour of feudal hospitality' (*MM* Oct. 1814, 297) and their 'feudal non-improvement' (*MM* 297) puts Highland society on a stage of development behind the rest of Britain. Without directly addressing Scottish-Enlightenment concepts, these appear to be the basis of reviewers' view of the Highlands (or, for some, their view of all of Scotland) as being still in a feudal stage, whereas the rest of Britain has developed on to a modern market economy. While this seeing the Highlands (or Scotland) in a previous stage could have led to a justification for conquering its society after the Jacobite rising to pull it forward into the modern world, reviewers appear to share Scott's divided attitude between admiration for that past society, its characters and attitudes, while at the same time realizing its incompatibility with the modern world.

That reviewers focus on the unfamiliar is further emphasized by the quotations they use from the novel, the majority of which deal with issues reviewers see as particularly Scottish, both Highland and Lowland. The passage most often cited is not one concerning the Highlands, which emphasizes that all of Scotland is interesting in its contrasts to England. Edward Waverley's entrance into the hamlet of Tully-Veolan is cited by five reviews (*CR, SM, Scourge, AJR, ER*) out of twelve, while a sixth describes Tully-Veolan as 'a truly Scotch village' (*Champ* 1814, 239). The actions of the novel are seen as particularly Scottish, such as the robbing of the Baron's cows and the ensuing reconciliation, which are 'extraordinary feuds' and 'not less extraordinary ... reconciliations' (*QR* 1814, 365), and it is these events that the plot summaries deal with, neglecting the story around Waverley. While plot summaries also emphasize historical events, and thereby the novel's instructiveness, it is the Scottishness of the events that is most dwelt upon, and it is their Scottishness at least as much as historicity that makes them unfamiliar and 'extraordinary'.

Reviewers' attitude to history and Scottishness appears paradoxical: on the one hand, the historicity of events and characters is emphasized; on the other hand, reviewers want to believe that the Scotland the novel describes is no less remote and romantic in 1814 than it was in 1745. Traits and characters that are perceived as particularly Scottish are seen as still existing, such as Davie Gellatly, who is a 'sort of personage ... but little known in England, yet in Scotland it *is* by no means uncommon. In almost every small town there *is* a sort of public idiot' (*BC* 1814, 205, italics mine). Highland landscape features frequently, which emphasizes Scotland's romantic qualities, as well as its eternal Scottishness, since landscape does not change. The unfamiliarity of the Highlands and their inhabitants is stressed through descriptions of their rudeness as well as splendour: they are 'savage and uncouth' (*SM* 1814, 529), 'stout' and 'wild highlanders' (*MM* Sept. 1814, 229), in a 'rugged scene' (*MM* 230), 'sublime, beautiful and picturesque scenery' (*Scourge* 1814, 293) and 'romantic glens' (*MM* Oct. 1814, 298) – all of which were then (1745) and are still (1814) far removed from any English reader's (or Lowlander's) experience.

Francis Jeffrey sees the work as revealing to himself and to the reader

> that in our own country [Scotland], and almost in our own age, manners and characters existed, and were conspicuous, which we had been accustomed to consider as belonging to remote antiquity, or extravagant romance. (*ER* 1814, 209)

The Scottish characters depicted in the novel are representatives of classes that are not antiquated, but either still existing or only recently vanished. Much of what is true for a village such as Tully-Veolan in 1745 is still true in 1814, in 'the more unfrequented parts of our country' (*ER* 213). He differentiates Scottish regions, so that rather than seeing the whole of Scotland as 'extraordinary', he limits it to its more remote parts. However, he and the reviewer in *The Scots Magazine*, the only two writing in non-English periodicals, give these parts more significance by seeing their manners and cultures as on a stage of development that 'the South' (*ER* 209) and 'all Europe' (*SM* 1814, 524) were at 300 years ago. While this takes the culture depicted out of the 'more unfrequented parts' of Scotland, the reviewers still do not see it as having any bearings on their own society. The principle is the same as with English reviewers: it is only other places and people that still exist as they were 70 years ago. Jeffrey thus realizes the significance of the past for the present, but does not take the next step and see his own society as a product of history. Regardless of whether reviewers distinguish regions within Scotland, they do not see the past depicted in *Waverley* as having any bearing on themselves.

Reviewers avoid any discussion of political issues. They do not mention developments in Scotland since the Forty-Five but ignore the government measures after 1745–46. These acts were meant to prevent another Jacobite rising and had the effect of undermining Highland culture and lessening the differences between Highlands and Lowlands, and therefore between

Highlands and the rest of Britain. By ignoring them, reviewers close the historical gap between Scotland in 1745 and 1814. This is where reviewers differ from Scott: the past that is depicted in *Waverley* is what reviewers, like Scott, admire, yet recognize as being incompatible with the present, but to most reviewers, the present means Britain other than Scotland, the latter becoming synonymous with the past. Scott, however, depicts the Scottishness of a particular time as well as a particular place. Claire Lamont points out that 'despite the fact that it was "Sixty Years Since" (almost seventy by the date of publication) the '45 was not an easy matter to treat in a novel. ... The delicacy was caused by the possibility of a lingering sensitivity to the political loyalties displayed in the novel.'[28] The few remarks that there are in reviews on the political implications of *Waverley* show reviewers' sense of this delicacy:

> There are certain feelings still alive, and a certain vigilance still awake, which render the avowal of a partiality for certain principles, and certain politics, though not unsafe, at least unpleasant and invidious. The author, however, has performed this difficult task with considerable skill and ability, steering clear of every thing which could give offence to the reigning family, and yet not disgracing himself by the sacrifice of truth. (*AJR* 1814, 218)

By not acknowledging the post-'45-measures and any changes in the society depicted in the novel, reviewers evade having to reveal any personal political preference. They prefer to focus on the timelessness of romance rather than the changes of realism. Scott has handled a subject in *Waverley* that reviewers do not want to handle, and has dealt with it in such a way as not to offend readers of either political conviction.

Ignoring change, and admiring the different, testifies to reviewers' desire to imagine an eternally romantic Scotland. A Scotland that has not developed makes the stage it was at in 1745 graspable for readers in 1814, since Scotland is remote, but reachable, and part of the same kingdom. Scott's fiction provides a concrete past, aspects of which readers can transport into the present. His works set unfamiliar but realistic characters in tangible and existing locations – in contrast to the improbable romances readers in 1814 were used to. In Scott's fiction then, realism and romance are no longer opposed to one another but combined, and it is precisely this unprecedented mixture of realism and romance that renders the works fascinating. Since the differences are those of location and culture more than those of history, it is possible to travel there and experience them, so that *Waverley*'s Scottishness contributes to the new concept of tourism. That one cannot only look at real romantic landscape but also at the sites of historical battlefields makes the past all the more real.

Romantic reviewers dwell on the existence of a wild, untamed country. To them, what Scott depicts is unfamiliar, grand, sublime: the opposite of the familiar scenes which Austen describes. Also, it is Scottish, rather than historical, and heroism and romance live on in Scottish culture. Reviewers' emphasis on the cultural distance between Scotland and England makes a nostalgic admiration of Scotland's romantic way of life possible because it detaches Scotland from English progress. That reviewers admire rather than look down on a society that is not as developed as their own shows their sharing Scott's sadness at what their society does not have, while at the same time realizing the inevitability of this lack. The Scottishness of the Waverley novels from the first is thus essential to their popularity in Britain: for English readers, Scotland can be experienced through the realistic depiction of people and places, but remains romantic. For Scottish readers, the same is true for the Highlands and more remote regions. For readers of both countries, the romance and heroism of 1745 still exists.

Criticism – *Guy Mannering*

Scott's second novel appeared in February 1815, in a first edition of 2,000 copies priced at 1 guinea (21 shillings), which sold out on the day of publication. It was noticed by 12 contemporary reviewing periodicals, which, as with *Waverley*, were many more Reviews than would have mentioned an average novel.

Though the overall verdicts on *Guy Mannering* are generally positive, the majority of reviews also include criticism, sometimes severe. Whereas in articles on *Waverley* reviewers approve of the combination of romance and realism, in reviews of *Guy Mannering* they object to the way the two genres are intertwined. Their criticism centres on the novel's use of astrology. Both Meg Merrilies and Guy Mannering predict Harry Bertram's fate, but it is only to Mannering's involvement that reviewers take exception. Mannering as an Oxford scholar of the late eighteenth century is well within reviewers' knowledge, even experience, and is therefore a figure of realism that they expect to act in a way they can recognize and approve of. That he should make use of astrology is a 'monstrous absurdity' (*QR* 1815, 507): he can have contact with the world of romance by travelling to Scotland, the land of romance, but he has to behave there as everywhere in accordance with his origin and time.

Meg also predicts the future. For her, reviewers find this acceptable: she is a figure of romance, and modes of behaviour belonging to that cast are therefore consistent with her character. As a Scottish gypsy matriarch she is exotic, and her actions and manners represent 'a class of people formerly so common in this country [Scotland]' (*SM* 1815, 609). Like ordinary characters of romance she is fictitious, but in contrast to them she represents a class of people that once existed. The novel's being set in the past as well as Meg's being a gypsy add to her exoticism. However, it is mainly her Scottishness that renders her different from English characters, just as in reviews of *Waverley*, critics emphasize characters' Scottishness more than their historicity. It is precisely the depiction of her romantic qualities that render the image a realistic one: her dealings 'may be true to nature, as the Scotch have not yet thrown off their belief in witchcraft, and continue bigots to the influence of second sight' (*CR* 1815, 601) – the Scots, not the gypsies. Where *The Scots Magazine* thus sees Meg as representing Scottish history, English periodicals, as in their articles on *Waverley*, again view Meg as part of a romantic Scotland that still exists. Meg's prediction is a particularly Scottish act, performed 'with all the ceremonials of the northern magic' (*NMM* 1815, 256).

Reviewers see *Guy Mannering* as belonging to the realistic cast. The incorporation of romantic elements renders it more interesting, and since the romantic characters too are perceived as realistic representations they do not impede the overall realistic mode. What reviewers object to as unrealistic, and therefore as incompatible with this work's truthfulness, is that both Meg's and Mannering's predictions come true. While one such prediction may come true 'by accident' (*QR* 507), so that the enlightened, non-romantic reader could still find the plot credible, 'no power of chance alone could have fulfilled the joint predictions of both Guy Mannering and Meg Merrilies' (*BC* 1815, 409). The author thus requires the reader to share beliefs that belong to the world of romance, and this is both absurd and 'contemptible' (*QR* 507). What renders Meg interesting is precisely that she works in a different set of beliefs from reviewers. They are more fascinated by her than by any other character in the novel. Generally, the further away from reviewers' own modes Scott's characters are, the more interested critics are in them. Again, it is therefore the exotic characters that feature most in reviews. In the delineation of the more familiar ones – Guy Mannering, Harry Bertram, Charles Hazelwood, Julia Mannering, Lucy Bertram – 'there is nothing very original or happy' (*SM* 609), and these characters are 'very little above the cast of a common lively novel' (*BC* 408). Just as in *Waverley* they were not willing to see any connection between *Waverley*'s Scotland and their own society, so English reviewers of *Guy Mannering* insist that Meg represents Scottish people, and Scottish reviewers point out that her Scotland is that of history. Both sets of reviewers are thus keen to emphasize the differences between Meg's world and their own. Early nineteenth-century readers cannot be expected to believe in the realism of a plot brought about by astrology because 'the time of the novel is not the dark ages, but scarcely forty years since, no aid therefore can be derived from the general tendency of popular superstition' (*BC* 409). However, there may be some readers who will be induced by the author's use of astrology to believe in its powers, so that its representation in the novel poses a moral threat. Indeed, the 'moral might ... [in history] have subjected the printer to an indictment for supporting astrology and witchcraft' (*AugR* 1815, 231). The depiction of romance as realism renders the realistic work fascinating and presents reviewers with the possibility of a more primitive and romantic society still extant close by. However, the realistic plot cannot hinge on elements belonging to romance. Yet these severe negative points are redeemed by 'the extraordinary merit of the work' (*NMM* 256) – though it is precisely this merit that 'will serve but the more to render [the work] injurious in this respect [superstition] to weak minds' (*NMM* 256). Only one reviewer, the one in the

CR, is negative in his overall verdict. All others find *Guy Mannering* 'interesting' (*NAR* 1815, 432) and derive 'pleasure' (*AJR* 1815, 544) and 'amusement' (*QR* 509) from the work.

While reactions to *Waverley* already show the eminent position of Scott's fiction, reviews of *Guy Mannering* emphasize this even more. The most important criterion in assessments of other contemporary novels is moral instruction. In articles on *Waverley*, reviewers change that to historical instruction. In articles on *Guy Mannering*, instruction does not feature at all and the work is criticized on moral grounds, which for any ordinary novel would have meant general unacceptability. Instead, reviewers praise *Guy Mannering* in spite of its potentially harmful influence, which testifies to the unimpeachable status of any work by the author of *Waverley*. Already at the time of the publication of his second work of fiction, Scott's status is such that even severe criticism does not influence his overall eminence. As with *Waverley*, reviewers are fascinated by the realistic depiction of the unfamiliar and place *Guy Mannering* high above any ordinary novel or romance. Scott's works are thus not judged within the novel-genre but in a class apart.

Story and characters – *The Antiquary*

The Antiquary came out in May 1816, in a first edition of an unprecedented 5,000 copies, at the raised price of 24 shillings (compared to *Waverley*'s and *Guy Mannering*'s 21 shillings).

Twelve reviews appeared. Critics do not pay much attention to the story lines of Scott's novels. As in reviews of Austen's novels, it is not the 'involution of the plot, variety of incident, or command over the stronger feelings of our nature, [but the] ... minute, happy, and frequently very humorous delineation of manners' (*MR* 1817, 39) that interests. While reviewers see Austen's novels as having hardly any plot at all, however, they regard that of *The Antiquary* as improbable, 'not sufficiently regular' (*AJR* 1816, 631) and in parts at least a 'miscarriage' (*ER* 1817, 200). Though a well-composed and interesting story line is usually a criterion novels need to fulfil to gain reviewers' approbation, critics are willing to overlook this perceived fault in both Austen's and Scott's works. Instead, they concentrate on characters.

Passages reviewers quote are indicative of their general focus. From these, it emerges that the young lover and heroine do not feature very much, that reviewers are more interested in Scottish lower-class characters, and that Edie and Oldbuck appeal most to reviewers.

Hero and heroine

Reviewers do not focus on the conventional lover-hero in Scott's novels that the romantic plot requires. Scott's novels often have multiple hero-figures, and in *The Antiquary* none of the characters combines the usual romance-hero traits of marrying the heroine, behaving in a heroic way, and exciting more interest than other characters. Critics therefore differ as to which character they regard as the hero, depending on reviewers' definition of the hero as the man who marries the heroine, the character whose name the novel bears or the one that interests most. They describe Lovel (MR, CR), the Antiquary, (AJR) and Edie (EM) as hero, so that Scott's novels once more go against fictional conventions.

Reviewers' choice of quotations shows that Isabella, the typical romance-plot heroine, features even less than Lovel. With one exception (MR), no quotations are included that are exclusively about either or both of them – if they feature, it is in interaction with other characters. Even the cliff scene, which shows Lovel in a typically heroic act rescuing the heroine, involves other characters' heroism. Reviewers are aware that the traditional young lovers do not excite their interest, usually not even enough for reviewers to criticize them. Yet few agree with the reviewer in the CR who finds fault with the author 'for not interesting the reader more in behalf of the hero and heroine' (CR 1816, 491); instead they focus on the characters that fascinate them: the unfamiliar and unusual ones. As with so many of Scott's conventional heroes, reviewers are not interested in the hero for himself but for the characters he meets and thereby introduces the reader to. It is because of this distribution of focus that reviewers do not pay attention to the story line: the plot mainly concerns hero and heroine, whom reviewers find neither heroic nor exotic enough to interest.

Lower-class characters

Passages quoted show that regardless of the political bias of the periodical, all reviewers apart from one (the conservative AJR) are interested in the lower-class characters and quote at least one passage that features them. There are more quotations about lower- than higher-class characters, though of course the reviewers themselves belonged to Scott's own social class. As most of the main characters of the novel belong to the higher classes of society and most of the minor characters to the lower ones, main and high and minor and low become almost synonymous terms. Rather than criticizing the inclusion of lower-class characters as reviewers might with other novels, they now find that drawing 'the subordinate characters ... with ... discrimination and variety ... is the true test of genius, and a distinguishing feature of [this] author' (BC 1816, 656).

Reviewers' praise of the inclusion of lower-class characters is based on their requirements for realism in fiction. With Scott, this realism comes to mean the realistic depiction of individuals representing social groups, as well as a realistic portrayal of society as a whole. Society can only be represented realistically if all its components are included. In reviews of *The Antiquary*, reviewers opine that the 'vulgar ... [are a] numerous and important class' (AugR 1816,

156), and therefore need to be not only included, but also realistically presented. Reviewers therefore praise the fact that lower-class characters are allowed real feelings and pathos: Steenie's funeral is an 'exquisitely pathetic' (*GM* 1816, 523) scene that 'come[s] home to our business and bosoms' (*AugR* 173), and his father's trying to overcome the loss is 'one of the most terrible scenes which domestic life presents; and it does not derive any factitious interest from the station of the sufferer: indeed the roughness of mind, incidental to such a condition as that of the fisherman, makes the effect doubly strong' (*MR* 51).

Edie and Oldbuck

Not only are lower-class characters allowed the same emotional range as their social superiors in Scott's novels, they also have the same intellectual range, and both are approved of by reviewers. The quotations reviewers select that show interaction between the classes are those that reveal the lower-class characters as clever and witty rather than inferior, especially in the scene where Edie proves the Antiquary wrong about the age of a ditch. He uses common sense, whereas Oldbuck's love of antiquity has blinded him, so that the socially higher character becomes a comic figure in this scene.

Reviewers draw parallels between Edie and Meg. Both are the most exotic characters in their respective novels, both are unfamiliar to reviewers, romantic, Scottish, and outside, or on the margins of, social class structures. Critics are laudatory about Edie, stress his Scottish qualities, and see these as realistically depicted. As in *Waverley* and *Guy Mannering*, romance thus becomes reality. Linking Edie and Meg shows reviewers' view of the characters as presenting a timelessly typical kind of Scottish people. Only one reviewer criticizes Edie as being 'unnaturally made the organ of ... bursts of moral eloquence and poetical feeling', and cannot understand why the author chose to put these 'into the lips of *an old beggar*' (*AugR* 176–7). That all other reviewers not only accept but praise Edie shows their willingness to welcome unconventional characters and practices in Scott's novels.

While reviewers thus see Edie as representing a type of character, their interest in the Antiquary is in him as an individual. He is variously compared to the Baron of Bradwardine, Dominie Sampson and Pleydel, and verdicts on him vary between 'the great blemish of the work' (*ER* 199), 'now and then a little tedious' (*CR* 499), incorporating 'many striking traits of originality' (*AJR* 628), and being 'very well drawn' (*AugR* 176). Like Edie, he interests because he is unfamiliar to reviewers, but, in contrast to Edie, not because he represents a socio-cultural group.

That the societies of Scott's fiction are different from reviewers' own is emphasized again and again. The cultural distance between Scott's characters and the reviewers themselves makes it easier for them to accept the introduction of various levels of society, as serious characters, into fiction. The approval of lower-class and unconventional characters also has to be seen in the context of the works' authorship, however: even if not absolutely certain that the novels are by Scott, reviewers know them to be the productions of a gentleman and therefore do not either fear or despise them.

Where similarities between Scott's characters and the reviewers' own society are admitted, this happens on a general level, never on a direct one. John Wilson Croker in his review commends Scott's realism in depicting real 'human beings' – an ability that is also characteristic of the 'greatest poet that ever lived – of Shakespeare' (*QR* 1816, 127). Similarly, the reviewer in *The British Critic* highly praises Scott's depiction of people: 'Real genius will follow nature into all her secret paths; real genius will present the living portrait of man, in all his varied forms, whether high or low, proud or humble' (*BC* 656). All Scott's characters contribute to the 'living portrait of man', so that this variety is necessary for a realistic depiction of society. Reviewers thus concede to a common humanity, but to no direct links with their own society. It is through geographical, historical, cultural and sociological distance that Scott's variety of characters can be admired: Edie's Scottishness is what makes it possible for reviewers to be interested in him and praise '*an old beggar*'. Unlike Austen's novels, in which readers recognize familiar characters, Scott's fiction fascinates because it opens an unfamiliar world.

Reviewers' tolerance – *The Heart of Mid-Lothian*

The Heart of Mid-Lothian was published in July 1818, as *Tales of My Landlord*, second series, in 4 volumes rather than the usual 3. The first edition comprised 10,000 copies at a price of 32 shillings. It was reviewed in 23 periodicals.

From *The Heart of Mid-Lothian* onward, Scott's novels are noticed by all kinds of periodicals, the most eminent as well as the more obscure, liberal and conservative, weekly, monthly and quarterly. The number of Reviews noticing each new Scott novel has by now doubled compared to periodicals discussing the first three Waverley novels, though the amount of critical attention paid to Scott's first fictional productions had already been unprecedented.

When Scott introduces a working-class heroine in *The Heart of Mid-Lothian*, reviewers praise Jeanie Deans more than they laud Scott's heroes and heroines that are in critics' own social rank. Jeanie is 'without beauty, rank, or any other quality to seize the imagination, [yet she] powerfully engages the reader's kindliest esteem' (*EclR* 1819, 430). Reviewers' interest in Jeanie shows again that the more characters differ from what critics are used to, both in their own lives and in fiction, the more captivating the characters become – whether Highland or Lowland, romantic or commonplace.

Like Edie, Jeanie is endowed with qualities not often found in working-class characters up to Scott, and critics praise her 'heroic generosity, and most invincible resolution' (*BR* 1818, 399), and her union of 'good sense with strong affections, firm principles and perfect disinterestedness' (*QR* 1821,

120). At the same time, however, her working-class status and Scottishness are emphasized through a repeated portrayal of her speech: more than half the passages quoted in reviews of the novel concern Jeanie, and with one exception always show her in interaction with other characters. Yet on a moral level, the same scenes show class boundaries to be non-existent.

Reviewers' discussion of Effie reveals how far their acceptance of lower-class characters goes. It is with regard to Effie that critics raise moral objections against the novel – but not on the grounds of her having sexually transgressed. Instead, it is her social rise to which they object. That Effie, 'the daughter of a poor, rude, vulgar milkman' (*BR* 403), becomes a lady, and a favourite of high London society, 'outrage[s] morality and probability' (*BC* 1818, 254). To have her move up the social scale, and from Scotland to England, threatens reviewers' own world and social hierarchy; to have her sexually transgress as a Scottish 'illiterate, giddy girl' (*BR* 403) does not.

Thus again, where characters are so far away from reviewers' own society that no connection between the two worlds needs to be drawn, reviewers accept both lower-class heroism as well as moral transgression, but where the novel's society moves too close to reviewers' home, they condemn.

Popularity – *Rob Roy*

The first edition of *Rob Roy* came out in December 1817 and comprised 10,000 copies – an extraordinary number for a novel, yet it sold out within a fortnight, at a price of 24 shillings and was immediately followed by an edition of another 3,000 copies.[29] By 1817 then, Scott's popularity had reached an immensity that readers could not be ignorant of, least of all the critics who reviewed the novel in 21 periodicals.

The extent of Scott's popularity poses new problems for reviewers. While they had hitherto been reluctant to review ordinary novels and had justified doing so by claiming to select suitable reading matter for the public, they could no longer draw on that justification for reviewing Scott's novels. Critics react by addressing the purpose of their reviews in the articles. Nassau Senior states that he 'cannot propose to draw the public attention to works, which are bought, borrowed, and stolen, and begged for, a hundred times more than [the periodical's] dry and perishable pages' (*QR* 1821, 109), and the reviewer in *The British Critic* goes into more detail to illustrate the novelty of this popularity:

> It is an event unprecedented in the annals either of literature or of the custom-house, that the entire cargo of a packet or smack from Leith to London, should be the impression of a novel, for which the public curiosity was so much upon the alert, as to require this immense importation simultaneously to satisfy. Yet such was the case with the tale before us: nor

were the expectations of the bookseller disappointed in the sale or circulation of his cargo, if to each copy, taking one with another, we suppose only thirty readers, we shall fall very short of the real number. (*BC* 1818, 528)

Reviewers are faced with a new situation, and continue to review Scott's novels in spite of the invalidity of their usual justification. They do not come up with a unanimous validation for reviewing *Rob Roy*. Their reasons vary between the novel's being so fascinating that it leaves reviewers 'no choice but to tell [the] readers what they all know already, and to persuade them of that of which they are most intimately convinced' (*ER* 1818, 403); the possibility that some readers may not yet know the work; the option that some readers may know it but will need critical guidance in order to appreciate it better; the feeling that the Waverley novels have inaugurated a new era of literature that needs to be recorded for posterity.

Not only do critics feel the need to justify the existence of their articles in a new way, but their reviewing practices also change. Because of the novels' unprecedented popularity, reviewers realize that even were they inclined to give a negative verdict, they would find it difficult, since 'few people have the courage to speak out' (*EdM* 1818, 41) against such an immense and united public opinion. While this consciousness does not stop the same reviewers from including negative points, they only criticize some aspects. As with previous reviews of Scott's novels, the overall verdicts unanimously elevate *Rob Roy* above all other novels, so that critics' judgements correspond with public opinion. The popularity of the Waverley novels leads to a new estimation of the public reception of a work, and grants the reading public a greater ability to judge a literary work. The former 'division between critical reputation and readerly demand'[30] that had caused Scott to distance his productions emphatically from the popular but disparaged Minerva novels had become reversed by 1817. Through Scott's novels, popularity had now become a sign of merit.

It is thus due to the novels' content and to public popularity that reviewers class the Waverley novels as a category of their own. Critics see the Waverley novels as responsible for their period having become 'an era never to be forgotten in the literary history of [Britain]' (*ER* 404). This attitude emphasizes again the extraordinary significance reviewers assign to these works, and shows how little the novels' faults matter: their imperfections can never impinge on their general greatness as literary and cultural phenomena. Reviewers discuss the works in a frame of reference that presupposes general agreement on the works' position as not comparable to other fiction – which also means that the usual set of novel criteria do not apply. They cannot 'speak more highly of [*Rob Roy*] than to say that it is worthy of his hand' (*LLG* 1818, 34), and maintain that 'this is not so good, perhaps, as some others of the family;- but it is better than anything else' (*ER* 403).

Critics' justification for discussing a Waverley novel is thus different from their reasons for noticing ordinary fiction. Reviewing practices, too, are different: for a novel this popular, critics are conscious of incurring animosity should they give overall negative verdicts. Articles on *Rob Roy* therefore testify to Scott's extraordinary position, as well as to reviewers' awareness of and dependence on public opinion and show that as regards the Waverley novels, critical and public opinion coincides. By the time *Rob Roy* appears then, the Waverley novels are in a class of their own and their status has become unattainable for any other novel.

Reviewers thus face a new phenomenon with Scott's novels, and they change their beliefs and criteria to accommodate them. While popularity had been a sign of bad quality, it was now regarded as a sign of merit. Aspects of the content of Scott's novels that broke the criteria hitherto used for the assessment of novels, notably the inclusion of lower-class characters and the absence of moral instruction, became acceptable, even expected, in Scott's novels. What reviewers require in a Waverley novel is the realistic depiction of romantic Scotland. Since novels by the author of *Waverley* are necessarily better than everything else, they are compared to each other, not to other fiction, and as such represent a class of their own.

* * *

Critics esteem Austen's works more highly than those of most contemporary novelists. However, they admire Scott's novels to an unparalleled degree – unparalleled not only by other novels but by any works of literature. External features of the articles emphasize this exceptional status: reviews of their novels are included more often, are longer, and are placed in a more prominent position than those on other novels. Austen's *Emma* was the only novel apart from Scott's *The Antiquary* to be reviewed in the eminent *Quarterly Review* in the space of a year (April 1815 to April 1816), and in an article of the same length as that on *The Antiquary*, which indicates the high esteem in which Austen's novel was held. However, external differences also make clear the scale of dissimilarity between the reputations of the two authors: while Austen's major achievement is an article in *The Quarterly Review*, Scott's novels are noticed by *The Quarterly Review*, *The Edinburgh Review* and all other major periodicals.

Contrary to reviewers' own statements about their articles' influence on readers, numbers and kinds of periodicals noticing a novel appear to have no influence on the sales figures of that novel. On the contrary, reviewers seem to follow public trends: *Waverley* sold unprecedented numbers before an unusually high number of reviews appeared, and that pattern is repeated with each novel: *Rob Roy*'s unheard of 10,000 copies were sold out within a fortnight, before reviews can have had any effect, and was noticed by more Reviews than had previously been thought possible for a novel. Similarly, *MP*'s first edition of 1,250 copies was disposed of within 6 months, in spite of no Review noticing this novel at all; and of *Emma*'s first edition, 1,250 copies were sold in 10 months, though this novel was reviewed in 8 periodicals.

Similarly, publishing arrangements appear not to have influenced sales numbers. Different publishers' imprints conferred different degrees of authority onto a novel. Yet when the more prestigious imprint of John Murray appeared on the title page of *Emma*, replacing Thomas Egerton's name on the title page of *MP*, this did not lead to an increase in sales numbers. In the same way, a publisher's buying the copyright to a novel would convey his belief in the novel's sales potential to a much greater degree than if the work was published on commission. Yet again, readers do not appear to have cared very much: though the copyright of *PP* had been sold to the publisher, that of no other of Austen's novels was, without *PP* selling significantly higher numbers as a result. Scott's *Waverley* was a first production by an anonymous author published on half profits, yet the scale of its sales numbers was unprecedented. Reviewers do not discuss publishing arrangements either, which further indicates the limited impact these had on readers.

Austen depicts a society with which reviewers are familiar, so that they can praise her realism. Scott introduces an unknown yet real world, so that critics' imagination is captured while their requirements for realism are also satisfied. Horst Tippkötter comments that the appeal of viewing the novels as a relation of facts should not be underestimated, as it is this which legitimizes the novels as useful literature. He describes *Waverley* as having been seen by contemporaries as a

> first-rate, captivating entertainment-novel, appearing with the verifiable claim to report the truth. ... the realistic core of the novel gave [contemporaries] a convincing alibi for the satisfaction of their need for entertainment, which would, for moral reasons, otherwise have been difficult to justify.[31]

What appealed most about Scott's novels according to Tippkötter, was the fact that they provided 'history as entertainment'.[32] Similarly Kurt Gamerschlag asserts that '*Waverley* was for many of Scott's contemporaries primarily a history of culture and society, interestingly told'.[33] However, as the assessment of reviews of Scott's novels has shown, though Scott depicts a historical Scottishness, critics do not so much emphasize the historicity of the society depicted as its Scottishness. It is the latter that keeps the Highlands (or, for some reviewers, all of Scotland) on a previous stage of social development. Historical instruction may have served as an initial justification for reading the novels, but it became an instruction about a different culture still extant. That reviewers, especially in *Guy Mannering* and *The Antiquary*, recognize characters as within their experience contributes to their interpretation of otherness as an otherness of culture, not of time. The Waverley novels combine social utility with entertainment, but significantly they also evoke a romantic yearning for the distant other. Reviewers intensify this effect by presenting the romantic as still living on in their own time, only removed from their own world by surmountable geographical distance. Because Scott portrays the romantic in a realistic mode, reviewers feel justified in admiring it. They can regard it as a means of opening their eyes to a world they are unfamiliar with, and as such contributing to society, especially as the cultures Scott's novels show are part of reviewers' own kingdom. Reviewers stress the distance between the culture Scott shows and their own, so that the instruction is not about what the Britain of the reader once was, but what parts of the Britain of the reader still are.

The publication of *Waverley* in 1814 not only changed perceptions of what the novel-form could do, but caused reviewers to apply new criteria. In particular reviewers' attitude to realism and imagination reveals that by 1818, Scott's novels have become the ideal by which all others are judged. Reviews of Austen's novels that appear before Scott's novels dominate the market praise her realism without hesitation. Adverse comments on Austen's novels are rare in these reviews, and generally confined to details. The reviewer in *The British Critic* of 1812, for example, asserts that in *SS*, 'there is a little perplexity in the genealogy of the first chapter, and the reader is somewhat bewildered among half-sisters, cousins, and so forth ... but for these trifling defects there is ample compensation' (*BC* 1812, 527). Where larger points come up, as in the *CR*'s remark that there is no 'newness' in the story of *SS*, the reviewer condemns readers for being 'insatiable after something new', rather than the author for failing to provide it. In 1818, it is not 'newness' in a particular story that is found lacking but the whole mode of more imaginary depiction in all Austen's fictions. Regarding it as a quality that the author is lacking ('in imagination, of all kinds, she appears to have been extremely deficient', *BC* 1818, 297), rather than relating it to an individual novel makes it a more serious criticism because it limits all her writings and thereby Austen's significance.

Through the influence of Scott's novels, the term imagination has acquired the additional, more specific, meaning of ability to create scenes in distant romantic places and times. Whereas 'want of imagination' (*BC* 1818, 298) has so far not featured in reviews of Austen's novels, though all her novels are in what reviewers regard as the imitatively realistic mode, this lack now becomes the 'principal defect of her writings' (298), showing that it is Scott's kind of imagination that is found wanting. Although the *British Critic* reviewer writing on *Northanger Abbey* and *Persuasion* recognizes himself that Austen's realism would not be possible in a more romantic mode, since it is precisely her want of imagination that 'enables her to keep clear of all exaggeration, in a mode of writing where the least exaggeration would be fatal' (298), he insists on lack of it as a defect. This insistence shows that by now, four years after the appearance of *Waverley*, the imagination evoked by the unfamiliar elements of romance has become such a highly valued ingredient of fiction that a novel that provides realism alone cannot go uncensored. Lack of imagination remains a major criticism of Austen's novels throughout the nineteenth century, testifying to the lasting influence of Scott's novels.

Scott's novels have thus changed the attitude of reviewers to realism and imagination in novels, to a degree that is self-contradictory: just as they object to *Guy Mannering*'s astrological dealings as unrealistic because he is an Oxford scholar and therefore within their experience, their praise for Austen's realistic depiction of the world they are acquainted with should exclude the simultaneous request for romance and appeal to the imagination – but it does not, showing the dominance of Scott's mode. In Scott, reviewers require romance and non-rationalism where the matters concerned are far away and unconnected with critics themselves, and expect their own world to be depicted as rational. Because Scott's novels provide romance while at the same time being written in a realistic mode, they can be enjoyed by readers who see themselves as rational members of an early nineteenth-century progressive and commercial society. Changes in reviewers' attitudes towards an emphasis on imagination in fiction generally thus again indicates that it was this, more than the historicity of Scott's novels as Tippkötter argues, that appealed to readers.

That Scott's novels had set new standards is also testified to by elements that are no longer insisted on in 1818, such as characters' nobility of rank. In early reviews of Austen's novels, the characters' being in 'genteel life' (*CR* 1812, 149) is commended. However, characters' social position is not even mentioned in reviews of her last two novels. In Scott's novels, characters from all social classes feature, even characters from outside the economic structure of society, or only tolerated on its margins. The old beggar Edie in *The Antiquary*, or the gypsy Meg in *Guy Mannering*, are given the same emotional and intellectual scope as characters from higher classes. For Scott's novels, the criterion of 'genteel characters' never exists: as soon as *Waverley* comes out reviewers take an interest in lower-class characters. This attitude is gradually transferred onto the judgement of other novels: not so much that inclusion of lower-class characters becomes a necessity, but that to focus exclusively on higher-class characters ceases to be a reason for recommendation. 1816 is a transitional period, so that a reviewer of *Emma* still laments that it 'has not the highly-drawn characters in superior life which are so interesting in "PP"' (*GM*, 1816, 248–9), while it is at the same time a sign of 'genius' that the author of *The Antiquary* includes such a variety of characters.

Reviewers emphasize again and again the distance between their own society and that of Scott's novels. It is because of cultural distance that critics can be as interested in the different social layers of the respective society as in the society itself. Social disparity between reviewers and characters is widest with characters on the margins of the social class structure and thus contributes to geographical and cultural distance. Edie's wit at the Antiquary's expense can be accepted because neither character bears resemblance to anything reviewers know. Austen's depiction of a society that is familiar means reviewers' demand characters' gentility, and they continue to do so for a few years after Scott's novels have introduced different levels of society, as serious characters, into fiction. That generally reviewer's own class is still the one they are most concerned with becomes obvious in statements such as the one quoted above, that what Austen depicts must have happened 'to half the families in the United Kingdom' (*BC* 1818, 297) – the whole population of the United Kingdom being apparently still limited to the classes that read. While beginning to accept the inclusion of other social classes in novels, reviewers' concept of realism is still confined to the depiction of their own class. (The concept of realism had developed to signify characters, rather than just 'probable incidents', only with the advent of Scott's novels: in early reviews of Austen reviewers do not describe her depiction of contemporary society as 'realism'.)

Reviewers' praising Austen and according her a higher position in 1818 than when she first published shows that although Scott as a novelist reigned supreme and set the standards, other modes were conceivable. Though there is a definite hierarchy, it does not follow that anything not Scott is bad: Scott is unreachable, but below him there are still good as well as bad novels, and since his works have raised the status of the novel generally, approval of a good novel is not as grudgingly bestowed as hitherto.

An exception to the general consensus of this hierarchy is the article in *The Edinburgh Magazine* on *Northanger Abbey* and *Persuasion* of May 1818. The reviewer also testifies to Scott's novels' supreme position, and shows an awareness of just how different Austen's and Scott's modes of writing are, but he is the first, and for decades the only one, to voice a doubt about the contemporary distribution of popularity. The reality of the times being so tumultuous has caused a desire for 'grand movements and striking characters' (*EdM* 1818, 454), but he predicts that

> the time, probably, will return, when [readers] shall take a more permanent delight in those familiar cabinet pictures, than even in the great historical pieces of our more eminent modern masters (454),

implying that Austen will overtake Scott in popularity, which, given their respective positions in 1818, is a daring prediction to make. The reviewer does not believe the absolute qualities of the texts to determine popularity, but the literary tastes of a certain culture at a certain time. Once these have changed, 'the delightful writer of the works now before us, will be one of the most popular of English novelists' (*EdM* 454). The critic thus sees the craze for Scott and the comparative obscurity of Austen as a phase, and with hindsight of 200 years' development of Austen's and Scott's reputations, his predicted outcome has come true, though it may have taken longer than he expected. However, he is the exception among reviewers; all others see Austen as being as popular as she deserves, and certainly do not imply anything about a possible temporariness of Scott's status.

That Austen's reputation increases over these years appears paradoxical, since the criteria applied to novels also develop. She fulfils more of the criteria applied in 1812 than of those used in 1818, when, due to the influence of Scott's novels, some of these criteria have changed. From the appearance of *Waverley* in 1814 onwards, reviewers' requirements of individual novels as well as their attitudes towards the genre as a whole change – gradually, since morality remains the most deciding criterion by which novels are judged, particularly those by women, and the genre itself, though no longer despised, was yet to develop into being esteemed. The genre's risen status makes higher praise more easily possible. Largely through the unfamiliar qualities of Scott's novels, reviewers have a more open attitude towards novels that do not fulfil all their criteria, so that Austen in 1818 can be more highly praised despite not meeting as many criteria as hitherto. That she is still accorded a high place, against, rather than in accordance with, some of the prevailing criteria, also testifies to reviewers' estimation of her.

In articles on Austen's novels then, the changes in reviewers' attitudes can be traced, but it is not her novels that change anything, since the requirements move away from what her novels provide, and towards Scott's. While reviewers judge Scott's works as a class apart, they increasingly see them as belonging to the genre of fiction. Only by belonging to the genre can they change its status the way they do, and the more reviewers come to call the works 'Waverley novels', the more the general status of the novel genre rises. Brian Southam's assertion that Austen's works 'revealed to the early nineteenth-century reading public that fiction was capable of unsuspected power, that it was to be taken seriously as a form of literature'[34] is thus an overstatement, made from a twentieth-century view of her significance, whereas evidence appears to bear out John O. Hayden's ambitious claim that 'Scott single-handedly revived the reputation of the novel'.[35]

Though the Waverley novels changed critics' attitudes to the novel-genre, the focus of reviewers is still only on content. Novels remain on the level of entertainment, instruction and utility and are not yet regarded as works of art that merit analysis of their artistic qualities. That Scott himself regarded novel-writing as not technically difficult and produced fiction at such speed would have confirmed reviewers' view of the genre. Reviewers therefore come to regard a novel as capable of being useful to society, but not as contributing to art. Their lack of interest in the analysis of a novel's art and technique means they are less capable of discerning the qualities and innovations of Austen's works than of Scott's. Yet reviewers' positive verdicts on both novelists show that they recognize the difference between other novelists and both these authors, even if they lack the vocabulary to describe their approbation for one of them. Reviewers focus on the content of Scott's novels and are fascinated by their scope. It is the novels' content and perceived high quality that causes reviewers to conjecture that they are by Scott, rather than rumours about their authorship necessarily leading to positive verdicts. While the names of other male authors occasionally feature in reviews, reviewers never consider the possibility of female authorship. The novels' historical, political, geographical and intellectual scope was such that reviewers believed the necessary pre-requisites could only have been acquired by a man. Austen focuses on subjects that reviewers deem appropriate for female authors, so that what reviewers regard as her strength – making domestic life interesting – is also what necessarily limits the significance of her works. Her novels are outstanding, but they are definitely within the ordinary category of the novel-genre, without the greater social significance that Scott's works offer.

Fiction had been regarded as a female-dominated field. Feminine writing and reading was seen as limiting the genre intellectually, so that its significance for anyone other than novel-reading young ladies had also been limited. Ferris argues that while up to the 1810s the literary sphere was a masculine field and therefore excluded the novel, *Waverley*

> was precisely the text to accelerate this process of incorporation, assuaging critical anxieties so as to allow the novel definitive if still uneasy entry into the literary sphere. As the product of a noted member of the republic of letters (Scott's anonymity was never an obstacle to his first reviewers) this text worked in complex ways not only to legitimate novel writing as a literary activity but to validate novel reading as a male practice.[36]

Reviews show that while the author's gender was the condition for the novels to thrive, allowing them to break out of ordinary novelistic rules in a way a woman's novels never could, it was through content, more than external circumstance, that they succeeded. The novels' possible connection with Scott, the most eminent poet of the time, is only discussed in reviews of *Waverley;* thereafter, the author's masculinity combined with masculine subject matter is sufficient to distinguish his works from other novels and Scott's name no longer needs to be explicitly featured. While Scott's possible authorship would have added excitement, it is because his novels gave readers matters beyond domestic morality, matters that concerned everyone, that reviewers praise them. Whereas the social utility of a woman's novels' was limited to domestic propriety and morality, a man's novels could merely assume domestic morality – both Flora and Rose are domestically admirable – and instead focus on instruction about different cultures.

As we have seen, contemporary reviewers' reactions to Austen's and Scott's texts depend almost wholly on critics' cultural context. Unanimity in criteria applied by critics and aspects omitted emphasize the shaping role of this context. Austen's works fit into the early nineteenth-century stereotype of female fiction, with necessarily limited social significance. Technical aspects are not discussed, nor are other issues that for modern readers of Austen's works are a matter of course – such as her satire. Reviewers' literary and cultural surroundings mean that her novels could not be regarded as great in the way Scott's works were. His novels did not fit the fictional stereotype. They satisfied readers' romantic yearning for a different world and at the same time provided a justification for being read and therefore reached a status beyond that of any ordinary fiction. The comparison between Austen's and Scott's reputations reveals how the Waverley novels shaped the cultural context into which Scott's own novels as well as those of his contemporaries were received. Though texts are read according to prevailing cultural values, this shaping power of the Waverley novels, as well as reviewers' appreciation of Austen, limited though it is, show that some intrinsic merit is in the text. The qualities of Austen's texts are acknowledged in spite of outer circumstances preventing them from being named, and from gaining outstanding success.

Chapter 3

Private Readers' Responses in Letters and Diaries, 1811–1818

Reviewing is a public activity, and does not necessarily reflect readers' private opinions; because of the low status of the novel in the early nineteenth century, the urge to disparage such works would have been greater in a public review than in a private comment. Also, reviewing was a male-dominated field, so that it does not reveal women's reactions. This study uses the more private sources of diaries and letters to investigate how far public and private responses differ, as well as looking at whether the private responses correlate with readers' social position and gender.

New books were only available to the well-off, so that the recorded comments on Austen's and Scott's works are also concentrated in that group. The comments drawn on are primarily printed ones, which represents another source of selectivity, towards the famous. Increasing literacy among working and middle classes did not mean access to new books, especially not to novels: while libraries may have provided members of the working classes with reading matter, this was not usually fiction. Also, working-class readers did not generally comment: literacy did not necessarily mean the ability to write; paper was expensive, and for people who did not travel there was little need to write. Both letters and diaries were very rare in the lower-class levels of society, so that the bias in the study of comments is necessarily towards the higher social classes.[1]

The chapter draws on the evidence of over 200 comments. Because of the inherently unsystematic nature of the material, the discussion has been organized by aspects commentators raise, rather than by novel, to assess commentators' responses to Austen's and Scott's novels in general. While analysis by aspect does not permit tracing a development, it allows for a comparison between the issues discussed about each novelist as well as to the issues reviewers raise. As with reviews, only comments on novels published up to 1818 have been included. The chapter also concentrates mainly on comments made up to 1818, but it includes some made between 1818 and 1832, the year of Scott's death, if made by people who were reading and writing at the same time as Austen and Scott.

The commentators

In order to give some idea of kinds of people who comment, a representative selection of commentators known has been listed below, divided by class, occupation, and gender. Addressees have not been included, as it is not always clear from the letter whether they would have known the novel concerned, but people referred to as having read or commented on them have been listed. Commentators have been divided into three groups: literati, members of the aristocracy, and members of the professional classes. If people belong to more than one group, they have been placed in the one that seemed more significant to their reading. Quantitatively there are of course many more comments on Scott than on Austen, the majority of which have not been discussed. In spite of not being comprehensive, the proportions of male and female readers in each of the groups have been indicated as this gives an idea of general trends.

Literati

Jane Austen	Walter Scott
	Jane Austen
	Joanna Baillie
	Fanny Burney
	Lord Byron
	Robert Cadell (publisher)
James Stanier Clarke (the Prince Regent's Librarian)	
	Henry Cockburn
Samuel Taylor Coleridge	Samuel Taylor Coleridge
	Archibald Constable
	George Crabbe
	John Wilson Croker
Maria Edgeworth	Maria Edgeworth
Thomas Egerton (publisher of *SS*, *PP* and the first edition of *MP*)	
Susan Ferrier (novelist)	Susan Ferrier
Henry Stephen Fox (novelist)	
William Gifford (editor of the *QR*)	

Jane Austen	Walter Scott
	Johann Wolfgang von Goethe
Francis Jeffrey (editor of the *ER*)	Francis Jeffrey
	Walter Savage Landor
	Matthew Lewis
John Gibson Lockhart (Scott's son-in-law, and himself a critic and novelist)	John Gibson Lockhart
Mary Russell Mitford (novelist)	Mary Russell Mitford
Thomas Moore	
John Murray (publisher of the *QR*, Byron's works, some of Scott's, Crabbe's, Southey's and Coleridge's work and of Austen's novels from *Emma* onwards)	John Murray
Henry Crabb Robinson (diarist)	Henry Crabb Robinson
	Charles Kirkpatrick Sharpe
	Mary Shelley
Richard Brinsley Sheridan (dramatist)	
	Sydney Smith
Mme de Staël	Mme de Staël
Walter Scott	
Robert Southey	Robert Southey
William Wordsworth	William Wordsworth
14 men, 4 women*	**18 men, 8 women***

* The group of literati is necessarily dominated by men: it includes publishers and reviewers, who read books as part of their job, and who are predominantly male.

Aristocrats

Jane Austen	Walter Scott
Lord John James Abercorn	
Lady Anne Jane Abercorn (friend of Scott's)	Lady Anne Jane Abercorn
Henrietta, Countess of Bessborough	
Lord Boringdon	
Lady Boringdon	
	Sir Alexander Boswell
	Duke of Buccleuch
Lord Broughton	Lord Broughton
	Lady Byron (formerly Anne Isabella Millbanke)
	Lady Charleville
Princess Charlotte	
Earl of Dudley	
Lady Jane Davy, wife of chemist Sir Humphrey Davy	
	William Erskine (later Lord Kinneder)
	Harriet, Countess of Granville
Lady Robert Kerr	
	Prince Pückler-Muskau
Prince Regent	
Lady Anne Romilly	Lady Anne Romilly
Lady Frances Shelley	
	Lady Stafford
	Lady Louisa Stuart
Lady Georgiana Vernon	
5 men, 9 women	5 men, 7 women

Professional classes

Jane Austen	Walter Scott
Cassandra Austen	
Henry Austen	
Mrs Charles Cage (the Cage family were in-laws to Austen's brother Edward Austen Knight)	
Mr Cooke (Godfather to Jane Austen)[2]	
Mrs Cooke	
	Revd Patrick Graham
	Mrs Grant
	Charles H. Hall
	Benjamin Robert Haydon (painter)
	Mrs Mary Ann Hughes
Margaret Mackenzie, daughter of Henry Mackenzie	
Anne Isabella Millbanke, future Lady Byron	
	John Bacon Sawrey Morritt (Scott's friend)
Mrs Pole	
Henry Sandford	
	Sophia Scott
Mary Somerville (scientist)	
3 men, 7 women	**4 men, 3 women**

Two initial conclusions may be drawn from these lists: As regards social distribution, there is no major difference between kinds of people who comment on the novels of Austen and Scott. While there are some literati who comment on Scott and not on Austen, several general readers comment on both authors. Both authors seem to have been well known enough to be read by the most important literati of their time as well as influential members of the aristocracy.

Despite novel-reading's being regarded as a predominantly female occupation, comments show that there are as many male as female readers. There is no significant difference between Austen and Scott as regards gender distribution of commentators. While it is not surprising that women would have read Scott because the great majority of literate contemporaries did, men reading Austen, a female novelist writing in a genre with a supposedly female readership, is perhaps a more unexpected result. The proportion of male and female readers of Austen's and Scott's novels indicates the popularity and prestige of these two authors. Comments reflect rather than influence readership, and male commentators especially may be less reluctant in a private letter to admit to having read a novel.

The comments do not allow for definite conclusions about general trends regarding a particularly English or Scottish readership, partly because the evidence in this respect is too personally connected to the two authors to admit generalization. Among Scottish literati, there are those who comment on both authors, and among the aristocracy and professional classes there are more Scottish commentators on Scott than on Austen. Most of these are Scott's acquaintances, however, so that one cannot conclude from the evidence of the comments that Scott's novels were more popular in Scotland than in England, or Austen's less known there than in England.

Generally one can conclude that, given the low status of the novel, the groups who comment on Scott and Austen, especially the group of literati with its predominantly male members and highly prestigious positions, reflect a reputation higher than that which reviews of novels would lead one to expect. Though only reactions to Austen and Scott have been looked at, and no statements can therefore be made about how comments on their works compare to those on other novelists, to be discussed in the private comments of some of the foremost literati of the time can be regarded as a sign of unusual esteem. Regardless of whether people comment positively or negatively, they obviously regard the objects they remark on as noteworthy. Discussing a novel in a letter indicates either a belief that the addressee will know the work in question, or a conviction that the novel is important enough to draw the addressee's attention to it.

There is therefore an inconsistency between reviewers' claims and readers' practices, so that literary reviews do not always reflect the private views of the critics. While reviewers still justify the inclusion of articles on novels in their periodicals with claims for variety and the need to protect a female readership from harmful publications, the fact that critics comment privately on them (even if they had to read them because they had to review them) reflects an interest beyond that displayed by professional reviewers. The people commenting on Austen's and Scott's works thus testify to the authors' prestige. For Austen especially it must be seen as an achievement to be thought worthy of being read and commented on in private letters or diaries, particularly by the same groups of people that discuss Scott's novels.

Anonymity and popularity

Austen's anonymity was both gendered and socially defined since *Sense and Sensibility* appeared as 'By a Lady'. Discussion of authorship of a novel shows a certain degree of popularity, especially at a time when anonymous novels were common. Either the person suspected of authorship or the novel or both must have been fascinating enough to provoke discussion. To attempt to discover who the author might be involves admitting to having read his or her work, considering it significant enough to mention and spending time and energy on the task. In contrast to reviewers of Scott's novels, reviewers of Austen's works are not interested in who the author might be. Making guesses concerning the unknown identity of an ordinary female novelist is beneath critics' formal notice, but not beneath commentators'. Mary Russell Mitford asks her friend Sir William Elford in November 1813: 'Pray, is not your neighbour, Lady Boringdon, an authoress? I have heard two novels in high repute (but which I have not read), "Sense and Sensibility" and "Pride and Prejudice" ascribed to her'.[3] By December 1814, three years before Austen's name officially appeared on the title pages of her novels, Russell Mitford has both read Austen's novels and found out who the authoress is. She writes to Elford that she 'quite agree[s] with [him] in preferring Miss Austen to Miss Edgeworth'.[4] Lord Broughton notes in his diary in October 1814 that his acquaintance Lady Boringdon 'is suspected of having written the two novels: "Pride and Prejudice" and "Sense and Sensibility"',[5] which indicates his interest in the novels as well as in his acquaintance, while the existence of the rumour shows that readers generally wanted to know who the author was. Margaret Mackenzie recommends *Pride and Prejudice* to her brother Hugh in 1813 and similarly indicates that interest in authorship is connected to interest in the novel:

> Do you ever read novels? Because we have been much pleased with one lately – *Pride and Prejudice*. It is published anonymously, but it is said to be by Mrs. Dorset, the renowned authoress of *The Peacock at Home*.[6]

This passage also again testifies to the gender assumptions about readers of novels – even in the son of the novelist Henry Mackenzie. Anne Isabella Millbanke writes to her mother in May 1813: 'I have finished the Novel called Pride and Prejudice, which I think a very superior work ... I wish much to know who is the author or *ess* as I am told'.[7] This letter again indicates that perceived quality leads to wishing to know the author.

As Austen was not a well-known literary figure like Scott, readers did not usually guess her identity. However, in September 1813, Austen writes to her brother Frank that 'the secret has spread so far as to be scarcely the shadow of a secret now'.[8] However far it had really spread, for it to have spread at all people must have been interested in the author behind the novels.

With Scott, too, authorship is discussed more by commentators than by reviewers. Scott's name features in most of those comments which make guesses as to authorship of the Waverley novels – increasingly with each novel. Austen, who led a country life outside the big literary circles of London and Edinburgh, is in no doubt about the authorship of *Waverley*. Writing to her niece Anna Austen in September 1814, she complains:

> Walter Scott has no business to write novels, especially good ones. It is not fair. He has fame and profit enough as a poet, and should not be taking the bread out of other people's mouths. I do not like him, and do not mean to like Waverley if I can help it – but fear I must.[9]

The degree of certainty might vary, but comments are usually more about the likelihood of the author's being Scott than guesses as to other possible identities. Lady Anne Romilly writes to Maria Edgeworth in November 1814 that 'Walter Scott, if he did not write it, certainly must have had a good deal to do with it, but there is a sort of note prefix'd to the last edition which they seem to say makes it very improbable that it should have been written by him'.[10] In February 1815 she writes: 'Surely there is no doubt but that Walter Scott is the principal Author of [*Waverley*]. The learned here do not speak of it as belonging to anyone else'.[11] In December 1816, Scott's is still the name that is principally associated with the novels, but even then Romilly is not entirely certain that they are written by him – though she, as well as the majority of readers generally, recognizes that *Tales of My Landlord* comes from the hand that wrote *Waverley*:

> Pray read 'Tales of my Landlord'. They are charming. I think there can be no doubt but that they are written by the *Author of Waverley* altho' it is not avow'd who that is. If it is not Walter Scott it is marvellous. I saw a gentleman the other day who told me that he had seen the manuscript in America in the hands of Walter Scott's Brother who there avow'd himself the Author-.[12]

Commentators thus spend more energy on the question of authorship and go on discussing it for longer than reviewers (the latter stop concerning themselves with authorship after *Waverley*).

Many of these conjectures are deferential and conclude that the novels have to be by Scott because they are of such high quality that 'there is but one person in the world able to write such works, and therefore they must be his'[13] – which again is similar to the argument put forward by reviewers. Frances Waddington remarks after reading *Waverley* that 'every part ... impressed upon us the conviction that we owe it to Walter Scott ... every perfection that shines forth in full splendour in this novel, is discernible in his conversation'.[14] Edgeworth herself writes to Scott in October 1814, saying *Waverley* had to be 'Aut Scotus, Aut diabolus!'.[15] Russell Mitford writes to Elford in October 1814:

> Have you read Walter Scott's "Waverley?" I have ventured to say "Walter Scott's", though I hear he denies it, just as a young girl denies the imputation of a lover; but if there be a belief in internal evidence it must be his. It is his by a thousand indications – by all the faults and beauties.[16]

Here she is comparing a novel to poetry, regarding them in this instance as similar, which in itself is an elevation for any novel. George Crabbe, too, votes 'with the Multitude',[17] who regard *Waverley* as written by Scott.

While these comments suggest that because the novels are good they must be by Scott, there is also evidence that this works the other way round – because they may be by Scott, and Scott is a highly esteemed poet, the novels must be good. Unlike Austen, Scott was already a well-known literary figure before he published novels. This fame rendered the question of whether the most popular poet of the age had written the most successful novels an exciting one for contemporaries. Though the comments on authorship of the Waverley novels do not directly refer to his poetry, comments such as the ones above reveal a preconceived image of the author of the novels that is already very positive. However, though a connection between Scott and the novels may have increased their fame, comments proving that someone read a Waverley novel because it is ascribed to Scott are rare. One such is by Matthew Lewis, author of *The Monk*, who writes in a letter to Scott in August 1814 that on 'hearing Waverley ascribed to you, I bought it and read it with all impatience'.[18] This being in a letter to Scott one cannot exclude the possibility of flattery on Lewis's part, so that even this comment does not prove the sequence to have been rumour, then reading. While reviews are rare that explicitly notice *Waverley* because of the Scott connection rather than for its public popularity or its internal qualities, the same is true for comments, so that the novels' fame caused interest in authorship, rather than vice versa. However, once read, conjectures as to possible authorship make discussion of the novels more exciting, so that their anonymity contributes to their fame. Henry Cockburn indicates that it was precisely the uncertainty of their authorship, and the possibility of their being by Scott, that made the novels exciting:

> If the concealment of the authorship of the novels was intended to make mystery heighten their effect, it completely succeeded. The speculations and conjectures, and nods and winks, and predictions and assertions were endless, and occupied every company, and almost every two men who met and spoke on the street. It was proved by a thousand indications, each refuting the other, and all equally true in fact, that they were written by old Henry Mackenzie, and by George Cranstoun, and William Erskine, and Jeffrey, and above all by Thomas Scott, Walter's brother, a regimental paymaster, then in Canada.[19]

This statement demonstrates the impact of Scott's novels, as well as the degree of uncertainty there was, so that it became impossible for a literary and educated person not to be acquainted with the Waverley novels.

Commentators are more willing to be guided by external evidence than reviewers are. In spite of belonging to literary circles, reviewers appear to have had to rely on 'internal evidence'. The 'northern literati are unanimous ... in ascribing part of it at least to the pen of W. Scott', writes the reviewer in *The British Critic* in August 1814,[20] and while he emphasizes that he cannot be a judge of this 'external evidence', as he is part of the literary world in the south rather than the north, he sees in his analysis of the content of the novel much to confirm this suspicion. Like other reviewers that discuss *Waverley*'s authorship, this reviewer justifies the discussion by making it a serious literary question through a comparison of the content of the novel with that of Scott's poetry. By contrast, John Wilson Croker is too uncertain to discuss *Waverley*'s authorship in his review of the novel, yet he is intrigued by the question and writes to a friend in 1817:

> The author is certainly Walter Scott, or his brother Mr. Thomas Scott. The internal evidence is in favour of the former, but his asseverations, and all external evidence, are for the latter. I cannot decide.[21]

This letter shows the different levels that an article in *The Quarterly Review* and a private letter have for Croker: while in the former, he discusses only what he knows, holding conjecture beneath the formal level of a reviewing article, in a letter he feels free to speculate.

In Britain, conjecture decreased with every new Waverley novel published. In continental Europe, authorship ceased to be doubted even sooner – in Germany definitely from 1822, when the novels began to have Scott's name on the title page.[22] References to Scott are frequent in German letters and literature of the time, such as E. T. A. Hoffmann having his characters discuss Scott's qualities as a novelist in his tale *Die Serapions-Brüder*,[23] first published in 1819–21, and Johann Wolfgang von Goethe on reading *Kenilworth* as his first Waverley novel in 1821 being aware that Scott is its author.[24]

Thus in spite of the anonymous publication of both Scott's and Austen's novels, Scott's name as well as the contents of his novels were factors contributing to making them exciting, while the response Austen's works received was entirely due to their content. Austen's name did nothing to recommend hers, even when it was eventually known. For both authors' works, authorship does not explain their success, so that readers' reactions to the content of Austen's and Scott's novels need to be assessed to understand the degree, and reasons for, both authors' popularity.

Apart from the discussion of authorship as a sign of popularity, and the kinds of people who comment on an author as a signifier of the degree of popularity, other important signifiers are the assumption of recognition in allusions to the novels and their characters, especially in letters. These differ from actual discussions of aspects of the novels as they usually link a real event, situation, or person to an equivalent in a novel. These allusions show a greater familiarity with a work than a comment written just after the perusal of a novel, both for the writer of the letter but also for its recipient, because it assumes recognition of what is referred to outside its context.

Where characters from Austen's novels are referred to in letters of the time, the references are usually explained. I know of only one example where no explanation is given. Scott's son-in-law John Gibson Lockhart refers to Austen's characters in an open letter to Lord Byron of 1821:

> Now tell me, Mrs. Goddard, now tell me, Miss Price, now tell me, dear Harriet Smith, and dear, dear Mrs. Elton, do tell me, is not this just the very look, that one would have fancied for Childe Harold? ... Poor Lord Byron! Who can say how much he may have been to be pitied? I am sure I would; I can bear with all Mr. E.'s eccentricities. ... What think you of that other [passage] we were talking of on Saturday evening at Miss Bates's? – Nay, smile not at my sullen brow, Alas! I cannot smile again.' I forget the rest:- but nobody has such a memory as Mrs. E.[25]

The passage shows that Lockhart expects most of the readers of this letter, including Byron, to understand the allusions. Also, the passage proves that Austen's characters, like Scott's, remained in the minds of those who read her. However, while Charles Beecher Hogan, in his desire to prove Austen's novels to have been very successful with their contemporary readers, uses this passage to prove that 'Jane Austen's name was, to the literary world of her day, a familiar one, and one that was held in esteem and affection',[26] Lockhart's is the only comment of this kind that I am aware of. All others explain the references, and of course neither Hogan nor I can give examples proving people being unfamiliar with her and therefore not citing her. Lockhart's comment shows that he expects Byron at least, as well as other readers, to recognize Austen's characters out of context.

Russell Mitford is more typical in her reference to a character from *Pride and Prejudice*, thinking it necessary to explain her source. Commenting on a letter she had received from an acquaintance, she writes to Elford in September 1818: 'I value it almost as much as Mr. Bennett [*sic*] (our dear Miss Austen's Mr. Bennett) valued the letters of Mr. Collins – a person whom, I think, my correspondent rather resembles.'[27] This shows that she expects the addressee to be acquainted with the novel intimately enough to understand her meaning, though she and Elford had of course exchanged letters on Austen already, referring specifically to *Pride and Prejudice* in one written in December 1814. However, a letter exchange four years previously is not necessarily a guarantee for recognition of the reference. Similarly, Maria Edgeworth writes to her stepmother Frances Anne Edgeworth in 1821 that Lady Catherine Bisset, whom she visited, 'is as unlike the Lady Catherine in Pride and Prejudice as you can conceive'.[28] Again, this shows that she would have expected her stepmother to have read and remembered the novel. While references to Austen's characters in contemporary letters thus exist, the characters are usually contextualized, which indicates the limits of the assumed familiarity.

Gender differences among commentators become apparent in comments about the availability and popularity on Austen's novels: it is mainly women who express the desire to obtain a novel. Anne Isabella Millbanke, the future Lady Byron, writes from London in 1813 that *Pride and Prejudice* is 'at present the fashionable novel',[29] which is supported by a comment by Charlotte Clavering who writes to Susan Ferrier in the same year that she 'should like amazingly to see that same "Pride and Prejudice" which everybody dins my ears with'.[30] Lady Anne Romilly writes that *Mansfield Park* 'has been pretty generally admired'[31] in London in 1814, and Lady Kerr reports that it is 'admired in Edinburgh by all the wise ones'.[32] Thus in abstract, without reference to the contents, it is female readers who are concerned with novels. However, Thomas Moore writes to Murray in December 1817: 'I heard a little of the new novel (Persuasion &c.) read at Bowood the other night, which has given me a great desire for the rest – Will you send it to Power's for us?-or, indeed, send it off at once here' (Bowood was the home of Lord and Lady Shelburne, Powers the music publisher who brought out Moore's songs.)[33] While this reveals that men, too, knew of the fashionable novels, it also shows that if men mention novels, it is for a specific purpose. Women are also involved in the practical aspects of novel-reading, however: Lady Abercorn writes to Murray in December 1817 about *Northanger Abbey* and *Persuasion*: 'Pray send us Miss Austen's novels the moment you can.'[34] Thus Jane Austen's novels imitate on a smaller scale the achievement of Scott's novels: to be discussed. These comments show that her novels were talked about and that it was desirable to obtain and to read them.

The popularity of Scott's novels was such that even people who had not read the novels knew and referred to the characters in his novels. John Keats, for example, had not read *Guy Mannering* by 1818 but, as Claire Lamont shows, he was familiar with the character of Meg Merrilies to the extent of deriving his own Meg in his poem 'Old Meg she was a Gipsey' from Scott's figure.[35] The contemporary reviewers of Scott's novel emphasize Meg in their articles; a play based on the novel was performed at the Theatre Royal, Covent Garden, in 1816, and again in 1817 and 1818. In addition, 'four paintings of Meg Merrilies, based either on the novel, or on Mrs Egerton's performance in the dramatic version, were exhibited in London between 1816 and 1818',[36] so that even people unfamiliar with the novels would have known their characters.

This familiarity also becomes apparent in contemporary letters, as characters are referred to with and without explanation; it is taken for granted that the addressee will recognize characters and their situations. The degree of familiarity is high, since even minor characters are evoked. In 1820, Lord Byron writes to Lord Broughton requesting his opinion of conflicting financial advice he has received and states that since he believes both his advisers, he is 'like Garschattachin – who wished to serve King George and King James both at once – so how shall I decide?'[37] The modern reader of Byron's letters and journals needs the editor's explanation that Byron assumes his addressee not to require: 'In Scott's novel [*Rob Roy*] Duncan Galbraith of Garschattachin, Major of the Lennox militiamen, captured Rob Roy after Rob had been deceived by Rashleigh Osbaldistone's treacherous message.'[38] References in Byron's letters to Scott's characters are frequent, and seem to be made regardless of whom he is writing to, which hints at his expecting almost all of his correspondents to understand such allusions. Jane Austen writes to her nephew James Edward Austen in December 1816, expecting him to have read the novel she is referring to, though she explains both character and novel:

> Uncle Henry writes very superior sermons. -You & I must try to get hold of one or two, & put them into our Novels; -it would be a fine help to a volume; & we could make our Heroine read it aloud of a Sunday Evening, just as well as Isabella Wardour in the Antiquary, is made to read the History of the Hartz Demon the ruins of St. Ruth – tho' I believe, upon recollection, Lovell is the Reader.[39]

Scott's contemporaries thus knew his novels intimately, so that even minor characters could be referred to out of context.

There are numerous references to the popularity of Scott's novels, and they indicate Scott's influence on the changing perception of the relationship between quality and popularity of a work. In July 1814, J. B. S. Morritt worries that *Waverley* may be too good to appeal to the stereotypical female novel-reader.

> Amongst the gentle class of readers, who swallow every blue-backed book in a circulating library for the sake of the story, I should fear that half the knowledge of nature it contains and all the Humour would be thrown away.[40]

He reveals the common assumptions about novels, and *Waverley* is of too high a quality to fit them. While this justifies his own enjoyment of the work, it also shows that for Morritt, popularity still has negative connotations, and a mark of quality is that it cannot become broadly popular. Coleridge shares Morritt's view of the impossibility of a work's possessing quality and popularity and implies that because of 'the present conditions and components of popularity, viz. to amuse without requiring any effort or thought, and without exciting any deep emotion',[41] Scott's novels are not of high quality. However, the majority of commentators use references to Scott's popularity to recommend one of the novels or to put their own verdicts into context, so that writers support their approval of the respective novel by referring to the general opinion. Maria Edgeworth writes to Mrs Ruxton in October 1814 that '*Waverley* was in everybody's hands. ... I am more delighted with it than I can tell you: it is a work of first-rate genius',[42] backing up her own approval of the work with public opinion. Sydney Smith writes in 1819 to Archibald Constable, Scott's publisher: 'Pray make the author go on; I am sure he has five or six more such novels in him, therefore five or six holidays for the whole kingdom',[43] indicating again Scott's overwhelming popularity.

For commentators even more than for reviewers, popularity becomes a sign of merit. Croker sends some of the Waverley novels to a friend and recommends them by saying that 'they are the most popular novels which have been published these many years; they are, indeed, almost histories rather than novels'.[44] In his review of *Waverley* he is more sceptical, arguing against the mixture of fiction and fact, yet in this letter, he recommends them apparently without hesitation. Even in a letter, however, Croker justifies his recommendation with the works' popularity as well as quality, and that quality manifests itself in their not really belonging to the novel-genre but to that of history. (The novels he recommends are *The Antiquary* and the first series of *Tales of My Landlord*, which makes his assertion that they are 'histories' seem all the more like a strained justification, since *The Antiquary* deals with almost his own time.) That Croker, who is not particularly positive about the Waverley novels in his reviews, obviously enjoys them enough to recommend them to a friend, shows again that privately reviewers were not as strict as they made out in their articles.

Criticism of the novels, too, indicates their immense popularity. It is rare, and where it appears commentators tend to disqualify their own opinion on the basis of the public fervour. Susan Ferrier writes that she has 'read "My Landlord's Tales" [first series], and can't abide them; but that's my shame, not their fault, for they are excessively admired by all persons of taste'.[45] Archibald Constable similarly declares that 'my opinion [of *HOM*] is of little consequence, as the public seems to be quite crazy for the novels of this author'.[46]

Realism

As in reviews, realism emerges from the comments as the aspect that most distinguishes Austen's from other novels. Readers remark on the newness of Austen's kind of novel and compare her novels to earlier and ordinary ones, especially to Gothic fiction. Mary Somerville in her *Personal Recollections* finds that the novels 'certainly formed a curious contrast to my old favourites, the Radcliffe novels and ghost stories', and she read Austen's novels because she 'had now come to years of discretion',[47] reading them for reflection rather than highly strung emotions. She regards them as the opposite of a wild, romantic, sentimental and mindless type of fiction. William Gifford, the editor of *The Quarterly Review*, comments in an 1815 letter that he also sees Austen's works as forming a contrast to the well-known patterns of Gothic novels:

> No dark passages; no secret chambers; no wind-howlings in long galleries; no drops of blood upon a rusty dagger – things that should now be left to ladies' maids and sentimental washer women.[48]

Gifford describes the novel as having undergone with Austen a development towards one of higher and more realistic quality. His comment shows the expectations with which a novel was met, and also gives hints as to the expected readership and thereby the status of the novel. Gentility was desirable not only in author and subject matter but also in readership, so that, again, quality is linked to a limited readership, though this time of class, not of gender. Linking in with Somerville's comment that describes Austen's novels as more mature and reflective reading, Gifford's comment elevates the novels above ordinary ones by inferring a more refined content that will lead to a more refined reading. Commentators see Austen's realism as more relevant to their own lives and therefore as more significant than the content of more romantic novels. While this also holds for reviewers, they emphasize the instruction that can be gained from Austen's novels because of the proximity of the subject matter to the readers. Commentators are more interested in the proximity itself as an unknown and entertaining experience, rather than its potential instructiveness. Lady Gordon comments that

> in most novels you are amused for a time with a set of Ideal People whom you never think of afterwards or whom you the least expect to meet in common life, whereas in Miss A-s works, & especially in MP, you actually live with them, you fancy yourself one of the family; & the scenes are so exactly descriptive, so perfectly natural, that there is scarcely an Incident of conversation, or a person that you are not inclined to imagine you have at one time or other in your Life been a witness to, born a part in, & been acquainted with.[49]

Realism is frequently bound up with character depiction, often by female commentators who identify with one of the female characters, making this an aspect where male and female readers differ. Princess Charlotte, commenting on *Sense and Sensibility* in January 1812, feels 'quite one of the company' and thinks herself and Marianne 'very like in disposition'.[50] Similarly, Maria Edgeworth finds 'the love and lover admirably well drawn: don't you see Captain Wentworth, or rather don't you in her place feel him taking the boisterous child off her back as she kneels by the sick boy on the sofa?'[51] Mrs Charles Cage is 'at Highbury all day, & can't help feeling [she has] just got into a new set of acquaintance',[52] while A. I. Millbanke finds *Pride and Prejudice* 'the most probable fiction [she has] ever read.'[53] The comments emphasize that to the great majority of Austen's contemporary readers the levels of society that she depicts were those to which the readers themselves belonged, and that the pleasure in reading her works was one of recognition, rather than of being introduced to something unfamiliar.

However, especially as regards characters, not all readers approve of Austen's realism. Some commentators regard it as rendering the novel trivial, because realism prevents the novel from dealing with 'grand movements and striking characters'.[54] A correspondent of Lady Charlotte Bury is ambivalent about this new kind of heroine:

> Formerly, in my time, a heroine was merely a piece of beautiful matter, with long fair hair and soft blue eyes, who was buffeted up and down the world like a shuttle cock, and visited with all sorts of possible and impossible miseries. Now they are black-haired, sensible women, who do plain work, pay morning visits, and make presents of legs of pork; – vide "Emma", which, notwithstanding, I do think a very capital performance.[55]

A realistic novel is thus seen as lacking something one would normally expect in a novel, while at the same time dealing with a type of heroine that this commentator is not quite comfortable with and recognizes as something new. Less ambiguously, Lady Frances Shelley writes to Walter Scott in 1819:

> A novel, like poetry, should have for its hero a person superior to the common herd of men – one who evinces a higher tone of feeling. [This] ... objection may be made to all Jane Austen's novels .... Surely works of imagination should raise us above our every-day feelings.[56]

She takes for granted that novels are 'works of imagination' because they are fiction, and they should deal with ideal characters and fictional events, as well as emotions that conventional romances would endeavour to evoke.

Several commentators regard a work of realism in general as almost opposed to a work that can interest. Wordsworth admits that

> her novels [are] an admirable copy of life, [but] he could not be interested in productions of that kind; unless the truth of nature were presented to him clarified ... by the pervading light of the imagination, it had scarce any attractions in his eyes.[57]

Mrs Guiton finds *Emma* 'too natural to be interesting',[58] and Lady Jane Davy does not like *Pride and Prejudice* very much as

> want of interest is the fault I can least excuse in works of mere amusement, and however natural the picture of vulgar minds and manners is there given, it is unrelieved by the agreeable contrast of more dignified and refined characters occasionally captivating attention.[59]

These commentators regard imagination as giving a work dignity that it cannot reach through the imitation of everyday life alone. The term has the connotations of creativity as well as of romance and the unknown, so that commentators' use of the word is similar to reviewers'. The statements also reveal, however, that Austen's novels are mainly read for entertainment.

Some commentators do not distinguish between the realistic depiction of 'vulgar' characters and bad, 'vulgar' depiction itself. Hannah Mackenzie likes *Pride and Prejudice* 'excessively only ... the heroine's a little vulgar'.[60] Similarly, Henry Crabb Robinson notes in his diary about *Emma* that 'we hear rather too much about fools: the kind-hearted but weak father, the silly chattering Miss Bates, who gabbles in the style of polite conversation and the vulgar impertinence of the Eltons'.[61] These comments link in with reviews of Austen's early novels that see characters in genteel life as a point of praise and vulgar or low characters as something to be criticized. A Mrs Pole remarks that

> there is a particular satisfaction in reading all Miss A-s works – they are so evidently written by a Gentlewoman – most Novellists [*sic*] fail & betray themselves in attempting to describe familiar scenes in high Life, some little vulgarism escapes & shews that they are not experimentally acquainted with what they describe, but here it is quite different. Everything is natural, & the situations & incidents are told in a manner which clearly evinces the Writer to *belong* to the Society whose Manners she so ably delineates.[62]

The comment shows realism to be defined as realistic imitation. Also, like reviewers, commentators see gentility of characters as reflecting positively on the work and its author.

Crabb Robinson also finds that realism limits the novel's capacity for beauty, while at the same time he praises 'the perfect truth of the painting' as *Pride and Prejudice*'s chief merit. 'The characters, tho' not ideal, ... [are] charming: The women especially are drawn after the life.... The heroines ... are as natural as beauties can be and as beautiful as any successful portrait can be.'[63] He contends that heroines can only be ideal or realistic, and is uncertain as to which of the two he wants them to be. His ambiguity is similar to reviewers' contradictory remarks in articles on *Northanger Abbey* and *Persuasion*, where they praise Austen's realism while at the same time, under the influence of Scott's novels, lamenting her lack of imagination.

Commentators as well as reviewers regard realism as the predominant quality of Austen's works and as what renders hers different from other novels. However, they fail to differentiate the two kinds of realism that they bring up: the conventional criterion of truth to nature and consistent representation of characters and events, and the aspect commentators perceive as new in Austen's novels, a concern with ordinary, everyday people and events. The extent to which individual readers are prepared to move beyond their conventional expectations and embrace what some perceive as a new kind of novel varies. Commentators are less unanimous than reviewers in praising Austen's realism and more often desire romance instead of realism. Reviewers' request for romance is ambiguous because it is combined with praise for Austen's realism. For both reviewers and commentators, Scott's novels have become the ideal because they combine realism with romance. Yet commentators and reviewers agree with Walter Scott's journal entry of 1826 that 'that young lady had a talent for describing the involvements and feelings and characters of ordinary life which is to me the most wonderful I ever met with'.[64]

As in comments on Austen's novels, Scott's realistic depiction of characters and events is commended and influences readers' verdicts on the works. As in reviews, the characters that feature most in the comments are the Scottish lower-class ones. Commentators are dissatisfied with Scott's heroes. Maria Edgeworth writes that 'the Admiral does not like [*Waverley*]; the hero, he says, is such a shuffling fellow.'[65] Similarly, Lady Anne Romilly writes about *Waverley* in 1814 that she does 'not like the hero',[66] and one year later again makes that point: 'as anything Walter Scott writes one never can feel great interest for the lover, which one certainly ought to'.[67] While raising the same point that reviewers make, she is more critical than they are in complaining that the hero is uninteresting. For her, amusement is the main criterion by which she judges individual characters and the novel as a whole, just as it was for commentators on Austen's novels. In both Edgeworth's and Romilly's comments, want of interest in the hero leads to a more negative estimation of the novel as a whole than the reviewers give.

Like reviewers, commentators are interested in what are to them the more unusual and new characters. Wordsworth asserts that 'infinitely the best part of "Waverley" is the pictures of the Highland manners at MacIvor's castle, and the delineation of his character',[68] and that 'the characters [in *Guy Mannering*], with the exception of Meg Merrilies, excite little interest'.[69] Lord Broughton says he and Lord Byron are 'struck with the soliloquy of the fisherman to his boat, in which his son had been drowned',[70] a scene that reviewers, too, are taken with and cite in their articles. As in reviews, lower-class characters' range of emotion is praised in the comments.

Contrary to the requests for gentility of characters in reviews and comments of Austen's early novels, commentators praise the wide social scope of Scott's works. Maria Edgeworth commends

> the various gradations of Scotch feudal character, from the high-born chieftain and the military baron, to the noble-minded lieutenant Evan-Dhu, the robber Bean Lean, and the savage Callum Beg. The *Pre-* the Chevalier is beautifully drawn.[71]

Also, neither reviewers nor commentators take exception to a working-class heroine. Benjamin Robert Haydon writes to Scott about Mrs Siddons' opinion that 'making Jeannie Deans interesting without personal beauty or youth was an instance of powers unexampled'[72] – not mentioning Jeanie's class origin. The reader's surprise at finding herself interested in an ordinary character underlines the expectations with which a fictional heroine in a novel was usually met. While with other novelists a lower-class character, particularly a heroine, would have been despised as vulgar and ungenteel, the praise given to Scott's characters emphasizes his extraordinary position as a novelist. Joanna Baillie writes to Anne Elliot in 1818 that 'Jeany Deans is allowed by every body to be the perfection of female virtue. It is indeed a character of great simplicity & strong rectitude & not over-strained in any of its virtues',[73] again not raising the issue of Jeanie's class. Like reviewers therefore, commentators not only accept a working-class heroine but are interested in her for qualities other than her class origin, so that the 'perfection of female virtue' is an example to all female readers, regardless of class. The condemnation of vulgarity in comments on Austen's novels renders it the more remarkable that readers approve of both Scott's lower-class characters and of his upper-class characters who behave in a vulgar way. With Austen's novels, the realization that a truly realistic novel cannot just deal with genteel characters is only partly there and certainly does not go beyond class boundaries, and an acceptance of a working-class heroine seems very far away – yet Jeanie Deans is highly praised when Scott introduces her. This change in readers' attitudes emphasizes Scott's impact on his contemporary readers.

Commentators testify to the same interest in what is furthest removed from their own everyday experience that reviewers show. Like reviewers, they accept belief in the supernatural as realistic in characters removed from readers' own, rational, spheres. Maria Edgeworth writes on finishing *Waverley* that she has to 'return to the *flat realities* of life',[74] which emphasizes her enjoyment of the romance parts of the novel. She recommends Fergus's heroism that approaches the sublime, and finds that the appearance of the Bodach Glass is not only 'perfectly natural' and 'a weakness quite consistent with the strength of the character', but so well related that 'the gray [sic] spirit ... thrills *us* with horror. *Us!* What effect must it have on those under the superstitions of the Highlands?'.[75] Her comments underline the difference she perceives between her society and that of the Highlands of Scotland, and, as in reviews, there is no indication of her believing this difference no longer to exist.

Commentators are less interested in the historical aspects of the novels than are reviewers. That entertainment is their main criterion again becomes evident: they comment on what fascinates them, not on what might instruct them, and they rarely mention history. Instead they bring up Scottishness repeatedly, both of location and especially of character. Crabb Robinson in his diary for 1817 comments on both Scottishness and history: 'Began *Old Mortality*, a delightful Scotch *Tale of My Landlord* by the author of *Waverley*. This is a capital historical picture of the state of religious parties at the latter end of the reign of Charles II.'[76] The novel is primarily Scottish and also historical. This order of what interests becomes more obvious in a later entry of 1821: *Old Mortality* 'is the first of the Scotch romances which I have begun to read a second time'.[77] It is chiefly the novels' Scottishness that renders them special. Other instances where history is commented on are also connected to Scottishness. Elizabeth Hamilton writes in 1814 that *Waverley* 'is quite Scotch, and gives such a picture of a state of society and manners now obsolete, as appears to me invaluable'.[78] She reveals a sense of *Waverley* preserving a memory of something that would otherwise get lost. Helen Darcy Stewart sees the society depicted in *Guy Mannering* as not yet vanished, commenting that the Scotch is pure and perfect. ... may I venture to mention, that what kills salmon, vol 2d p. 65, is not a *waster*, but a *leister*; that it is not *Staneshie*bank fair, vol 2d p. 17, but *Stagsshei*bank; vol 2d p. 52, it is a *whin* of the billies, when it should be a *wheen*, vol 2d p. 186, for '*dooms likely*', it ought to be '*doons likely*'; these are indeed trifling errors. Scotland is truly indebted for the preservation of its language and manners to such a portrait painter.[79]

She believes the language and manners of Scotland are in danger of being forgotten, but her familiarity with both, and her correcting the Scotch suggests it to be still existing rather than being history, so that it is the present that is preserved rather than the memory of the past. Byron asserts that *Waverley* is 'all easy to me – because I have been in Scotland so much – (though then young enough too) and feel at home with the people lowland & Gael'.[80] This statement shows that Byron assumes a reader's potential difficulties with *Waverley* lie in the reader's unfamiliarity with the novel's Scottishness, rather than with its historicity. One can travel there and learn to 'feel at home' with Scottish speech still, not just in the past. These comments confirm the contemporary belief in the absolute truth of Scott's realistic depiction of Scottish characters, which is further substantiated by one of the few comments from a member of the working classes: an anonymous Scottish shepherd writes to Scott in 1820 that he is 'astonished, perfectly astonished, how ye have acquired the Scottish dialect and phraseology so exactly'.[81] While those reviewers that mention the use of Scottish dialect condemn it as 'unintelligible to four-fifths of the reading population of the country',[82] commentators are positive about it as enhancing the realism of the Scottish scenes.

In retrospect, too, the novels' Scottishness is what contemporary readers remember as having found most striking. Henry Cockburn in *Memorials of his time* remembers how

> in 1814 Scott published Waverley – the first of those admirable and original prose compositions which have nearly obliterated the recollection of his poetry. Except the first opening of the Edinburgh Review, no work that has appeared in my time made such an instant and universal impression. The unexpected newness of the thing, the profusion of original characters, the Scotch language, Scotch men and women, the simplicity of the writing, and the graphic force of the descriptions, all struck us with an electric shock of delight.[83]

Not only does Cockburn compare *Waverley* to *The Edinburgh Review* in its impact and therefore takes the novel out of its genre, he also carefully avoids the term 'novel' and substitutes it with 'prose composition', as well as emphasizing that these were 'original prose compositions', which would already have distinguished it from the majority of novels. The novel's newness is its main asset, and that consists of its Scottishness – language, characters, description – with history not being mentioned.

Both English and Scottish commentators thus focus on Scottishness and thereby render the historical aspects less important. Some make the Scottishness of Scott's novels one of their own day, as reviewers do. The non-Scottish commentators focus on the differences between their own and the depicted society, thereby closing the gap of history and making the differences primarily geographical ones. For them, the novels are appealing because they show unfamiliar romantic scenes and societies that are nevertheless real. Scottish commentators, too, do not focus on historicity, but on recognizing manners and speech, thus again making the societies Scott depicts still exist. For them, Scott's realism is similar to Austen's because it is one of recognition. What captures all commentators is thus not historical events but the people, their manners and speeches. Even for the Scottish commentators, however, the highland scenes would have borne the same romantic impact that it had for English readers, so that for them, Scott combines the unfamiliar with the recognizable.

In contrast to Austen's works then, Scott's novels offer romance and the unfamiliar – realistically depicted. His depiction of what is unknown subject matter adds to the novels' newness, whereas Austen's domestic realism, though in itself perceived as new, has the opposite effect of making her subject matter familiar to contemporary readers. Although the shepherd's comment indicates that Scott's readership extended beyond the upper and middle classes, this was exceptional and the great majority of commentators belonged to the upper classes. They would therefore feel at home in the circles Austen describes. Scott's novels include characters and scenes unfamiliar to all readers because they are more varied, as well as some that certain readers would recognize. Austen thus offers recognition only, Scott romantic newness to everyone, in combination with realism or recognition. As in reviews, it is the novels' contents that determines judgements, not their technical aestheticism. The emphasis on the factual basis of Scott's novels that characterizes reviews of Scott's novels is only borne out in the comments as regards the realistic depiction of Scottish manners and speech, not as regards historical events. Tippkötter's assertion that Scott was popular primarily as a historical entertainer is thus not confirmed in comments on Scott's early novels.

Instruction and amusement

As regards the criteria of instruction and amusement, differences emerge between commentators and reviewers. The general stereotype was that novels would provide amusement only, and it was mainly this lack of useful instruction that gave the genre such a low status. For reviewers, moral instruction was therefore the most important criterion for the assessment of a novel. Ann Jones in her *Ideas and Innovations* stresses that 'a good moral tone was often allowed to excuse any number of artistic flaws, while no amount of artistry could justify a novel without a moral purpose'.[84]

In contrast to reviewers' focus on morality, commentators, who are usually more open and less morally strict in their utterances, admit to liking novels because they provide 'mere amusement'. With few exceptions, they are not concerned with the novels' morality. Russell Mitford lauds Austen precisely because she 'preaches no sermons',[85] while the Earl of Dudley approves of Austen 'never plagu[ing] you with any chemistry, mechanics, or political economy'.[86] However, this also limits the novels' significance. Commentators like Crabb Robinson, though praising Austen's works highly, do so not within the novel-genre as a whole, but within a specifically female part of that, regarding *Pride and Prejudice* as 'one of the most excellent of the works of our female novelists'.[87] Seeing the novels as devoid of any instruction means that these readers do not give the novels the same status that some reviewers assign to them. Reviewers' emphasis on moral instruction, the only kind of instruction they think possible in female-authored novels, bestows importance beyond mere amusement on Austen's works. By contrast, comments are to a greater extent than reviews characterized by expressions such as 'finely written',[88] 'much entertained',[89] 'charming',[90] 'delightful';[91] *Pride and Prejudice* is regarded by Gifford as 'really a very pretty thing',[92] and by Richard Brinsley Sheridan as 'one of the cleverest things he ever read'[93] – clever, but not intellectually challenging. Russell Mitford recommends Elford to 'go for amusement to Miss Edgworth and Miss Austen'. This comment is followed by 'how delightful is her "Emma"! the best, I think, of all her charming works'[94] and reveals the category in which Austen's novels are placed. The majority of commentators are positive about her novels, but it is praise along these lines, marked by a sense of no real possibility of greatness in this genre. Seen in this context, even comments such as Mr Cooke's calling *Mansfield Park* 'the most sensible novel he had ever read'[95] underline the generally low status of the genre as sense is not something he would expect in a novel. Anne Romilly finds that *Mansfield Park* is justly admired, as

> all novels must be that are true to life as this is . . . . It has not, however, that elevation of virtue, something beyond nature, that gives the greatest charm to a novel, but still it is real natural every day life, and will amuse an idle hour in spite of its faults.[96]

Austen's domestic and therefore feminine realism is also what limits her in commentators' eyes. Even in 1833, by which time the novel was no longer a female-dominated genre, the editor of the Bentley 'Standard Novels' edition of *Sense and Sensibility* writes in his preface:

> Miss Austen is the founder of a school of novelists; and her followers are not confined to her own sex, but comprise in their number some male writers of considerable merit.[97]

He emphasizes that men have not found it degrading to use Austen's mode of writing, thus attempting to elevate her by taking her out of the female canon, so that while the status of the novel rose during the Romantic period, writing of women was throughout assumed to be necessarily of lower quality than that of men. Ina Ferris's assertion that the 'male canon ... coincides with the "highest" form of novel'[98] therefore holds, but, as reviews and comments of Scott's novels show, only once Scott's works are definitely placed in the novel-genre, which was not the case by the end of the 1810s.

As in reviews, it is therefore Austen's gender that is perceived as informing and limiting her subject matter. Her novels are charming, but they are not great. These comments testify to readers' view of the novel-genre as well as to Austen's status within it, and while her prestige is lower in comments than in reviews, her popularity is equal in both.

In contrast to commentators, reviewers insist on instruction as a legitimization for a novel. For both commentators and reviewers, however, a work's significance is bound up with its instruction and morality. Austen herself finds *Pride and Prejudice* 'rather too light & bright & sparkling'.[99] The few comments there are on morality confirm the definition of morality as essentially domestic, and therefore specifically related to female behaviour and female writing. Romilly commends *Mansfield Park* as having 'a good strong vein of principle running thro' the whole',[100] so that for commentators, too, morality is defined as filial obedience and feminine propriety, and moral instruction in a novel comprises the presentation of young women as modest and obedient to their parents, chaste before marriage and faithful after it, the obligation of parents to instil these virtues, and showing that any characters who fail these standards suffer for it.

The manliness of author and content in Scott's novels' means neither reviewers nor commentators insist on moral instruction in them. Because public morality was not considered as such, reviewers see no moral instruction in *Waverley* and therefore focus on its historical instructiveness. Commentators judge the novels by their entertainment value: Sydney Smith writes that *The Heart of Mid-Lothian* is "excellent, quite as good as any of his novels .... It made me laugh, and cry fifty times, and I read it with the liveliest interest".[101] It is primarily the enjoyment of having romance realistically depicted and being introduced to a new world that renders the novels popular, rather than the wish to be instructed.

The discrepancy between reviewers' focus on instruction and readers' focus on amusement confirms the contemporary stereotype of novels being read primarily for entertainment rather than for instruction. However, in contrast to the contemporary stereotype of a typical novel-reader, comments reveal that both men and women read novels, and find similar aspects appealing. While reviewers may publicly set themselves up as selfless social benefactors who select suitable novels, thereby running 'the risk of being poisoned [them]selves, to save [the readers] from the risk of being so',[102] readers privately emphasize a novel's ability to interest and entertain above its inclusion of a moral or historical lesson. The immense success of Scott's novels therefore gives some idea of what amusement comprised for most nineteenth-century readers.

One of the factors usually seen as contributing to a novel's entertainment is its story line. Commentators and reviewers are similar in their remarks on the thin story line of Austen's novels. Susan Ferrier finds *Emma*

> excellent; there is no story whatever, and the heroine is no better than other people; but the characters are all so true to life, and the style so piquant that it does not require the adventitious aids of mystery and adventure,[103]

thus emphasizing that Austen's novels have qualities other than the conventional ones. However, lack of story also leads to negative comments, such as Austen's friend Miss Bigg's objecting to *Emma* because of 'sameness of the subject (Match-making) all through'.[104] On the whole, commentators as well as reviewers do not seem to mind the novels' lack of a gripping story line but find compensation in other aspects, which shows willingness to receive a different kind of novel positively. As with comments on Austen's novels, the story in Scott's works is often criticized, but usually in the context of general praise for the respective work. Fanny Burney comments in her notebook that *Old Mortality* 'has more sterling merit ... than any modern one of its species that has fallen in my way, yet its story is conducted without interest'.[105] As with Austen, positive comments specifically about the story are rare, though Baillie asserts that 'the story of Guy Mannering is more uniformly animated and entertaining [than that of *The Antiquary*]'.[106] For neither author is story perceived as the quality that entertains.

Genre and reputation

Austen's status can also be measured by the authors she is compared to in comments – specifically Scott, as the most prestigious and popular contemporary novelist. Most comments that draw a comparison between Austen and Scott prefer her novels to his or see them on an equal level, which indicates that comparisons the other way round, of readers preferring Scott over Austen, were taken for granted and did not have to be mentioned. Occasionally readers do spell out their preference of Scott, such as Henry Crabb Robinson who indicated in a letter of 1819 to Mrs Pattison praising *Pride and Prejudice* before writing 'since my return I have been reading, however, a still better book that you have probably already read – *The Heart of Midlothian*'.[107] However, that some readers at least see Austen and Scott on the same level testifies to an unusually high prestige for Austen while at the same time confirming Scott's overwhelming position. Sarah Harriet Burney writes in 1816 about *Emma* that she has 'read no story book with such glee, since the days of

"Waverley" and "Mannering", and, by the same Author as "Emma", my prime favourite of all modern Novels "Pride & Prejudice"'.[108] Lady Abercorn writes to Murray in 1817 that 'Lord Abercorn thinks [Miss Austen's novels] next to W. Scott's (if they are by W. Scott); it is a great pity that we shall have no more of hers.'[109] Jane Austen's brother Henry's friend Henry Sandford reports that while he sat in a coach with Robert Southey, Sandford quoted from one of Austen's novels, upon which Southey immediately exclaimed

> 'that's in Miss Austen's Novels'. 'What' said I to Southey, 'Do you know Miss Austen's works?' 'Do I know them' replied S-. 'Sir, It would take me to the top of that hill before I could tell you whether I had rather be Author of Miss Austen's novels, or Walter Scott's.'[110]

Southey is still full of praise in a letter of 1830. Austen's novels are 'more true to Nature, and have (for my sympathies) passages of finer feeling than any others of this age',[111] so that he again places hers above Scott's. A letter from another Austen brother, Charles James, to his sister relates an incident concerning Henry Stephen Fox:

> Books became the subject of conversation. I praised Waverly [sic] highly; when a young man present, observed that nothing had come out for years, to be compared with Pride & Prejudice, Sense & Sensibility &c. As I am sure you must be anxious to know the name of a person of so much taste, I should tell you it is Fox, a nephew of the late Charles James Fox [the politician].[112]

Jane Austen's mother Cassandra writes to her grand-daughter Anna Lefroy in 1814 that *Waverley* 'has afforded me more entertainment than any modern production (Aunt Janes excepted) of the novel kind that I have read for a great while'.[113] While she is of course not an impartial judge of her daughter's works, her comment again indicates that entertainment was the main criterion by which readers judged fiction.

Scott's novels are judged in a class of their own. They are compared to one another as a measure of quality, and only occasionally to the works of Fielding, Smollett, and Sterne – and very rarely to contemporary novels. Lady Louisa Stuart places the first *Tales of My Landlord* 'above Guy and Monkbarns, but *Waverley* being my first love, [I] cannot give him up'[114]. Byron asserts that '"The Antiquary" is not the best of the three [W, GMann, Ant] – but much above all these last twenty years – saving it's [sic] elder brothers',[115] William Godwin regards *Guy Mannering* as 'on the whole inferior to Waverley; but [he has] since read the Antiquary, which [he judges] superior to both'.[116] Helen Darcy Stewart is explicit: 'I cannot say I prefer [*The Antiquary*] to its elder brothers; but Mr. Scott can only be compared to himself.'[117] While opinions about which is the best Waverley novel thus vary, the general consensus is that no other novel can compete with them and that, therefore, any comparison to a work other than by the author of *Waverley* is irrelevant.

There is a distinction between those commentators who see Scott outside the genre, like Cockburn, and those like Byron and Broughton, who see his novels as 'better than any other of our times',[118] and thus at the top of, but still within, the novel-genre. Morritt finds that *Waverley* 'deserves a place among our standard works, far better than its modest appearance and anonymous title-page give it as a novel in these days of prolific story-telling',[119] showing the contemporary insecurity about *Waverley*'s generic category. Commentators emphasize the difference between Scott's works and ordinary fictional productions. While, according to Broughton, novels usually deal with love, Morritt states that *The Antiquary* is a 'very good novel' because there 'is no love in it, and absurd womankind do not play too distinguished a part'.[120] He thus emphasizes the masculinity of the novel, and the fact that it only deals peripherally with love implies that it focuses on more sensible, male topics, going against the conventional sentimental feminine novel that has romance in the form of a romantic love-story at its heart. Scott's romance is of a different kind, one that fascinates because it takes readers away from what they are familiar with, and yet a romance that appeals to the imagination without dealing with the far-fetched and improbable. Byron's and Helen Darcy Stewart's use of 'brothers' for 'novels' might also be motivated by the connotations of a male author. Morritt legitimizes his wish to see *Waverley* outside the novel-genre by insisting that Scott's 'manner of narrating is so different from the slipshod sauntering verbiage of common novels, and from the stiff, precise and prim sententiousness of some of our female novelists'.[121] Instead, as Ferris points out, *Waverley* is seen as possessing 'the literary and gentlemanly quality of "style"'.[122] Ferris sees this as expanding the novel-genre beyond what it had meant hitherto, and legitimizing it as a gentlemanly and literary activity. While this was the effect in the long run, the immediate response of readers such as Cockburn and Morritt appears to have been an attempt to take *Waverley* out of the genre precisely because they saw it as going beyond what 'novel' meant to them. It took more than the first of the Waverley novels to change the perception of the genre's possibilities and its prestige.

* * *

Brian Southam's assertion that up to 1870, she 'remained a critic's novelist – highly spoken of and little read'[123] is not true for the early nineteenth century. Contemporary readers of Austen's and Scott's novels are similar in their judgements of the two authors. While the great majority of commentators belong to the same social classes and some similarity of opinion could therefore be expected, their unanimity as regards both authors emphasizes that readers judge according to their cultural context, as part of their interpretive community. Comments show that both men and women read novels, and that verdicts of male and female readers do not differ from one another. Their cultural and social surroundings thus appear to determine their readings more than their individuality.

Similarities between readers become apparent both in the aspects they raise and in those they do not mention. Whereas twenty-first-century readers enjoy Austen's satire as one of her main assets, contemporaries seem unaware of it, and similarly, early nineteenth-century readers of Scott do not discuss politics, revolution or the significance of the past for an understanding of the present.

Reviewers and commentators generally raise similar aspects of the novels. Again, they belong to the same social class and the same cultural surroundings, but the purposes of the discussions are different because one is a public communication and the other a private one. Some differences therefore are discernible between reviewers and commentators as regards the hierarchy of criteria applied to novels. While reviewers emphasize morality and instruction as a novel's most important asset to legitimize their discussion of a novel, commentators focus on entertainment, generally without attempting to legitimize their reading. Scott's statement in his review of *Emma* that novel-reading is one of those 'vices in civilized society so common that they are hardly acknowledged as stains upon the moral character, the propensity to which is nevertheless carefully concealed'[124] thus appears to hold: in a diary entry or letter to a friend, no justification is necessary, and in many cases it is assumed that the correspondent will have read the novel in question too.

Commentators are not interested in the potential moral instruction of Austen's novels. While reviewers see her novels as conveying moral instruction, which gives them significance and raises them above other novels, commentators prefer her to other authors on the basis of the amusement her novels offer. With Scott, reviewers stress the instruction of both history and Scottishness, whereas commentators do not pay attention to history, and they focus on Scottishness because they find it fascinating, not because it might have instructive value. Reviewers' focus on instruction emphasizes that the need to legitimize the discussion of a novel is greater in reviews than in comments. With Austen, reviewers' need to justify their articles is greater than with Scott because Austen is within the novel-genre, so that in reviews of her novels the issue of instruction is more prevalent than in articles on Scott's novels. As regards instruction then, the difference between commentators and reviewers of her novels is greater than that between commentators and reviewers of Scott's novels, emphasizing that he is outside any conventional criteria. With Scott too though, reviewers are more concerned than commentators to show the novels' seriousness.

Not only are commentators similar to one another in applying entertainment as the main criterion, they are also entertained by the same qualities in fiction. In Austen's novels, the pleasure is one of recognition, and thus of character description, dialogue and realism, and in Scott's, it is one of excitement and newness that appeals to the imagination and is yet a truthful depiction, and thus again one of character description, dialogue and realism – combined with wide social and geographical scope.

Commentators do not mention reviewers' verdicts, which makes something of a mockery of reviewers' self-assigned roles as the public's moral guardians. However, commentators refer to the popularity of an author with the general reading public. This focus gives significance to the judgement of the reading public at large, and emphasizes that especially in the case of Scott, reviewers were part of a trend and followed the public's verdict, rather than the public following their judgements. The immense popularity of Scott's novels thus changes the relationship between readers and reviewers as well as leading to a reversal in contemporary assumptions about the connection between popularity and quality.

The general unanimity of response shows that Scott's novels became so immensely popular because they met the needs of the time. They gave readers what they longed for: romance that was yet realistic, about people belonging to the same kingdom yet far enough removed to make them interesting and new rather than threatening, and masculinity of author and content that made this wide scope of subject matter possible. The focus of both reviewers and commentators is on content, so that while Austen's new kind of domestic realism is perceived as rendering her novels high quality, it cannot convey the same level of newness and therefore excitement that Scott's novels evoke. Her femininity combined with her limited social and geographical scope restricts the excitement the novels can give, though it also makes them charming and amusing. For reviewers, her feminine subject matter prevents intellectual utility; for commentators, it prevents larger scope and therefore greater entertainment. While readers' gender thus did not influence reading, authors' gender did. The comparison of Austen's and Scott's contemporary reputations shows that what readers wanted was realistic romance and newness of content.

The study therefore confirms the theoretical perception of Jauss and Iser that was taken as the approach for the project: reception depends on the interaction between a text and its readers at a given time in a given cultural community. It is possible to identify the historical horizons of expectations against which the reading encounter with the text occurred so as to produce reception.

Part 2

The Victorian Response

Chapter 4

Editions, 1832–1912

This part considers the availability of the two authors' novels in Victorian times, first in terms of the books and editions produced for sale, and then in terms of their accessibility to multiple readerships through lending institutions.

A key indicator of readership is numbers of copies sold, although there are problems about turning production figures into readership figures, since books were shared privately as well as through libraries. Plenty of information drawn from archival records is available in print for the first half of the nineteenth century. There are also scattered indications for the later decades, although nothing consolidated for the period when Austen and Scott were entirely in the public domain and sold competitively by various publishers simultaneously. Books can be sold over many years after they are printed, there was a big second-hand market, and we do not have quantitative information on the large numbers of copies printed abroad, particularly by the Paris offshore pirate Galignani, that reached readers in Britain in considerable numbers.

What is beyond question is that, in terms of numbers of copies, Scott outsold Austen by a wide margin throughout the period. However, for the purposes of tracing changing perceptions, production data are hard to interpret. For investigating comparative trends, magnitudes are less important than relativities. I have therefore made the main unit of measurement the 'edition', not so much in the bibliographical sense as a description of the physical book, but as a publishing term for issuing or reissuing a title, irrespective of method of manufacture. 'Edition' therefore here means a formal relaunch of an author's work. The choice of edition in this sense, for the purposes of the study, gives a precise measure of how often an author was deliberately relaunched, when, and of the time gaps. It gives a potential measure of changing producer perceptions at any level of production.

In the early nineteenth century, printing was still very largely a handcraft. An edition and an impression were therefore usually the same thing, since to keep the type standing for possible later reprinting was in most cases impracticable. Occasionally, with popular works, several impressions might be printed off the same type, such as the first and second impressions of the eighth edition of *Waverley*.[1] In contrast to impressions, which are an exact reprint of the original edition, issues differ in some respects from this edition, but are still from substantially the same setting of type, so that they, too, only existed for popular works in this era of movable type.

As the century progressed, printing became more mechanized. Printing presses developed into being powered by steam, and stereotype was invented. Casting a duplicate plate of the original page, which could then be kept and reused in the future, meant avoiding having to reset the type for a reprint. Stereotype therefore greatly facilitated reprinting and considerably reduced its cost, but made the task of a bibliographer more difficult: the same setting of the text could now be used in volumes which might otherwise look very different through added illustrations, different title pages or bindings. Stereotype also allowed one setting of type to be repeatedly used over several years. A. & C. Black's 1877 edition of the Waverley novels in four volumes is textually the same as their 1867 Copyright Edition: the only difference between the two is the order of the preliminary pages containing portrait, title page, contents, Scott's 1829 advertisement and his dedication of the novels to the King; yet the two issues are marketed as two editions.[2] The difference of ten years between original edition and reissue was made possible by stereotype.

To compile lists of all formal relaunches of Austen's and Scott's novels in Britain between 1811 and 1912, I drew on various bibliographies, library catalogues and commercial catalogues. Since Scott's works in particular confirm the inverse relationship between cheapness and survivability, commercial catalogues proved a helpful addition. Sources primarily used to draw up the lists of editions were the catalogues of the British Library and the National Library of Scotland, as well as Gilson's bibliography of Austen that takes her publication history up to the late twentieth century, Todd and Bowden's bibliography of Scott editions published in his lifetime, and Cadell's 1847 catalogue of editions of Scott's works.[3] Until 1847, the data is therefore complete for both authors, but for the later period, when the novels were coming out of copyright, the information is more scattered and harder to interpret, so that I inspected a large proportion of the 176 single and 75 collected editions personally. The lists show comparative trends, since the bibliographical difficulties that exist apply throughout the century and for both authors.

The only kinds of editions that have been differentiated throughout the century are collected and single editions. I have defined as collected editions any complete set of novels of an author published under the same publishing agreement and in the same format, even in cases where I know that the novels were also available individually, such as the 1833 and 1870 Bentley editions of Austen's novels and all editions of Scott's novels, at least up to 1847.

For an author to be accorded a collected edition is *ipso facto* a sign of canonical status. Very few authors of the Romantic era were accorded that honour at least until the twentieth century. This was not just a function of reputation. When copyright ownership was spread it was hard for British publishers to gather all the copyrights. (This was one reason why editions by offshore pirates like Galignani were often better than the British editions.) In terms of being accorded a collected edition early, Scott was fortunate in that the publishers had bought all the copyrights. In the case of Austen, copyright was more scattered: until 1832, the copyright to *Sense and Sensibility, Mansfield Park, Emma* and *Northanger Abbey and Persuasion* belonged to Jane Austen, and to Henry and Cassandra after her death, while that of *Pride and Prejudice* belonged to her first publisher Thomas Egerton. As the copyright was owned by more than one person, there could not be a collected edition of her works, especially after Austen's change of publisher from Egerton to Murray. Richard Bentley bought the copyrights belonging to Henry and Cassandra Austen in 1832, and that for *Pride and Prejudice* from Egerton's executors in 1833 and promptly brought out a collected edition in the same year.

When Scott's and Austen's novels were first published, the intellectual property regime conferred only a relatively short period of copyright (28 years until 1808, with changes in 1814 to make it 28 years or the lifespan of the author, whichever was the longest). An 1842 Act introduced a long copyright (42 years or the life of the author plus 7 years). The effect was that the times at which Austen's and Scott's novels entered the public domain, and therefore the extent to which they could be competitively reprinted, and the price of access, depended upon the vagaries of the copyright regime and the date of death of the authors. For *Sense and Sensibility, Pride and Prejudice* and *Mansfield Park* the copyright lasted for 28 years, according to the 1814 Act. They had been published in 1811, 1813 and 1814 respectively, the copyright therefore expiring in 1839, 1841 and 1842. *Emma* and *Northanger Abbey and Persuasion* had been published in 1815 and 1818 respectively. They were therefore due to go out of copyright in 1843 and 1846, which was prevented by the 1842 Act, that extended the copyright of *Emma* until 1857 and that of *Northanger Abbey and Persuasion* until 1860.

Relating publishers' relaunches of Austen's and Scott's works indicates comparative developments over time. Figures 4.1 and 4.2 show numbers of editions per decade throughout the nineteenth century.

Both graphs appear at first to indicate that Scott's popularity was immensely high throughout his lifetime and then decreased in the middle of the nineteenth century to rise again just after the centenary of his birth in 1871. For Austen, the graphs together show a low but steady number of publications and an increase towards the end of the century. However, these developments have to be seen in relation to nineteenth-century copyright laws. The 1829–33 Magnum Edition of Scott's novels, on which all subsequent editions until the late twentieth century appear to have been based,[4] went out of copyright from 1871 to 1875. The end of copyright of Austen's novels was more scattered, occurring between 1839 and 1860.[5] Bentley was the copyright holder for all Austen's novels from 1833 onwards. As the individual novels went out of copyright, other publishers brought out single editions, which can be traced in Figure 4.2: in the period of 1843–52, just after the copyright for *Sense and Sensibility, Pride and Prejudice* and *Mansfield Park* has expired, there are eight new editions of an Austen novel, none of them by Bentley. Similarly, for the period of 1853–62, during which the copyright for *Northanger Abbey and Persuasion* expired, the three editions shown in Figure 4.2 were published not by Bentley but by Routledge.

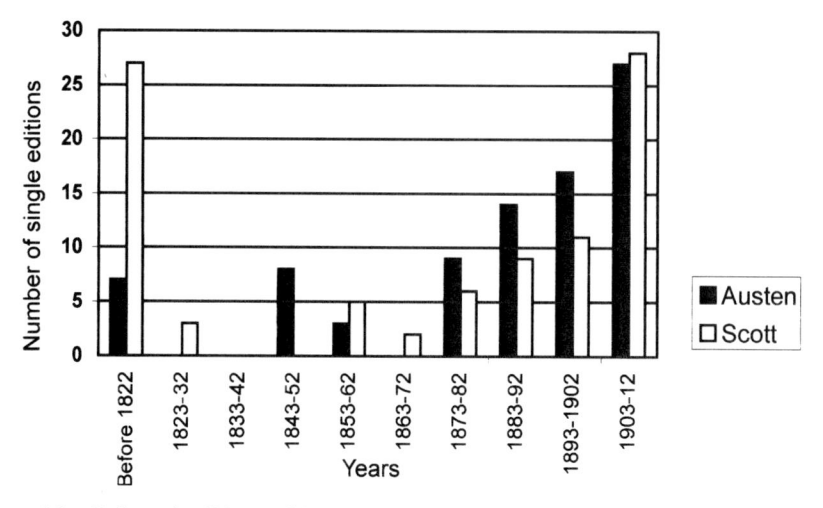

Figure 4.1 Collected editions of Austen's and Scott's novels

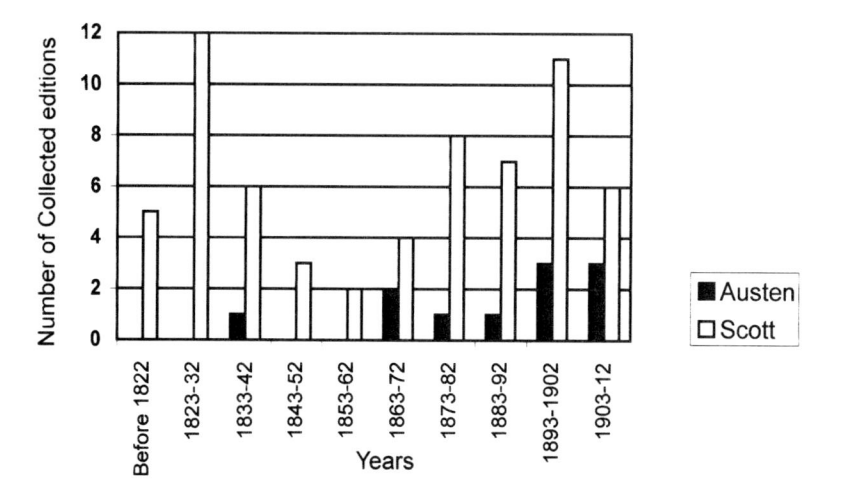

Figure 4.2 Single editions of Austen's and Scott's novels

Figure 4.1 shows collected editions of Austen's and Scott's works. Figure 4.2 shows single editions and includes all six Austen novels and the first seven novels by Scott, from *Waverley* to *The Heart of Mid-Lothian*, to make a comparison between the two authors possible. Abridged editions have been excluded; reissues have been excluded if marked as such in catalogues by publishers.

For collected editions, the date of first year of the edition has been used to determine the decade into which it was placed in the graph. In Figure 4.2, several novels published together were counted as one edition (e.g. *The Black Dwarf* and *The Tale of Old Mortality*, which before 1832 appeared together as the first *Tales of My Landlord*, and after 1832 usually appeared separately. Similarly, *Northanger Abbey* and *Persuasion* have been treated as one entry when published together).

By 1870, the copyright of all Austen's novels had expired, so that Bentley as well as Chapman & Hall bring out a collected edition of her works, which explains the gap for the period of 1863–72 in the single editions graph. It appears as if interest until 1870 was low, though existent, and only increased once Bentley published the *Memoir*, the first full-length biography of Austen, written by her nephew James Edward Austen-Leigh.[6] However, when reissues are taken into account, the two decades preceding 1863–72 show Austen to be more widely read: there are ten reissues of her novels between 1843 and 1952 (as well as the eight new editions shown in Figure 4.2) and five between 1853 and 1962 (as well as three new editions), compared to no reissues between 1863 and 1972.

While studies hitherto have seen the *Memoir* as the turning point in Austen's popularity, creating interest in her works,[7] editions do not point to the *Memoir* leading to any significant increase in popularity. Since two publishers bring out a complete run of Austen's novels (which were also available individually), the *Memoir*'s impact was in the initiation of a move from individual to collected Austen editions, rather than in an immediate increase in numbers of Austen publications. Both collected editions emphasize each individual volume's being part of a series and thereby draw attention to the author. Bentley inserts a half-title reading 'Austen's Novels', with the individual novel title underneath. Chapman & Hall introduce the first volume (*Sense and Sensibility*) on the title page as 'By the Author of ... ' listing all Austen's other novels.[8] The volume also contains Henry Austen's 1818 Biographical Notice with his 1832 addition, which Bentley's 1870 edition does not – assumedly because of the latter's simultaneous publication of the *Memoir*. However, the *Memoir* only renders biographical information given with the text of the novels superfluous if Bentley can presume that readers will be interested enough in the author of the novels to wish to know more about her life and read an entire *Memoir* rather than a short biographical introduction. The *Memoir* therefore reflects rather than initiates interest in the novels. Collected editions accentuate the author through emphasizing her entire work, so that they, as well as the *Memoir*, indicate that interest in the novels has become high enough for readers to want to know about the author.

The evidence of single editions also suggests that the *Memoir* did not cause an instant upsurge of interest in Austen's novels. As Figure 4.2 shows, the decade of 1843–52 sees almost as many new publications as the decade immediately following the publication of the *Memoir*, 1873–82, so that it is only from 1883 onwards that Austen rises higher in popularity than she had ever been before. Editions therefore – like library catalogues – indicate that her popularity develops gradually, rather than being marked by turning points, so that the *Memoir* comes as part of an upward trend.

Respecting Scott's novels, the expiry of copyright is yet more evident in the graphs than that of Austen's works because of the higher numbers of editions involved. The Magnum Edition of Scott's works was published by Robert Cadell, from 1829 to 1833. Under the 1842 Act it remained in copyright until

1871–75. Copyright was held by Cadell until his death in 1849, following which it was purchased by Adam & Charles Black.[9] No single editions were published in the two decades after Scott's death by either Cadell or Black, and they remain scarce until the very end of the century.

Numbers of collected editions are immensely high during Scott's lifetime, partly because there could not be many reissues of a collected edition since new novels kept being added. Few collected editions appear mid-century, though the ones that do comprise up-market as well as cheap ones.[10] The publication events on the expiry of the Magnum copyright indicate that readers demanded Scott novels. Rather than the mid-century dip in editions pointing to a decrease of Scott's popularity, it shows that the market was saturated with reprints of the Black editions: as soon as the copyright expires a variety of editions by several publishers appear. Different kinds of editions hint at publishers expecting readers of various social classes and tastes to be interested in an author's works. These editions therefore indicate which readers were catered for, as well as what innovations new publishers brought in.

Ten editions appear from 1871 to 1880, four by A. & C. Black and six by as many new Scott publishers, so that the former copyright holders still publish more Scott than anyone else. In view of A. & C. Black being at an advantage in comparison to any new Scott publishers because they as the former copyright holders would have had stereotype plates for the novels, the fact that so many new publishers wanting a share in the market emphasizes Scott's popularity.

- 1870–71, Centenary edition, Edinburgh: A. & C. Black (25 vols)
- 1870–79, Popular edition, ed. Revd P. Hately Waddell, Glasgow: D. Wilson & T. & J. Lochhead (25 vols)
- 187?–187?, Waverley Novels, London: John Dicks (32 vols)
- 1873–74, Pocket edition, A. & C. Black (25 vols)
- 1875–76, Waverley Novels, London: Routledge and Sons (25 vols)
- 1876, Waverley Novels, ed. Revd P. Hately Waddell, London and Edinburgh: William P. Nimmo (13 vols)
- 1877, The handy volume Waverley, London: Bradbury, Agnew & Co. (25 vols)
- 1877–79, The illustrated Waverley novels, London and Belfast: Marcus Ward & Co. (25 vols)
- 1877–78, Illustrated edition, A. & C. Black (25 vols)
- 1877, 'Author's edition entire', A. & C. Black (4 vols)

Blacks' Centenary Edition of the Waverley Novels came out in 1870–71, reaching completion in the year other publishers would be allowed to begin publishing the Magnum texts. The timing indicates that the Blacks had expected the upsurge of editions that takes place in the 1870s and therefore testifies to Scott's popularity in the preceding decades. The Centenary purported to be closer to Scott's 1829 intentions than any previous edition: when the Blacks bought the copyright for the Magnum, they also acquired the Interleaved Set of the Waverley Novels in which Scott had made his final corrections and notes on the texts. The Advertisement to the Centenary claims that 'in printing this New Edition of the Waverley Novels, the Publishers have availed themselves of the opportunity thus afforded them of carefully collating it with the valuable interleaved copy in their possession'. In fact, as Claire Lamont points out, the Centenary *Waverley* 'contains only three new notes attributed to Scott, all of them trifling'[11] – Blacks' advertisement yet shows that they market their editions as the ones closest to the author's original. Also, claiming to make changes to the copyright text that had been overlooked is a way of bidding for an extension of the copyright – which, however, was not successful.

The other innovation with which A. & C. Black hoped to trump other publishers was their inclusion of notes by David Laing, whom they introduce as 'one of the few surviving friends of the Author'. This again emphasizes their exclusive access to the author's intentions. They include a dedication: 'To Mary Monica Hope Scott of Abbotsford this Edition of the Novels of her Great-Grandfather Walter Scott is dedicated by the Publishers'. In case 'Abbotsford' is not enough to make readers realize the link to Scott, A. & C. Black clarify the dedicatee's exact relation to the novelist, and again accentuate their own special relation to Scott. The name of the edition itself emphasizes the author, since it draws attention to his birth rather than that of the novels. Furthermore, A. & C. Black include a portrait of the author and subscribe it with a Scott autograph: 'Yours very truly Walter Scott'. This not only stresses the author as the originator of the novels but also establishes a bond between author and reader, so that it is for and to the reader of Blacks' edition that Scott is writing. The Centenary incorporates all material that Scott had added in 1829–33 to the Magnum: his advertisement, his 1829 General Preface, the 1829 introductions to the individual novels, Appendices to the General Preface, the Author's Dedication of the Magnum to the King, a glossary and notes. It also includes Scott's 1814 preface to the so-called 'third edition' (really second edition, second issue) of *Waverley*, as well as material not by Scott: notes (interspersed throughout the text) and an index to the novels. Among all the Scott material that of David Laing is hardly noticeable, so that Blacks' purpose in using Laing appears to have been mainly to increase their emphasis on their exclusive access to the author.

Subsequent Black editions repeat and add to these features. Even their cheaper editions include Scott's portrait and all his 1829 material. However, the publishers drop the editor and the notes he had added to the Centenary and rely on the purity of Scott's own voice in all their future editions, whether cheap or expensive. They also do not value Scott's notes and changes that they had added to the Centenary. The 1873 Pocket edition is externally a different affair from the Centenary, fitting double the number of lines onto smaller pages, yet it retains all Scott's 1829 material as it had appeared in the Magnum. However, instead of keeping those of Scott's notes that had been newly added from the interleaved set, the Pocket Edition cuts or shortens them: the sentence at the beginning of the second chapter of *Waverley*, ('It is, then, sixty years since Edward Waverley ... ') in the Centenary carries a note after 'since', reading 'the precise date (1745) was withheld from the original edition, lest it should anticipate the nature of the tale by announcing so remarkable an era'.[12] In the 1873 edition, the sentence does not carry a note and instead includes a short explanation in brackets, reading 'It is, then, sixty years since (1745) Edward Waverley ... '.[13] Since the Waverley novels are historical they do not need to be updated for new generations of readers, but there was a particular problem with the beginning of the first volume of *Waverley* that offers a long disquisition on the title, and contains allusions to the novels of the eighteenth century that Victorian readers might have found puzzling. Also, that work depends upon understanding voices from two chronological periods, 1745 and 1814. A. & C. Black made no attempts to help new readers but relied entirely on the texts themselves. The four-volume 1877 edition dispenses with the note completely. This edition is in fact an exact reprint of the 1867 Copyright Edition – apart from the order of the preliminary pages – which indicates that the changes the Centenary had brought in were not regarded as important to either text or readers.[14] The four-volume 1877 edition is a cheap one, with small print, two columns per page and more than seventy lines per column, yet again it includes all the author's 1829 introductory material. As well as incorporating illustrations of scenes in the novels, many of the interspersed images show details about the author and his life. The title page of volume I shows 'Sir Walter's Hat and Stick', volume IV shows the dog 'Maida. Sir Walter's faithful and much loved friend'. The higher-quality 1877 Illustrated Edition intensifies this focus on the author through illustrations by including images of Scott's belongings throughout the text, such as a picture of the 'Author's Chair' heading the 1829 advertisement or one of the 'Author's Volunteer Helmet' ending the first chapter. Like all 1870s Black editions, the 1877 Illustrated includes all Scott's 1829 material, this time so spaciously printed that the text of *Waverley* does not begin until page 91.

The Illustrated, like the Centenary, also makes use of autographs. The first chapter in both editions is headed 'Waverley or 'tis sixty years since' in Scott's hand. However, whereas in the Centenary it takes up three lines ('Waverley | or 'tis | sixty years since') in order to fit between the bears of the gate of the Baron of Bradwardine's manor house (see Figure 4.3), the Illustrated dispenses with the bear gate and therefore fits the heading into two lines ('Waverley | or 'tis sixty years since') (see Figure 4.4). Iain Gordon Brown points out that the autograph occurs in Cadell's 1842–47 Abbotsford Edition of Scott's novels and is

> a fabrication, made up from one or other occurrence of the name of [Edward] Waverley in the novel manuscript, the subtitle 'or 'tis sixty years since' being in some way mocked-up by the engraver as the phrase does not, in fact, occur in the surviving portion of the manuscript extant in 1842.[15]

The Blacks not only use the already existing 'facsimile' but further edit it to fit the size they want in the respective edition (down to cutting off the last line of 'since' in the earlier one). The individual autograph words are exactly the same in both editions. The inclusion of these autographs again testifies to the Blacks' emphasis on authenticity (paradoxically so, since their autograph is 'mocked-up'), on the connection between text and author, and on the exclusive closeness that they have to the author as possessors of the manuscript and 'true' owners of the copyright.

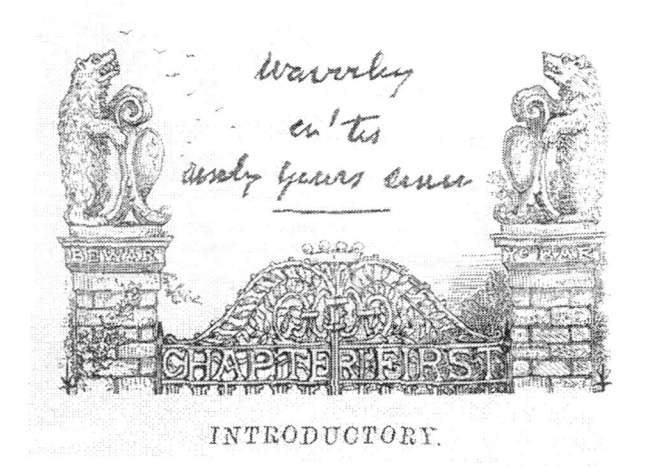

Figure 4.3 Heading for the first chapter of *Waverley* in A. & C. Black's Centenary edition of 1870–71 (enlarged)

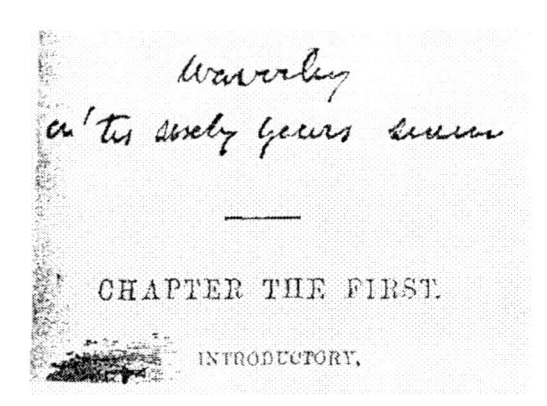

Figure 4.4 Heading for the first chapter of *Waverley* in A. & C. Black's Illustrated edition of 1877 (enlarged)

In the 1877 Illustrated Edition, A. & C. Black state in the Advertisement that the illustrations used as well as the format in 48 volumes is that of the Abbotsford Edition, which they refer to as 'the Author's Favourite Edition'. They do not give the date of the Abbotsford (1842–47) since Scott had been dead for a decade by the time it came out and could not possibly have judged it. It is another attempt at proving their closeness to Scott's tastes and intentions.

Of the other six editions that appear in the 1870s, after the novels enter the public domain, five distance themselves from Black's. Only the 1875 Routledge (begun in the year the last Magnum copyrights expired) attempts to copy the Black editions by producing an edition very similar to the Centenary.

D. Wilson & T. & J. Lochhead's Popular Edition and W. Nimmo's edition are textually exactly the same, without being acknowledged as such. The only difference is that Nimmo halves the number of volumes by combining sets of two novels in one volume. The edition is edited by the Revd P. Hately Waddell, which already distinguishes it from Blacks' claim of authentic purity. The half-title reads 'Waverley Novels: Popular Edition; Rev. P. Hately Waddell, Editor', and does not give Scott's name, nor does the title page. The edition includes a preface and an essay on 'Walter Scott as a Novelist' as well as a glossary by the editor. The glossary is divided into sections of 'Scotch', 'Latin', 'French', and 'Italian' and explains people as well as expressions. The edition dispenses with all 1829 preliminary material provided by Scott and also cuts most of the 1829 notes. It consciously distances itself from the Black editions' pure Scott and instead provides external information about text and author. Marcus Ward's 1877–79 edition similarly counters Black's. It also begins with a 'Memoir' of Scott by an editor, and excludes most of Scott's 1829 material. Illustrations in all of the non-Black-editions tend to show scenes from the novels, such as that on the title page of Wilson & Lochhead's edition showing 'Tully-Veolan: A Scottish Manor-House Sixty Years Since', rather than images of the author's belongings. The author is still emphasized in these editions through the editors' essays, but the focus is more on the individual text than in Black's editions and author's life and text are more clearly divided. Also different from Black's editions is Bradbury, Agnew & Co.'s 'The Handy Volume "Waverley"' edition of 1877. The volumes measure only 12 cm in height, fit 36 lines onto the page, and follow the title page immediately with the first chapter of the novel, thus dispensing with all introductory material. The *Waverley* volume has 'Introduction and Notes' at the back (the 1829 General Preface), which is prefixed with an editor's note: 'For the Convenience of the Reader, the Author's last General Introduction has been slightly abridged' (536), which further indicates a different implied reader from both Blacks' and other publishers' editions. Dicks, too, distances his edition from Black's, though he includes all Scott's introductory material and makes a point in his advertisements of there being 'no abridgement, no re-editing'. Yet the readership Dicks addresses is a different one from that of Blacks' editions: the main object of Dicks' Waverley Novels is cheapness, the volumes are paperbacks, with tiny type and two columns per page.[16] The price of access to Scott's novels fell steadily throughout the century, but while the lowest price before Dicks' edition had already been very low at 6d (0.5s), Dicks managed to halve this yet again, selling the volumes at 3d (0.25s) each. This price meant the Waverley novels were available extremely cheaply by any standards.

All 1870s publishers except Routledge distance themselves from the previous copyright holders' strategy, mostly by accompanying Scott's texts with an editor's explanations. Instead of stressing purity, these publishers market their editions as being tailored to a late-nineteenth-century reader.

All these editions are collected editions. As Figure 4.2 shows, very few single editions appear in the 1860s and 1870s. The insistence on publishing collected editions of Scott explains why there are no editions other than Black's (with the single exception of an 1868 edition of *Waverley* in lithographed shorthand[17]) before the expiry of the Magnum copyright in spite of the original texts of the Waverley novels having gone out of copyright individually throughout the preceding decades – that of *Waverley* since 1856. Editions tend to read both on spine and specially inserted title page 'Waverley Novels' and then give volume number and individual title. This shows the novels to be part of a whole, thereby again connecting author and texts as well as making a collected edition the only valid way of reading 'Scott'. Holding the copyright to Scott's authoritative collected edition would then be sufficient for them to remain the only Scott-publishers because no publisher would want to bring out the earlier individual texts. Though some of the other publishers' editions also stress each novel's being part of a series, this is never as strong as in A. & C. Black's. The latter's marketing strategy appears to have been extremely successful: though the anonymous author of *Adam and Charles Black* claims that 'when the copyrights of the earlier Waverley Novels expired, the market was soon flooded with cheap reprints',[18] this is not borne out by the evidence. No publishers except the copyright holders bring out Scott editions throughout the 1840s, 1850s and 1860s, until the expiry of the Magnum copyright, and, as Figures 4.1 and 4.2 show, the great majority even in the 1870s are collected editions.

That there are hardly any single editions of any of Scott's novels either before or after the expiry of the Magnum copyright, and thus of neither the 1814 nor the 1829 texts, indicates that Scott's novels are marketed as a collected entity only. There is evidence that some Victorian readers did reread all the Waverley novels again and again. Ruskin, for example, read them so frequently that he complained of being too familiar with them, and Leslie Stephen read them aloud to his family as a continuous process, starting all over when finished.[19] The absence of single editions indicates that it is not the 1829 additional material that readers insist on but the collected edition of the novels. A. & C. Black therefore abandon the interleaved set as a marketing tool: while it renders individual texts more authentic it does not emphasize the texts' collective nature. Similarly editions such as Wilson & Lochhead's Popular one exclude all Scott's Magnum non-fictional material – but print a collected edition. Individual texts are of no interest while collected editions emphasize the author because they represent his whole fictional oeuvre.

Variety and numbers of publishers and editions show the demand for Scott's novels to go up rather than down towards the end of the century. Figures 4.1 and 4.2 indicate that readers tended to buy collected editions of Scott's works and individual editions of Austen's, which suggests that a collected edition of Scott's works was still an essential component of every household library. Concerning single editions of their works, numbers of titles of her works overtake his before mid-century and stay higher throughout since, in spite of the individual works of Scott going out of copyright long before the Magnum, they were not republished. More single editions of Austen than of Scott indicate that he was being read almost exclusively in collected editions, testifying to his status being higher than hers. (Also, Figure 4.2 only includes a quarter of his novels – the first seven – whereas it shows all of hers.) This difference between editions readers prefer shows the respective status of Austen and Scott: while the complete works of Scott were compulsory for any reader, Austen's individual novels were pleasant additional reading.

Editions suggest that Scott's cultural status remained undiminished throughout the century. The variety of kinds of editions indicates that his popularity with all social classes also continued unreduced. Austen slowly gains on Scott in both popularity and status: absolute numbers of publications of her novels rise as well as numbers of collected editions. St Clair observes that Routledge's cheapest Austen editions, reduced eventually from 2.5 to 2 to 1 to 0.5 shillings in the late nineteenth century, sold not much better than the more expensive editions.[20] Austen therefore – unlike Scott – remained an author mainly for the middle classes.

Regarding collected editions, Scott remains well ahead of Austen throughout the nineteenth century. While she appears to attain a status half as high as his by reaching 50 per cent of numbers of collected editions of his in the decade of 1863–72, this is in fact due to copyright: the Magnum was still in copyright, her novels were not. As soon as the Magnum copyright expires, collected editions of his novels soar. However, though collected editions of both authors' works go up from the 1870s onwards, Austen is gaining on Scott: hers increase proportionately more than his. In the decade of 1873–82, the first in which all novels of both authors are out of copyright, numbers of collected Austen editions are at only 14.3 per cent of Scott's. In the following decades, this rises to 36.4 per cent and reaches 50 per cent between 1903 and 1912.

Chapter 5

Library Catalogues, 1832–1912

The nineteenth century was a period of rapid growth in literacy and reading so that by the end of the century almost everyone read. This growth in reading was accompanied and assisted by an increase in book lending institutions. Robin Alston has collected the names of 7,683 libraries that existed in Britain between 1800 and 1850, compared to 3,071 between 1700 and 1799.[1] However, the information we have does not yet enable us to plot net growth,[2] nor have the figures been related to the increase in population, which quadrupled between 1700 and 1900. Yet the main patterns are clear: there is a surge in commercial and private libraries in the second half of the eighteenth century, followed by a less rapid growth later, the invention of Mechanics' Institutes' libraries in the 1820s, and a drastic change in the later nineteenth century when free public libraries were established in every substantial town.

Private subscription libraries regarded themselves as too serious to include novels. However, Scott's novels were held by many of them. He therefore led the way in being accepted into the masculine libraries, establishing his form of novels as serious reading and raising the status of this type of literature across all classes of the reading public. Among the reasons why they were able to cross that boundary was the universal judgement that they were, without exception, morally admirable.

Mechanics' Institutes and similar institutions were designed for the education of the working classes. Since they largely depended for their support on upper- and middle-class benefactors, they were careful to avoid potentially controversial publications, as regards both politics as well as literary status. Novels were therefore usually excluded. Yet, like subscription libraries, many gradually acquired Scott's novels. A few even obtained his fiction during his lifetime, such as Keighley Mechanics' Institute or Morpeth Mechanical and Scientific Institute Library, which underlines the extraordinary contemporary status of Scott's fictional works almost outside the novel-genre. Later on in the nineteenth century, Mechanics' Institutes increasingly held Scott's works, indicating that Victorians, too, believed in the morally instructive nature of his novels.

Figure 5.1 is composed of data drawn from 119 library catalogues in Britain dating from 1814 to 1912. Information was obtained either by direct consultation or by correspondence with librarians. The 119 catalogues assessed belong to 103 different libraries since most libraries' records are not fully extant, often because the libraries themselves no longer exist and only some of their records have been passed on to other institutions. In many cases I have therefore been able to include only one catalogue per library rather than a continuous run.

All kinds of libraries from everywhere in Britain were included, without selection by type or region, the only criterion being whether they held any novels at all. The question then asked was whether they held one or more novels by Austen or Scott, so that Figure 5.1 does not indicate how many or which novels a library held. The catalogues were placed in order by date, then grouped into periods of 20 years (except the first period, which was ended in 1832, the year of Scott's death): 1814–1832, 1833–1852, 1853–1872, etc.

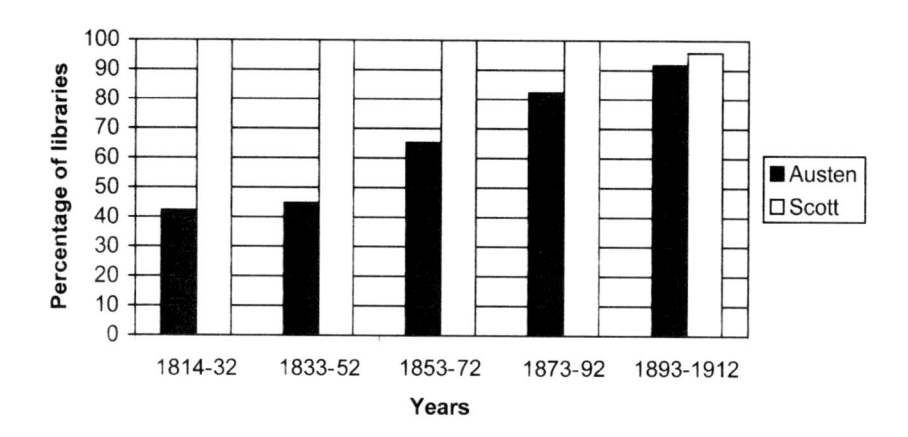

Figure 5.1 Library Holdings of Austen's and Scott's Novels

As Figure 5.1 shows, Scott's novels were held by all libraries that hold any novels at all until the very end of the nineteenth century. Decrease in popularity is more difficult to trace than increase because libraries are unlikely to have disposed of Scott's works immediately, even if they perceived him as having become less popular. However, the graph also includes newly founded libraries and new acquisitions of older ones and therefore testifies to Scott's popularity remaining on a similar level throughout the century. The number of libraries holding Austen novels steadily increases throughout the century, indicating a continuous upward development rather than any sudden changes.[3]

In general, circulating libraries discarded most novels once they had done their circulation, and replaced them with newer titles. That Austen and Scott feature in the catalogues of newly founded as well as long established libraries throughout the century indicates that their novels were not so disposed of but had a continuous readership as new cohorts joined the libraries. Unlike the normal flow of fiction through the circulating libraries therefore, Austen and Scott did not become out of date.

Library holdings, like editions, suggest that the 1870 *Memoir* was part of an upward trend, rather than being a turning point in Austen's popularity: it appears at the end of the period that shows the biggest increase in Austen's popularity yet. Between 1853 and 1872 five libraries out of twenty-three obtained her in or after 1870, so possibly as reaction to the *Memoir*, but the others had already acquired her during the 1850s and 1860s. The nature of the increase of library holdings in this period thus indicates a slow and steady rise of Austen's popularity, rather than showing sudden changes motivated by a specific event.

Only one library catalogue out of the 119 investigated does not hold any novels by Scott though it does hold some other fiction, including the complete novels of Austen: the Bath Royal Literary and Scientific Institution. There are local factors at work here: Bath had many circulating libraries from which this institution was different in its aims, and Bath was becoming a city associated with Austen and the characters in her novels. Still, that any library should acquire Austen and not Scott had been unthinkable throughout the nineteenth century.

Chapter 6

Victorian Reviews and Criticism, 1865–1880

The first full-length biography of Jane Austen appeared in 1870. The 1871 centenary of Scott's birth was commemorated with a Scott Centenary Exhibition, held in Edinburgh for several weeks. The copyright to his novels expired between 1871 and 1875, so that both authors' fictional works were now out of copyright and free for publishers to bring out. All these events feature in reviews:[1] Austen and Scott, although they were by now long dead, continued to attract a continuing flow of critical comment by reviewers, editors, educationalists, biographers and writers of literary history. But do critics of this period share the opinion of the public as testified to by library holdings and editions, showing an ever increasing popularity for both Austen and Scott?

Since Victorian readers always came to Austen after having read Scott, for this time period it is appropriate to reverse the previous order.

Walter Scott

Biography, morality, genius, unconscious genius

Critics of Scott fall into two categories: those that see work and man as directly reflecting one another, which for the period in question is the majority of reviewers, and those that discuss work and man separately, criticizing one but not the other. While the first group realize Scott's many capacities, they maintain that life and works are too closely connected to be analysed independently. 'From every point of view – as a man of letters, as a man of business, and a gentleman – Sir Walter Scott was the ideal of a brave and honest Englishman' (*GM* 1871, 292), his character making it impossible for him to write 'a single line to unsettle any man's faith, or to corrupt any man's principle' (*GM* 316). Reviewers justify equating the man's morality with that of the novels because 'the Waverley Novels ... represent the man' (*LQR* 1872, 41). Julia Wedgwood in the *Contemporary Review* of 1878 asserts that it is Scott 'who holds the key that lets the weary spirit out of its dungeon of petty cares and gnawing anxieties into a sunny garden' (*ContR*, 1878; cited from reprint in Hayden's *CH*, p. 513) – Scott the man, not just his texts. Though 'others, no doubt, have taught us more ... [Scott gives us] that sense of transplantation to another soil' (*ContR*, *CH*, p. 513) from where the reader returns with a refreshed heart.

Scott does not need to include open didacticism, because the readers gain access to his healthy personality through his works.

It is a sign of Scott's natural genius that his works are 'genuine outpourings of the man' (*Month* 1871, 262), both when the man is healthy and when he is sick, which 'is not so with inferior minds' (*NC* 1880, 955). John Ruskin asserts that because 'the whole man breathes or faints as one creature ... [Scott] never has a fit of the cramp without spoiling a chapter' (*NC* 955). Scott's later works, therefore, necessarily get weaker, since his physical health declines. Ruskin maintains that many scenes in these later works are

> signs of the gradual decline in the force of intellect and soul ... the mean anxieties, moral humiliations, and mercilessly demanded brain-toil, which killed him, show their sepulchral grasp for many and many a year before their final victory ... [lowering some of his novels] into fellowship with the normal disease which festers throughout the whole body of our lower fictitious literature. (*NC* 948)

Rather than denying that some of Scott's works contain weaknesses, Ruskin sees the decline as showing the truthfulness of Scott's works because it proves the connection between them and Scott the man. This connection enhances the quality of Scott's earlier novels which are necessarily healthy in their effect on the reader as the outpourings of a healthy mind and soul. Also, Ruskin is blaming circumstances and the merciless demanders of brain-toil for the decline of Scott's novels, which leaves the status of their author's genius untouched. 'Simplicity of genius' (*NC*, 955) is therefore a positive asset, since it is a sign of moral integrity, opposed to artificiality. Faults in the novels can be excused through reverence for the man.

The second group of reviewers attempt to distinguish man and work in their analyses, with varied success. Margaret Oliphant in *Blackwood's Edinburgh Magazine* admits that because of Scott's 'great sweetness of temper' (*BEM* 1871, 232), she cannot 'take him to pieces in cold blood' (*BEM* 251-2). She does not distinguish man and work even while trying to do so, so that criticism of the works becomes synonymous with taking the man to pieces. Even Leslie Stephen, who might have been expected to resist the construction of Scott as a champion of Victorian Christianity, finds criticism of Scott 'painful ... [because] he is one of those rare natures for whom we feel not merely admiration but affection, ... that kind of warm fraternal regard' (*Cornhill*, 1874; cited from Hayden's *CH*, p.441). Stephen assesses the artistic qualities of Scott's novels and comes to the conclusion that they have been overrated; yet he, too, gives Scott more significance than that which Stephen's own technical discussion appears to merit, and connects author and work after all: on reading some of Scott's works, 'we feel ourselves transported to the "distant Cheviots blue" .... The pleasure of that healthy open-air life, with that manly companion, is not likely to diminish' (*Cornhill; CH*, p. 458), so that Scott's lesser works can be redeemed through the healthiness of his best works. The difference between Stephen and reviewers who do not distinguish man and author is that Stephen sees Scott's works as strong or weak independently of the author's physical health, whereas most reviewers, if they admit weaknesses at all, do so with regard to those novels that Scott wrote under physical and mental strain.

Reviewers regard Scott not only as a genius, but also as the model of Victorian, Christian, masculinity: dutiful, diligent, modest, frank and unselfish. These manly qualities make him unique among geniuses: he is not occupied with himself, and reviewers 'cannot say this of any of his great contemporaries' (*ContR; CH*, p. 500). Scott's 'was not ... the mind of a mere dreamer or poet' (*QR* 1868, 20), but he lived in the buzz of family and society and was 'first of all things a man before ever he was a poet!' (*BEM* 243). Scott, like an ordinary and dutiful man who does not request privileges for himself, toiled to pay off the debts that others had caused while 'his poetic contemporaries ... were preaching to the world the necessity laid upon it of providing a peaceful nest and a sheltered life for the man of genius' (*BEM* 243). The extent to which his manly sense of duty colours Victorian reviewers' judgements of his work is emphasized by their comparison of his character to Shakespeare's. According to Oliphant, writing himself out of debt 'is what Shakespeare would have done. And Scott did it – and no one else' (*BEM* 242). To state what Shakespeare 'would have done' shows how closely connected are genius and personal goodness in reviewers' eyes. Because his genius is only comparable to Shakespeare's, Scott's personality, too, can only be compared to Shakespeare's. By the nineteenth century, Shakespeare was universally regarded as the supreme writer of the nation and Oliphant assumes that, as such he must have had a matchless personal character. Association with Shakespeare redeems treating writing as a trade:

> Scott, it seems, wrote for money ... and did not Shakespeare do pretty much the same? ... there seems to be no reason why the desire of a good house at Stratford should be intrinsically nobler than the desire of a fine estate at Abbotsford. (*Cornhill; CH*, pp. 445–6)

Writing for money to pay off debts becomes an act of heroism and is in no reviewer's eyes something to be criticized, but for the majority makes criticism of the novels so written impossible. Writing for profit, and thereby for the public instead of for his own edification or for art, emphasizes his being a man as well as a writer and underlines that he possesses a human quality that is lacking in other geniuses. His manly virtue is part of the moral lesson of his works. The man who worked 'as never man worked before' (*BEM* 256) employed his genius to meet 'the duties and amenities of extra-literary life [more] than any man who ever seriously was author' (*LQR* 52). Scott's personality takes precedence over his writings: his being a man and a writer, and humble in spite of his great genius and success, makes his works so wholesome

Scott's novels and the concept of the novel as art

Reviewers' perception of Scott as a man colours every assessment of his works. Critics do not address the definition of a novel directly, nor do they consider his contribution to the novel as an art form in any but the most general terms, usually not even examining the historical novel. For most of them, morality remains the most important assessment criterion, through author and content, not form, though realism (connected to historical truth and characters) also features as a criterion. Because reviewers see it as a sign of greatness that when he 'took up his pen it was not to think, but to write' (*GM* 307), they necessarily neglect artistic considerations and technical finish. His speed and his not having an artistic aim is proof of the greatness of his natural genius and does not incur criticism, since one 'may well doubt whether much labour would have improved or injured him' (*Cornhill, CH,* p. 446). The use of the personal pronoun even when the novels are discussed again emphasizes the man. What would provoke censure with other authors is not only excused in Scott but adds to his greatness, since it is not for 'such a crowned and reigning soul that laws of art were made. Let us be bound by them, who are as other men – but not our sovereign' (*BEM* 252). Both Shakespeare and Scott are seen as being above criticism, and some reviewers find that they are so closely connected one cannot condemn one without having to condemn the other too: 'both Shakespeare and Scott are benefactors too great for us to "pick spots on" without much ingratitude' (*LQR* 37). Both are 'poets and heroes who are above comment – men who can do no wrong' (*BEM* 252).

It is deliberately not through an assessment according to the usual rules of art then, that critics defend Scott's high position. Apart from his qualities as a man, critics instead focus on the content of the novels, again testifying to the prevalence of moral over purely artistic criteria. The focus on content makes a close connection between works and their author easier. Wedgwood writes about the qualities needed not by a novel but by an author: a novelist needs

> the balance of genius and good sense – the harmony of a cool shrewdness of intellect and a glowing fervour of imagination ... and from the first [Scott's] dramatic sympathies array themselves on the side which judgement condemns. Thus the double feeling supplies the place of impartiality, and art has the mellowing atmosphere it needs. (*ContR, CH*, pp. 512–13)

Wedgwood does not absolutely exempt Scott from all artistic rules, but bends them to fit him. The argument is coined towards morality, since it shows readers to align their sympathies with Scott to the losing side, while seeing the necessity of the victory of the cause supported by judgement.

Where critics discuss his contribution to the development of fiction they do this in general terms and assume that it was not his aim to contribute to the art of the novel. Robert Louis Stevenson in The *Cornhill Magazine* of 1874 sees Scott unconscious of 'so lightly initiating' a literary movement (*Cornhill*; cited from reprint in Hayden's *CH*, p. 477). The reviewer in The *London Quarterly Review* concedes that there are novels that he deems

> higher in artistic form and ... individually greater than any one work of Scott's ... [but] should search, without hope of success, through the whole world of fictitious literature for an artist whose single hand did as much for his department of art as [Scott's]. (*LQR* 41)

Again, this shifts the focus from the work to the author, and emphasizes the entirety of Scott's fictional opus. This effect is strengthened by the lack of focus on any individual work in most reviews: they deal with the entire fictional oeuvre rather than one novel. This is again similar to editions, the great majority of which came out as collected, rather than single, editions. Reviewers deal with characters generally, who embody a morality that reflects Scott's own, but not with a concept of art.

Realism, realistic characters, historical accuracy

The majority of reviewers discuss realism in their articles, defining it as truthfulness, as opposed to artificiality, and usually focusing on this in relation to the depiction of Scott's characters. Critics see realism and romance as being successfully combined in Scott's novels. More than the detail of the individual character depictions they praise his scope, comparing his works to Shakespeare's. Some see Scott's realism as inferior to the 'impetuous ideal realism of Shakespeare' (*LQR* 41), while others assert that only Scott and Shakespeare are capable of depicting realism in all classes. Whereas other novelists are limited in their realistic depictions to their personal experience, critics emphasize Scott's wide social and historical range, unusual 'even with novelists of genius' (*BEM* 248). It is Scott's realistic depiction of 'English life' (*ContR*; *CH*, p. 505) that makes him greater than all. The emphasis is again on scope, which matters at least as much as the quality of individual depiction.

Critics experience Scott's characters as 'living images ... who are human and complete' (*LQR* 36) and refer to them as if they had lived: Diana Vernon '*was* a girl of a very powerful mind and unusual literary accomplishments' (*Macmillan's*, 1870, 285, emphasis mine). The reviewer advises female readers, however, that 'before you imitate her manners, be sure that you possess her brains' (*Macmillan's* 285). Reviewers do not condemn those of Scott's characters who behave outside the boundaries of Victorian propriety, nor do they regard them as unrealistic, both of which are facilitated by the novels' having been written and set in the past. Reviewers all agree in seeing Scott as 'the undisputed parent of a whole population full of enduring vitality' (*Cornhill*; *CH*, p. 450), differing only in whether they include all his characters in this group. Male characters are usually regarded as more realistic than the female ones, lower social classes more so than Scott's own class, and subsidiary characters more so than heroes.

Dialogue is especially commended as enhancing Scott's realism, which is one of the few points made about Scott's technique. It shows that critics are alert to artistic elements, but tend not to raise them in connection with Scott's novels unless they are positive. Ruskin states that 'few authors of second or third rate genius can either record or invent a probable conversation in ordinary life' (*NC* 947) – but Scott of course has that ability.

Though reviewers do not discuss the genre of the historical novel, some are concerned with historical accuracy in the novels. Again, their assessments demonstrate their desire to judge Scott's works positively: they defend his inaccuracies as being due to the time in which he wrote, finding that to look

> at the Scotch novels, as we do now, with a microscope, we are able to detect inaccuracies of costume and historical solecisms which [contemporaries] ... must of necessity have missed. But these inaccuracies and violations of art are, after all, but trifles. (*GM* 310)

Instead of criticizing Scott for the inaccuracies, the reviewer draws attention to the 'scrupulous nicety with which he hunted up his facts' (*GM* 309), so that the man's conscientious efforts are more important than the result in the novels.

Popularity and status – reviewers' direct comments and other evidence

The development of Scott's critical and public popularities does not exactly correlate. Though his public popularity as testified to by editions and library catalogues remains high, critical popularity is no longer unequivocal. Reviewers begin to voice criticism of Scott's works – tentatively, excusing faults in his novels, or finding them unimportant, but nevertheless discerning them. Where critique is voiced, it is always about technique, never about content. Some critics also perceive a decline in Scott's public popularity (though without stating on what evidence their perceptions are based), and while most of these vehemently defend the greatness of Scott's works, they nonetheless reveal an awareness that not everyone shares their esteem.

Reviewers can be divided into two groups: those that perceive changes in Scott's public popularity and those that consider him as being as popular as always. Within the first group one can distinguish those that agree with a diminishing popularity and give reasons for their argument, and those that entirely disagree and want to keep Scott on his pedestal.

As early as January 1868 *The Quarterly Review* complains that 'Scott himself, both as a man and as a writer, seems to be in danger of passing – we cannot conceive why – out of the knowledge of the rising generation' (*QR* 1). This statement shows that in estimating Scott's popularity, critics are concerned with both man and works. Stephen perceives that 'the great "Wizard" has lost some of his magic power, and ... the warmth of our first love is departed' (*Cornhill; CH*, p. 440). Like the reviewer in the *QR*, he believes the shift in taste to be generational – but he gives both generations' opinions validity by investigating the real and perceived qualities of Scott's works. Neither of the two reviewers says how they perceive these changes. Stephen asks whether Scott will entirely disappear, something inconceivable to most reviewers.

A reviewer writing in the *London Society* about the Scott centenary celebrations at Edinburgh in 1871 reports how fellow journalists pretend to knowledge of Scott's works while in fact never having read 'a single novel of Sir Walter's straight through in the original' (*London Soc* 1871, 276), using a '"Handbook to the Waverley Scenes"' (*London Soc* 276) to write articles on Scott. Similarly, Stephen wonders how many of those attending a recent Waverley Ball in costume 'were able to draw upon the stores of their memory, and how many were forced to cram for the occasion?' (*Cornhill; CH*, p. 440). These observations indicate the still very high status of Scott's works with both reviewers and public, and the need for any educated person to be acquainted with him. They also show that these reviewers believe the reading of Scott's work to have become a duty rather than a pleasure to some. The public and critical decrease of popularity appears to have begun, though decrease of public popularity is not as yet generally discussed in writing nor is it evident in edition numbers or library holdings. Scott's cultural status is as high as ever, so that these reviewers perceive a discrepancy between Scott's high cultural status and less high popularity.

While some reviewers sense a decrease in Scott's popularity, the majority do not. The reviewer in the *LQR* even maintains that Scott's popularity 'still goes on strengthening and spreading in influence' (*LQR* 59). Reviewers still assume all readers to be intimately acquainted with Scott's novels and allude to them out of context without explaining references. Henry F. Chorley for instance, at the end of his article on Jane Austen and Mary Mitford, finds Mitford exceptional 'especially in the quarter of [the world of letters] inhabited by those whom one Jonathan Oldbuck scornfully called "the women-kind"' (*QR* 1870, 218).

The decline of Scott's public popularity perceived by some reviewers is, if accurate, not dramatic. Apart from editions and library holdings, entries on Scott in *Notes and Queries: A Medium of Intercommunication for Literary Men, General Readers, etc.* testify to how much Scott is still in the public mind. *Notes and Queries* consists mostly of letters and comments written by members of the public rather than professional reviewers. Almost every issue of the weekly periodical prints something in connection with Scott in the 1860s and 1870s, varying from discussions of 'Sir Walter Scott's physique'[2] and the shape of his head – again compared to Shakespeare – via publication numbers of his works over a particular decade,[3] debates about his misquotations,[4] the display of a letter by Scott,[5] the discussion of geocentric constellations at the time of his birth[6] to discussions of his popularity. In a letter appearing in *N&Q* in 1874,[7] Jonathan Bouchier agrees, though unwillingly, with a lecture William Gladstone had given in 1868, in which Gladstone had asserted that 'we did not in these days appreciate this great writer as we ought, and that newer literary fashions had for a while (but only for a while) obscured his splendid fame'(1); but Bouchier finds that 'there is still a remnant left in the land who have not bowed the knee to the false deity of sensationalism' (2). Readers are assured of Scott's superlative position by the editorial comment that follows the letter: they

> need not fear for the great object of their admiration ... the successive cheap editions of Scott's Novels are so many proofs of his undying popularity ... [as are the] new dramas founded on his works. (2)

Writer and editor are aware of changes in Scott's popularity, but both want Scott to retain his popularity.

The majority of reviewers do not write about changes in Scott's public popularity. His relevance is 'beyond times and seasons' (*BEM* 229), and 'what he was to his contemporaries he may well be to us and to our children's children' (*LQR* 36). As Stephen explains Scott's diminishing popularity by condemning aspects of the novels, the reviewer in *Month* gives reasons for Scott's consistently high reputation, among them the linking of 'the national history to the local scenery ... [and the depiction of] the courage and manly virtues of the past' (*Month* 283). Again, his reasoning does not always distinguish man and novel, which contributes to his positive verdict.

The Scott Centenary Exhibition

The Scott exhibition of 1871 was an emanation of the time as well as helping to form it. The organizers modelled their exhibition on one celebrating Dante that had been held in Florence in 1865, which had lasted only three days. 'What Dante was and is to Italy and Florence, Scott was and is in many ways to Scotland and Edinburgh',[8] wrote Sir William Stirling Maxwell, a member of the organizing committee, in April 1871, voicing a view that was shared by many of his contemporaries. The exhibition was about life and works, displaying busts and portraits of Scott as well as manuscripts, early editions, and illustrations to Scott's poetry and prose. The exhibitors were pleased with the success of the undertaking: 'Upwards of 12,000 persons visited the Exhibition during the period it was open.'[9]

Jane Austen

Biography and morality

Victorian readers came to Austen always after having read Scott. His status was absolute, hers needed to be related to that of other authors.

Austen the person as well as Austen the author feature in articles on her and her works, but critics emphasize Austen's works more than they do Scott's. This focus on her works takes place in spite of many of the articles appearing in connection with the *Memoir* of 1870, when a more exclusive focus on Austen's biography might have been expected since it was the first full-length biography to appear on Austen. This emphasis on the text while also taking into account the author is again similar to what the evidence of editions suggests. The majority of Austen editions are individual publications of her novels and therefore stand on their own, but the two collected editions published in 1870 stress the author through printing the entirety of her works. With Scott, the majority of editions are collected. The kinds of editions of the two authors' works therefore reflect the degree of emphasis on the author, while also showing the increase in interest in Austen as a person.

While reviewers consider Austen's character, they do not discuss her life as they do Scott's. Her life was less eventful and she was a woman. Reviewers focus on the stereotype familiar from conduct literature: the character of a dutiful, kind, domestic daughter, sister and aunt. Unlike Scott, Austen is a woman, whose life was 'without incidents or passions' (*Academy*, 1870, 118).

As with Scott, reviewers continuously connect life and work, but rather than connecting biographical events or the author's physical health to the general quality of the works, they draw direct parallels between Austen and her characters, most often with Anne Elliot. A. I. Thackeray asserts that 'Anne Elliot must have been Jane Austen herself' (*Cornhill* 1871, 166), because of her sensitivity and womanliness. Though Austen bears characteristics of both Anne Elliot and Elizabeth Bennet, Richard Holt Hutton sees her as closer to Anne, who

> is a far more perfect lady, has far more of the grace and refinement which we find from this short biography were the most distinguishing characteristics of the writer ... [as well as] health and spirit ... high breeding and gentleness of nature ... refinement, playfulness, and alertness, rather than depth of intellect. (*Spect* 1869; cited from reprint in Southam's *CH*, vol. *II*, p. 163).

Hutton's description of Austen already typifies one of the main differences between Victorian assessments of Austen and Scott: Scott's genius is never doubted, even where his novels are criticized, whereas Austen can never be on the same intellectual level because she is a perfect lady. Her productions cannot have an equal social impact and are not comparable in strength to Scott's manly works, which is a view similar to that of Austen's contemporaries, only now it is connected to biography. Critics emphasize her womanly nature and benevolence and see this reflected in the novels. Personal qualities and those of the writer are not distinguished: she is 'so graceful, so affectionate, so fine in observation, so exquisite in touch, so real in her knowledge of the secrets of the human heart' (*QR* 1870, 204). Thus with Austen, too, the novels are judged through her personality, but reviewers only have the *Memoir* and the novels to judge from, rather than major events that would shed light on her character, so that they create an image of her as an ideal Victorian lady, just as Scott becomes an ideal Victorian gentleman.

Irony in Austen's works had been overlooked for most of the nineteenth century. As Joseph Cady and Ian Watt point out, the first critic to discuss Austen's irony is the Shakespeare scholar Richard Simpson in his review of the *Memoir*.[10] Even those critics that now see her novels as containing elements of criticism and irony still regard the woman as sweet and philanthropic, which, as with Scott, demonstrates critics' desire to approve of the author's personality when praising the works, especially with a female author. She has to be above all womanly, hence where Austen's novels are regarded as including cynicism at all it is 'female cynicism which ... is something altogether different from the rude and brutal male quality that bears the same name' (*BEM* 1870, 294). Oliphant perceives Austen's work as 'cruel in its perfection' (*BEM* 300), but offers two excuses for this, thereby making it still possible to regard the author as sweet, gentle and feminine. Though there is cruelty in the novels, this is 'fine-stinging yet soft-voiced contempt ... [and] gentle disdain' (*BEM* 294), which is the natural result of the observations with which a 'young woman, with no active pursuit to occupy her, spends, without knowing it, so much of her time and youth' (*BEM* 294). Women nowadays could find ways of improving their minds, but these opportunities 'were rare in Miss Austen's day' (*BEM* 294–5). Female cynicism is thus the result of the times not offering women more wholesome occupations, not of Austen's character. Though her work is a 'pitiless perfection of art ... [she] was in reality quite unaware of its real power ... [because] genius ... goes a great deal deeper than conscious meaning' (*BEM* 301–2). As such, cynicism can be seen as the result of her unconscious genius, without diminishing the gentle femininity of the woman, so that genius becomes a term distinct from feminine qualities.

Anne Isabella Thackeray asserts that Austen's heroines 'have a certain gentle self-respect and humour and hardness of heart' which enables them to take love lightly, and which modern heroines do not possess. Again, this trait is due to 'the spirit of the age', and again, it does not mean that 'Jane Austen herself was incapable of understanding a deeper feeling' (*Cornhill* 166). Thackeray, like Oliphant, employs the technique also used in articles on Scott of holding responsible the times in which the authors wrote for traits of their novels that reviewers do not want to ascribe to the authors' personalities. That Austen's heroines are seen as representing her when they are soft and womanly, but not where they are hard or pert, reveals the extent to which Victorian reviewers mould the author to fit their preconceptions about essential femininity.

Austen's womanly qualities make her exemplary, and she is praised for these as one of those women who 'raise and ennoble all those who follow after, – true, gentle and strong and tender' (*Cornhill* 167). With Austen, reviewers are interested in physical and mental endowments: they describe her as 'healthy' (*FR* 1870, 191) in body and heart, 'personally ... most engaging' (*QR* 203), 'at least pretty' (*FR*, 189), selfless and genteel. As with Scott, personal qualities dominate over literary ones. Like Scott, Austen is an ideal not primarily because she wrote high-quality novels, but because her novels are an image of her own pure self as imagined by the reviewers. It is through her person that her novels make readers 'feel happier and better for the goodness and charity which is not ours, and yet which seems to belong to us while we are near it' (*Cornhill* 167). Her moral integrity reflects onto the reader. Austen's 'cheerful healthy tone, the exquisite purity, and the genuine goodness which are reflected in every line she wrote ... [leave the reader] amused, refreshed, benefited' (*FR*, 191). She is thus presented as a role model for women of her class.

Austen-Leigh insists that 'there was scarcely a charm in her most delightful characters that was not a true reflection of her own sweet temper and loving heart'.[11] He presents Austen as a kind and sweet woman who wrote novels almost by accident, certainly without an artistic concept. Instead, they reveal her moral principles: the novels

> were not written to support any theory or inculcate any particular moral, except indeed the great moral which is to be equally gathered from an observation of the course of actual life – namely, the superiority of high over low principles, and of greatness over littleness of mind.[12]

He presents her as not having given her writing undue importance but as always having put her domestic duties first, which encourages the image of her necessarily producing what she sees, filtered through her own moral consciousness: 'whatever she produced was a genuine homemade article'.[13] Her general benevolence prevented her from ever playing with the 'serious duties or responsibilities [of everyday life], nor did she ever turn individuals into ridicule. ... She was as far as possible from being censorious or satirical'.[14]

In Austen-Leigh's biography, Austen becomes a woman adorned with every female virtue who also happens to write novels. Reviewers react to the *Memoir* in four main points, largely by accepting his version: his insistence of the novels reflecting Austen's character, connected to that her general benevolence and sweetness of character, her having written without an artistic concept, and her not having put her novels before her domestic duties. They accept the points regarding Austen's character without hesitation, but differ as regards Austen's artistic consciousness. The *Memoir* thus not only gave reviewers the opportunity to write on Austen, but gave them the image of the woman they had been lacking: just as they emphasized Scott's personal qualities before those of his novels, so they could now approve of Austen's feminine virtues.

Realism

Victorian reviewers' treatment of Austen's realism is similar to that of early nineteenth-century reviewers. They praise the realism of her novels, especially that of 'ordinary people in ordinary circumstances' (*LQR* 1872, 43), while at the same time censuring the lack of romance (as opposed to ordinary everyday life), holding even the most perfectly executed realism insufficient as a substitute. With Scott, reviewers find not all characters equally realistically drawn; with Austen, they praise the execution of all of them as perfect, but complete perfection is not as significant as portraying an ideal mixture of romance and realism.

Victorian reviewers differ from their predecessors in their criticism that Austen's novels 'do not stir the deeper passions' (*FR* 190). Whereas Scott's works transport readers and make them feel empathy, the love in Austen's novels is 'rather an adjunct of the sober common sense than of the impetuous and passionate side of the soul' (*NBR*, 1870; cited from reprint in Southam's *CH*, vol. I, p. 245). While reviewers are critical of her novels' entire lack of emotion, some, such as the one in *St Paul's Magazine*, compare the lack of sentiment in her works favourably with other novels, commending the 'total absence of the delirious excitement which distinguishes the novel writing of the present day' (*St Paul's* 1870; cited from a reprint in Southam's *CH*, vol. I, p. 228). However, he also claims that Austen's realism leads to a 'starving of the higher imaginative faculties' (*St Paul's* 235), so that for him, too, a perfect depiction of the quotidian is no substitute for a romantic appeal to the imagination.

Austen's characters are 'familiar acquaintances, who are ... more alive to us than a great many of the people among whom we live' (*Cornhill* 158). They gain a timeless quality that their author does not possess, since faults in the novels have to be attributed to the author's times. Though Austen's realism is praised, it also emphasizes her limits in two ways: it draws attention to her lack of romance and passion, and because the focus of reviewers' praise of the novels' realism is on the characters, it emphasizes her limited social and temporal range. This limited scope prevents her novels from containing instruction – other than through the author's moral integrity – which limits their social relevance.

Reviewers come up with various justifications for this perceived fault, all connected either to Austen's times or her sex. 'At the time in which Miss Austen wrote, high thinkers – for even Scott was not a high thinker – did not write novels' (*EWDM* 1866; cited from reprint in Southam's *CH*, vol. I, p. 204), so that instruction would not have been expected. Similarly, Austen's limitation to only one topic is 'probably a true picture of village life in England half-a-century ago, and perhaps even now, though the feminine sphere of thought and action has greatly enlarged with the progress of education' (*St Paul's; CH*, vol. I, p. 232). Again, the reviewers' own times are regarded as superior to Austen's. Richard Simpson sees Austen as 'obey[ing] the adage, "ne gladium tollat mulier"' ('Let the woman not carry a sword', *NBR; CH*, vol. I, p. 264). Instead of condemning her limitations, he praises her for her consciousness of both the limitations of her abilities and the boundaries of female prudence, justifying her by rendering her literary boundaries those of feminine propriety. Writing within these becomes a virtuous necessity for a perfect lady, and it is as a lady that ignorance of "the great political and social problems" (*NBR; CH*, vol. I, p. 250) of her day can be excused. However, the same excuse nevertheless limits the author.

Because of the novels' limited scope reviewers see them as being 'of a very unambitious character' (*Month* 1870, 372). Only because of Austen's limits is her artistic perfection possible: 'the very narrowness of her range enabled her to concentrate her intellectual vision upon the few types of character which she did meet' (*FR* 188), so that while the circumstances of her life are responsible for the limitations of her novels, they also make her perfection possible by preventing her energies being spent on scope. Reviewers regard wide range more highly than technical perfection in a limited thematic field. Stephen voices this most decidedly:

> [while] allowing all possible praise to Miss Austen within her own sphere, [he] should dispute the conclusion that she was [because of her great literary skill] entitled to be ranked with the great authors who have sounded the depths of human passion, or found symbols for the finest speculations of the human intellect, instead of amusing themselves with the humours of a country tea-table. Comparative failure in the highest effects is more creditable than complete success in the lower. (*Cornhill* 1876, 324–5)

The complaint that Austen's novels came under as soon as Scott's novels first appeared still determines the extent of reviewers' admiration. Her realistic depiction of a section of society cannot compete with the all-encompassing realism of Scott, and, by now, Dickens or Thackeray. It was the pervasive, unexamined, assumptions that a woman author was essentially different from a male author that led some writers, such as the Brontës and Mary-Ann Evans, to assume masculine names in order to offset them and be taken more seriously.

Even where reviewers do not censure Austen's novels, they yet see her realism in opposition to that of Scott, so that because 'her subjects were not grand ... the employment of unusual art [was] requisite in order to make her work readable' (*EWDM; CH*, vol. I, p. 204) – readable, but not equal in significance.

Novel as art, Austen's genius, female boundaries

What is also striking about the comparison is that reviewers unanimously describe Austen's novels as art and, connected to that, present her as a conscious composer of art rather than as an unconscious genius like Scott. Reviewers find that

> her just sense of proportion never deserts her, no one portion of her work is ever suffered to bear down another, the action is always easy, the progress of the narrative is always smooth, the writer never gets in the way of her characters, they are never interfered with by unnecessary reflections, the business of the scene is never disturbed by useless interjections from the dramatist. (*St Paul's*; *CH*, vol. I, pp. 227–8)

The shift from her qualities to those of her novels in this passage emphasizes that they are her conscious products, as does the reference to her as a dramatist since it implies deliberately directing characters. The results of 'the technical dexterity of her workmanship' (*Academy* 118), her novels are perfections of composition and contain none of the faults that some criticize, some love, but all excuse in Scott. Her perfection also limits her: it proves her conscious composition, the opposite of the Romantic notion of an unconscious genius whose workings are unaccountable. Her strength lies in

> the perfect power she has over her wit. . . . she is never carried away . . . she is always perfectly calm, perfectly self-conscious. Her great characteristic is patience, which is notoriously a surrogate genius, the best substitute for it which nature has contrived. (*NBR*; *CH*, vol. I, p. 252).

'Poetic genius is denied [her]' (*NBR*; *CH*, vol. I, p. 252), instead she labours over her compositions, but she labours with 'an incommunicable gift of humour' (*Month* 1871, 310), and 'a gift for telling a story' (*Cornhill* 162). She thus possesses talents, but she employs them consciously to achieve the perfect art she composes. This is the main point of deviation between reviewers' and Austen-Leigh's accounts of Austen, a writer whose excellence is involuntary. Without using the word, Austen-Leigh is moving the argument on that she was a spontaneous genius, like Scott.

Reviewers tend not to refer to her as a genius, and if they do, they limit the extent, calling her a 'real genius in her own line' (*Month* 372). She is too feminine to be genial: 'Miss Austen's nature was not of the highest type; she was not poetical, she was not philosophical, she was not even very noble or highminded; she was amiable and ladylike' (*EWDM*; *CH*, vol. I, p. 203). Austen is held up as an example to the

> scores of young ladies who are at the present moment anxious of rushing into print as novelists . . . to follow her at least in the exercise of [industry

and observation] ... and sparing no pains in cutting down, refining and polishing. (*Month* 310)

While this reviewer regards Austen's humour as 'impossible to purchase' (310), her attitude and mode of composition are graspable and therefore imitable. Because her novels are the result of labour as well as genius, some of their aspects at least can be copied, which is where reviewers' perception of Austen differs fundamentally from that of Scott, whose genius is regarded as inimitable.

Austen fits the ideal Victorian work ethic that is so emphasized in articles on Scott since what she wrote 'was worked up by incessant labour into its perfect form' (*NBR; CH*, vol. I, p. 253). What in reviews of Scott had to be made up by his quantity of labour because the writing itself came so easily to him, is in articles on Austen seen in her labouring to perfection over every detail, 'with a reverence for art itself, and a disregard of immediate popularity as aim' (*EWDM; CH*, vol. I, p. 207). For Scott, reviewers claim the opposite, and writing for money is acceptable. For Austen, it is a virtue that she does not write for money, particularly because she is a woman. While her assiduous writing leads to only six novels, it is yet an equivalent model to what Scott represents: a benevolent soul working hard to achieve an ideal – a literary one in Austen's case, one of honour and manly duty in Scott's.

Austen's femininity makes her writing incompatible with that of men. The reviewer in the *EWDM* 'will not compare her to men, for she never aimed at writing like a man' (212). Her work is superior to that of other women writers, since 'in the art of weaving a narrative Miss Austen is still pre-eminent among women' (*Times* 1866; cited from reprint in Southam's *CH*, vol. I, p. 198). It is in comparison to men that art alone is not enough: 'as a matter of art, Miss Austen's novels are more perfect than Thackeray's, but they are far from containing as many separate excellencies' (*Academy* 118); yet 'by the side of "Emma" and 'Persuasion", [Fanny Burney's] "Evelina" ... as a work of art, is coarse and farcical' (*QR* 200). The confinement to art is therefore seen as a feminine quality; greater scope, intellect, moral and social significance as masculine attributes. This distribution determines the status of the respective novels as well as judgements of the authors' capacities.

Comparison with Shakespeare

What Austen's novels are most praised for in reviews is their realistic character depiction, and it is in this that Austen is linked to Shakespeare, which testifies to her high regard with critics. However, they always make clear in their comparisons that it is only in this one aspect that she can be compared to him, so that 'she is as true to nature (in her limited acquaintance with it) as Shakespeare himself' (*Chambers's* 1870, 153). Again, the personal pronoun is used though the novels are under discussion, which emphasizes her sex and her limitations.

The Shakespeare scholar Richard Simpson in his review of the *Memoir* compares Austen to Shakespeare extensively – her works as well as her abilities and methods, but not, as reviewers do when linking Scott and Shakespeare, her characteristic behaviours. 'It is clear that she began, as Shakespeare began, with being an ironical censurer of her contemporaries' (*NBR*; *CH*, vol. I, p. 242), by being a critic, who then developed her artistic faculty. Simpson is not only the first critic to discuss Austen's irony, but he emphasizes it by linking it to Shakespeare. Simpson asserts that she deserves to be called a 'prose Shakespeare ... [because] within her range her characterization is truly Shakespearian; but she has scarcely a spark of poetry' (*NBR*; *CH*, vol. I, p. 243). The link to Shakespeare is limited at the same moment as it is being drawn, which testifies to the weight a comparison to him bears. Simpson allocates her so high a place in literature on the merit of her characters, and though she is also deficient in other aspects, it is her lack of a wider variety of characters that limits her most, precisely because the depiction of characters is her greatest strength. While Simpson thus laments her lack of character diversity, he also sees this as an inevitable limitation because she is a woman: 'her benevolent judgement [does not] allow her to paint [rascals]' (*NBR*; *CH*, vol. I, p. 246). Conscious irony in a lady is only possible to a limited extent.

Austen's popularity and status

Evidence in the articles suggests that reviewers are acquainted with most of Austen's works, since mentions of characters and subject matter occur frequently, and mistakes are rare. Where mistakes occur they tend to be of minor significance, such as the reviewer in the *EWDM* writing that 'Catherine pays a visit to Bath on the invitation of the Thorpes' (*EWDM*, *CH*, vol. I, p. 205; in fact the Allens). Articles appearing after the publication of the *Memoir* (1870) also show knowledge of that work and of Austen's life as there given.

The majority of reviewers believe the public not to be familiar with Austen's novels and include explanations of characters and circumstances referred to, such as that

> Mr. Tilney and his sister [are] the children of General Tilney, a rich and proud man, who [is] being deceived as to [Catherine's] fortune by the representations of John Thorpe (the fast Oxonian whom we have already introduced to the reader) (*EWDM*; *CH*, vol. I, p. 205),

or, more judgemental, introducing Frank Churchill as 'the confidant of Emma's suspicion ... , a young careless coxcomb, little fitted to receive any sort of confidence from any young woman' (*St Paul's*; *CH*, vol. I, p. 232).

A few reviewers mention characters assuming that the reader will know them, such as Thomas Kebbel's proving that Austen's characters are more successfully commonplace than George Eliot's:

> A Mr. Bennet, a Mr. Woodhouse, a Mrs. Norris, or a Mrs. Allen, a Catharine [sic] Morland, an Eleanor [sic] Dashwood, are characters, not only common enough in themselves, but common to the experience of all educated people. (FR 191)

With Scott, popularity concerns both works and author, whereas with Austen reviewers primarily discuss the novels' popularity. That popularity mainly concerns the novels testifies to her status throughout this period as not having reached a level at which the person matters without the works, as is the case with Scott.

Reviewers are all concerned with how well known Austen's works are among the public, though without citing evidence to support their opinions. However, the fact that they discuss this issue already indicates a changing popularity. Critics who assume that the novels are not widely popular give two main reasons for this. One is that because the novels' emotional and thematic range is limited, they can never become more popular than they are; the other, usually connected to the first, is that only cultivated people can appreciate Austen's high skill. Oliphant states that 'it is scarcely to be expected that books so calm and cold and keen, and making so little claim upon their sympathy, would ever be popular [with the general public]' (*BEM* 304), since an admirer of Austen's novels needs 'a certain amount of culture and force of observation' (*BEM* 304). Similarly, the reviewer in the *EWDM* warns that only if 'you can appreciate subtle strokes of character, ... can take pleasure from fineness of workmanship and have patience to examine it, [did] Miss Austen ... write for you' (*EWDM; CH*, vol. I, p. 201). Austen-Leigh in the 1870 *Memoir* introduces R. H. Cheney's notion of seeing it as a 'test of ability, whether people *could* or *could not* appreciate Miss Austen's merits',[15] so to find this kind of argumentation after 1870 is less remarkable than to find the same idea in the *EWDM*'s review of 1866, which would suggest that Austen's status remained largely unchanged by the appearance of the *Memoir*, at least initially. Thus, while reviewers unanimously regard critical popularity as a sign of high literary quality, some, such as Oliphant and the reviewer in the *EWDM*, see Austen's limited public popularity as evidence of her literary excellence.

Where reviewers do not agree that appeal to a limited readership attests to merit, they do not see it as a sign of poor quality either. James Payn in *Chambers's Journal* links Austen to Shakespeare in their not being read by the public, insisting that this is not to the authors' 'discredit': 'if it were not for quotations, extracts in school-books, and occasional dramatic representations, the public at large perhaps would know very little of Shakespeare' (*Chambers's* 158). Quality and public popularity are not connected. Whereas with Scott, his vast public popularity over decades is repeatedly cited to prove his superiority, the logical inversion, that a lack of popularity means mediocrity, is not applied.

The converse argumentation for Scott and Austen – broad appeal as attesting excellence, versus limited appeal as either a proof of value or as not signifying – shows that there is no general concept of the relation between public popularity and quality. It also shows reviewers' wish to regard both authors' works as high quality.

Direct statements showing reviewers' belief in Austen's popularity with the public are rare, and only occur after the publication of the second edition of the *Memoir* in 1871, which included hitherto unpublished works by Austen. Hutton writes that 'the public have been so long and so eagerly expecting' these materials (*Spect* 1871, 891), whereas in his review of the first edition he makes no mention of general readers, only of critics. Leslie Stephen, in an article on 'Humour' of 1876, brands the term 'Austenolatry' (*Cornhill* 324), already with its connotations of 'intolerant and dogmatic' readers (324), which implies professional as well as general readers. The fact that Stephen uses Austen as an example of the kind of humour of which he disapproves, and also that he deprecates all who have a taste for her kind of humour, suggests some degree of public popularity at least.

Reviewers agree on seeing Austen's popularity as having developed since her novels first appeared, so that she is now more recognized than she had been by her contemporaries. Just as the majority of reviewers of Scott believe that he will always maintain his high status, the assumption with Austen is that 'the sobriety of her fiction which prevented it from making any sudden sensation, secures to it a permanence of approbation' (*St Paul's, CH*, vol. I, p. 226). Reviewers argue that now the novels' artistic qualities have been recognized, these will ensure continued appreciation – though this will never include the public at large. Austen's depictions are ageless, and in 'the test of time ... art will make up for the want of force' (*NBR; CH*, vol. I, p. 265). Rather than, as with Scott, wide popularity after one hundred years being a proof of quality, it is the endurance of the novels with only a few readers that shows merit.

It is in this limited sense of readership also that the word 'classics' is used in the articles: 'Her works have become classics, and it is now the duty of every student of recent English literature to be more or less acquainted with them' (*BEM* 305), so that 'classics' does not mean wide popularity, but popularity with 'students of literature'. Chorley asserts that Austen's novels 'will be read so long as any one cares for English domestic fiction', and, though she was not properly appreciated during her lifetime, he is

> proud to believe, that in England at least, everything which is real makes a way, not to be closed up, but to be widened as years go on .... These quiet novels have become classics. So much can hardly be said for the other [early nineteenth-century] female novelists. (*QR* 200)

Like other reviewers, Chorley sees the fact that it has taken until now for people to appreciate her as she ought to be appreciated as reflecting well on his age, making his own generation the first of many to honour her work. He also applies Austen-Leigh's 'Cheney-test' and sees appreciation of Austen's novels as 'a new test of ability' (*QR* 196), so that readers of Austen now become 'ablest judges' (196). Also, Chorley again judges her firmly within a female, limited category, so that even as a 'classic' she remains a certain kind of classic, and her novels will not be read as long as anyone cares for fiction, but as long as 'any one cares for domestic fiction'. These statements reveal a sense of her status having developed between the early and the late nineteenth century. Reviewers' pride in appreciating Austen reveals that they perceive these changes as recent ones.

There are, however, reviewers that testify more directly to recent developments, such as Payn, who asserts that Austen's works

> are very seldom bought. There is no such a thing as a cheap edition of them – that is, *really* cheap – in existence; and considering she has been dead these fifty years, the fact is conclusive against her popularity. (*Chambers's* 158).[16]

This statement carries a footnote, reading 'Since this paper was written, a cheap edition of Miss Austen's work *has* appeared'. Only two editions appear in 1870, the year his article appears in, so that the edition Payn is referring to is presumably Chapman & Hall's, priced at 2–2.6 shillings depending on binding. This price was still high above '*really* cheap' editions of Scott's novels. Nevertheless, by Payn's own criteria, the appearance of this edition means that Austen is becoming more widely popular, but this was still mainly among the middle classes. The development is a gradual one, since she is not yet in the public mind in any way comparable to Scott: I found no entries on her in *Notes and Queries* prior to December 1884.

Hutton, in 1869, can already state that he finds quoting authorities on her superfluous, because 'no one with a grain of literary sense doubts her wonderful originality and artistic power. To dispute it now is simply to prove that the disputant does not know what he is talking about' (*Spect, CH*, vol. II, p. 161). He writes this immediately on the appearance of the *Memoir*, so before it can have had any large impact. Hutton believes criticism to have developed into appreciating Austen and feels himself superior to anyone who does not realize her skill. Even Stephen, who condemns her most of all the reviewers, does not doubt her ability:

> To deny Miss Austen's marvellous literary skill would be simply to convict oneself of the grossest stupidity. It is probable, however, that as much skill may have been employed in painting a bit of old china as in one of Raphael's masterpieces. We do not therefore say that it possesses equal merit. (*Cornhill* 324)

Direct comparisons of Austen and Scott

Even if past its peak, Scott's critical popularity remains supremely high throughout the period. Reviewers usually see Austen as approaching him, possibly exceeding him in some aspects, particularly in her character depictions, but being unable to compete with him on any larger scale. Scott 'has achieved the most natural amalgamation of the romantic and the real' (*St Paul's*; *CH*, vol. I, p. 235); Austen offers realism only. His wide range leads to a more realistic image of the world. The depiction of a section of one social class at a particular time can never be as relevant and instructive as the depiction of all social classes over centuries. Also, reviewers complain that she can only appeal to the reader's head, not heart, whereas Scott appeals to both reason and emotion. Where Scott is referred to in articles on Austen, it emphasizes her strengths by showing where she is as good as or better than Scott, which gives her prestige but also stresses her limitations. The major points of criticism about Austen's novels are seen as being fulfilled in Scott's, so that his novels, as in the early nineteenth century, still represent an ideal, though no longer exclusively nor in all aspects.

Scott is also frequently mentioned in articles on Austen as having judged her favourably, which testifies to his continuously high status as a literary authority. It also shows that Austen is still on a level where authorities' praising her is needed to confirm the status reviewers assign her. Reviewers repeatedly mention that Austen recognized Scott as the author of *Waverley*, by which they praise her powers of perception and again connect literary and personal skills.

Austen's featuring in articles on Scott is more unexpected than his appearance in articles on her. It is evidence of her being known to a certain extent, even where she is brought in to enhance Scott's qualities, as in the *London Quarterly Review*. The reviewer is very clear about the hierarchy between Austen and Scott:

> The art so exquisitely practised by Jane Austen, within strait enough intellectual limits, and without any deep perceptions of human passion or any wide knowledge of the human heart ... will never countervail, for the uses of our youths and maidens, [Scott's] art (*LQR* 1872, 43),

because Austen is not alone in having done her kind of art well, whereas Scott did 'magnificently what no one else has yet approached him in' (*LQR* 43). The vehemence of the reviewer's argument, his absolute statements and the denial of significant qualities in Austen, while yet referring to her, in themselves testify to her risen status. Austen's art cannot be useful to the younger generation, whereas Scott offers moral, healthful reading and 'noble manliness' (*LQR* 40). Again, she is seen as lacking in scope, romance and morality.

Oliphant states that while Scott was 'helped in the origination of [the modern novel by] Miss Edgeworth, Miss Austen, Miss Ferrier, [they] rose with the greater magician, like secondary moons round a planet' (*BEM* 1871, 230); and she later asserts, as if to prove the hierarchy just drawn, that 'nothing of any weight or importance in the shape of fiction had appeared between "Waverley" and "Sir Charles Grandison" ' (*BEM* 245). Though Oliphant gives Austen credit for originality and contributing to the development of the novel in general, she leaves no doubt as to who is the greatest novelist of all.

The review that most favourably links Austen and Scott appears towards the end of the period, in 1879, and is not specifically about either author. In an article in *The Quarterly Review* on 'The Reflection of English Character in English Art', the reviewer links the two authors by seeing them each as the best in their domain. Scott's field is that of history, romance and realism; Austen's that of the novel of manners, focusing on character rather than incident, and her genre therefore gives 'new opportunities to female genius' (*QR* 1879, 98). Though still distinguishing male and female genius, the reviewer does not deem female genius impossible and no longer by definition inferior. He argues that 'with Sir Walter Scott and Miss Austen the art of novel writing in England reached its meridian' (98). He lists Dickens, Thackeray, Eliot and Reade as inferior to both Austen and Scott, which shows acceptance of Austen's mode of writing. As well as male and female writers being potentially equal, a novel with a more limited range can be better than one with a wide scope – an opinion unthinkable a decade earlier. Both Austen and Scott are thus given as high a position as possible as the best of their literary class, but because Austen stays in the female domain of the novel of manners, her limitations, though not discussed, are implied – not least in the reviewer's fervent statement that

> could we suppose ourselves condemned to solitary confinement, and our supply of books restricted to the works of a single writer, who would not choose for his companion 'the author of "Waverley"'? (97)

Part 3

The Later-twentieth-century Response

Chapter 7

Editions, 1913–2003

By plotting the numbers of publishers' relaunches, we can trace the comparative status of the individual works of the two authors in the marketplace during the whole period from 1811 till 2003. For the twentieth century, as for the earlier period, I use relaunches in preference to editions to take account of the fact that existing stereotype and electrotype plates were sometimes used. We can also trace the number of collected editions, a measure of the extent to which publishers believed that the market was interested in the whole oeuvre and an indication of their canonical status as classics. The results are summarized in Figures 7.1 and 7.2.

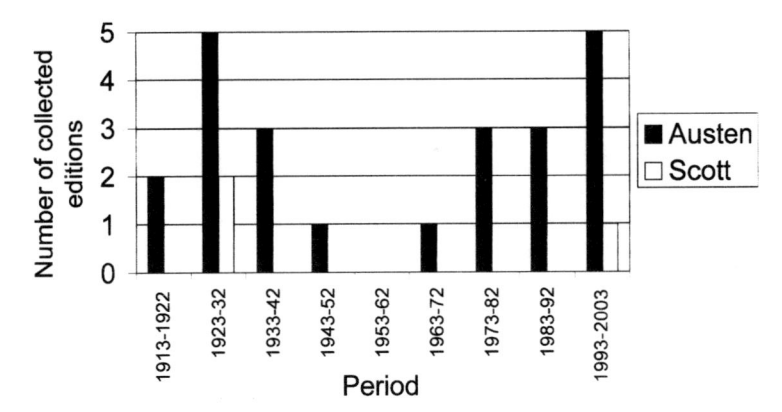

Figure 7.1 Collected editions of Austen's and Scott's novels
Figure 7.1 shows collected editions of Austen's and Scott's works in the twentieth century.

The key event during the post-First World War years, and one which explains the apparently strange U shape in Figure 7.1, was the publishing of R. W. Chapman's collected edition of Austen's novels in 1923. Chapman's edition includes a textual apparatus, maps, explanations of early nineteenth-century customs and vocabulary, etc. He gives Austen the kind of treatment until then reserved for ancient Greek and Latin classics, and a handful of English authors such as Shakespeare and Milton. Austen therefore not only achieves a belated fully canonical status but becomes the first ever British novelist to have her works published in a textual edition.

The care that is taken over Austen's texts compared to no attention being paid to which version of Scott's texts is read indicates the two authors' different critical status. These findings are consistent with assumptions hitherto made about when Scott's reputation decreased, usually somewhere between 1870 and 1885,[1] but definitely before 1900.

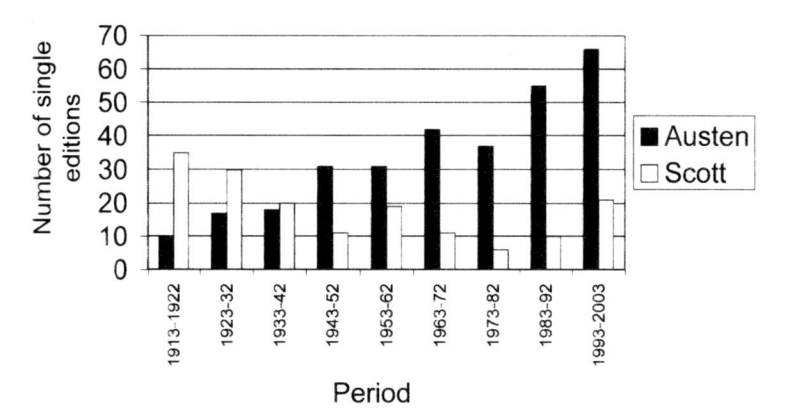

Figure 7.2 Single editions of Austen's and Scott's novels
Figure 7.2 shows single editions of all completed novels by Austen and Scott.[2]

However, Figure 7.2 shows the importance of distinguishing between public and critical reputation: while Scott's critical reputation goes down towards the end of the nineteenth and the beginning of the twentieth century, single editions intimate that Scott's public popularity stays higher than Austen's until the 1930s – much longer than is generally assumed. The Scott titles published also suggest that his popularity continues with a broad readership: between 1913 and 1932, 23 out of Scott's 27 novels appear in at least one edition.[3] Reading Scott has not yet become focused on a few titles, as it would in later decades. Nevertheless, the earlier trend of Austen rising in esteem relative to Scott carries on constantly, and after the crossover in popularity, the gap between the two authors continues to widen during the years of economic depression, the Second World War, and postwar austerity. The turn of the twentieth century, however, sees a change in the trend of Scott's popularity: the Edinburgh Edition of the Waverley Novels is inaugurated, the first collected edition of Scott's novels to appear since 1932 and the first textual edition of his fiction ever, indicating Scott's increased critical status.

Chapter 8

Media Reception and Cultural Status, 1990–2003

Newspaper articles testify to an author's literary reputation with the public as well as to cultural status. They aim at a non-specialist audience, and reflect what readers want to be informed about, thus shaping as well as representing public opinion. They are therefore in some respects the equivalent of the anecdotal comments in the early nineteenth century, though on a much larger scale.

Articles that do not have either author as their main focus but mention him or her peripherally in the context of something else reveal more about this author's cultural status than articles focusing exclusively on the author. Peripheral references reveal what an author denotes and what kind of acquaintance with work and person can be taken for granted. The study therefore includes articles concentrating on Scott or Austen as well as articles that refer to them peripherally. Newspapers included are *The Times,* the *Independent,* and the *Guardian,* chosen to give a spectrum of political stance. A longitudinal study such as is offered in this chapter would not have been feasible before now, since looking for articles of this kind is only possible through electronic databases, notably *LexisNexis,* that permit word searches.

Walter Scott

Newspaper articles on Walter Scott can be divided into two main groups: those that focus on his works or on him as a writer, and those that bring him in as culturally and historically important without directly connecting this to his literary output. The majority of articles that feature Scott between 1990 and 2003 are articles not on him alone but on other issues, featuring Scott only in passing. The views expressed in articles focusing entirely or peripherally on Scott are similar to one another.

The three papers investigated do not differ in their ways of presenting Scott. Also, in spite of all three being national papers, articles on Scott tend to be written by Scotsmen, which already puts him in a Scottish, rather than British, category.

Scott the Writer

Few articles are devoted entirely to Scott as a writer. I have found none for the years 1990–92, five in 1993, and only two between 1994 and 2003, testifying to Scott's low literary popularity. The year 1993 sees the launch of the Edinburgh Edition of the Waverley Novels (EEWN) with the publication of *Kenilworth, The Tale of Old Mortality* and *The Black Dwarf*, so that exceptions to mentioning Scott peripherally occur mostly in connection with this.

The appearance of these articles reflects what Figures 7.1 and 7.2 indicate: there is a minor upsurge in interest in Scott's novels from 1993 onwards, so that the EEWN motivates reaction from both newspapers and publishers. However, the great majority of allusions to Scott as a writer or to his works occur in articles on other topics, such as the Edinburgh Festival, other writers, literary history, genres and technique.

The underlying assumption in all articles is that readers of the articles will not be acquainted with Scott's novels. The only 1993 article that discusses an individual novel rather than concerning itself with the EEWN as a general fact is revealingly entitled 'On The Shelf; Books: Kate Saunders thrills to Sir Walter Scott's swashbuckling *Old Mortality*' (*ST*, 16 May 1993), already indicating that Scott's novels are perceived as unread and as adventure stories.[1] Articles portray the EEWN as an attempt to 'make Scott fashionable' (*ST*, 15 Aug. 1993). They sensationalize Scott's novels, however, suggesting little knowledge of the texts in either this or any previous edition. The EEWN 'is likely to surprise readers with its pace, liveliness and occasional vulgarity' (*T*, 17 Aug. 1993), as scholars have unearthed the 'real' Scott from the original manuscripts, which had been the victims of censors for two centuries. Articles make out that Scott is unread because his novels had been repeatedly subject to censorship, though in fact no changes had been made to the texts since the Magnum of 1829–33 apart from abridged editions, and these had not been motivated by censors. The concept of censorship appeals to journalists, since what was censored in the nineteenth century for its vulgarity may precisely be what most interests now so that 'anyone who dismisses the classic novels of Sir Walter Scott as staid and boring should think again' (*T*, 17 Aug. 1993). Censorship makes the new edition more of a sensation, restoring 'Walter Scott's prose ... to full sexual vigour' (*Ind*, 17 Aug. 1993). Journalists render Scott's novels more interesting by this implied comparison to the censored works of authors in any totalitarian regime and thereby add to the sensation of their news by appealing to readers' sense of their own social and literary freedom. Articles remain vague about just what Scott's literary qualities are, showing that the writers themselves, as well as the readers, possess little knowledge of the novels.

Articles rarely mention individual novels, and where they do they are careful to mention author and novel together. Iain Martin starts his article off with 'Sir Walter Scott, the 19th century novelist who created *Ivanhoe* and *Rob Roy*' (*T*, 1996), significantly choosing *Ivanhoe* and *Rob Roy* as examples, the only two

Scott novels with titles that also exist as 1990s films.[2] While the knowledge that Scott was a novelist is usually presupposed, any detail of works or even which century he lived in is not.

Knowledge about Scott the writer is vague, often legendary. Journalists all have an image of Scott as prolific, referring to his productiveness admiringly as well as disparagingly. One journalist looks up to Scott as having written 'over 70 novels' (*Ind*, 9 Oct. 1994), (in fact less than 30). Another sees Scott's fecundity as having led to his novels 'clogg[ing] up the pores of the second-hand book trade' (*Ind*, 7 Feb. 1996) – though it is not the number of novels written but their popularity in the nineteenth century, leading to the publication of vast numbers of copies, that is responsible. Scott's fecundity adds to the image of his unreadability by implying the impossibility of ever getting through all his works. Scott's writing off his debts is another such legend, and the amount of his debts becomes even more colossal than it really was (about £120,000), being inflated to his having 'ended up £5 million in debt' (*G*, 17 Feb. 1997). In a similar vein are statements such as 'the novel was virtually created in its modern form by Sir Walter Scott' (*ST*, 9 Aug. 1992), while comments such as 'the novels of Sir Walter Scott were even more gripping collected in a single volume than they had been in their initial magazine instalments' (*Ind*, 11 May 2001) demonstrate the unreliable nature of most knowledge even about, not just of, Scott's works. While knowledge of Scott's novels is thus neither expected in the readers of the articles nor present in the writers, articles testify to an indefinite sense of Scott as a somehow significant writer.

The image of Scott's novels given is that they are not worth reading. Their main quality is seen in their being romantic, and romantic is defined as not realistic, out of date and not relevant for today. Reading his works reflects on the reader as being 'as quaint ... as anything produced by Walter Scott' (*Ind*, 16 Aug. 1997). His novels are seen as idealizing the past 'with their yearning for some golden age of bloody chivalry' (*Ind*, 25 Jan. 1996). Their historical subject matter adds to journalists' perception of Scott as backward looking. Romantic and historical settings are seen in opposition to dealing with the present. They are connected to the novels' Scottishness, which facilitates articles' tendency to present all Scott's novels as Scottish. The vagueness with which the novels are referred to also makes it easier to present him as always writing about romantic Scotland, and if a novel is specifically mentioned that does not deal with Scotland, such as *Ivanhoe*, it is its romance and adventure character that is emphasized, so that the image of Scott the Scottish romantic can be retained. Journalists thus shape the novels to fit their image of Scott and his works. They ignore the fact that he is not a militant Scottish nationalist but addresses questions of nationhood and nationalism, and how to retain national identity within a larger unit. The topicality of these issues would render him relevant for today, but articles insist on presenting Scott as backward looking.

The few writers who regard Scott's novels as topical invariably see the works as favouring national unity and Britishness. Not only do the writers regard the novels as approving of the Union, but also see Scott as having appropriated Scottish as well as British tradition into his works. Allan Massie states in the *Sunday Times* that

> nobody can doubt the intensity of Scott's attachment to Scotland, ... [yet] he found no difficulty in associating himself with 'the mightiest chiefs of British song'. [Massie doubts if he] could find a Scots poet to express similar sentiments today (*ST,* 6 Jan. 1991),

and thereby gives Scott political insight and tolerance even above modern Scottish writers. Scott's being romantic and out of date is bound up with his being Scottish; as soon as he is either seen as British or as writing with British relevance, he becomes more topical.

Some articles give Scott's style as a reason for the unreadability of his novels though these statements, too, are vague. One writer praises a radio adaptation of *Waverley* as better than the novel because 'the story comes across as livelier and more plot-driven when not bowed down by the weight of Scott's prose.' (*Ind,* 4 Jan. 1994). Journalists such as these see his novels as containing exciting adventure stories, but his way of telling as too slow and heavy to make the novels attractive. Slowness adds to the works' quaintness, so that the works are unreadable 'unless you're in prison or just fantastically old' (*Ind,* 12 Aug. 2001). Late-twentieth-century readers cannot be expected to spend their precious time on Scott, and a 'Londoner's experience' of Scott's works in particular is necessarily negative because of a fast-moving lifestyle that Scott's works do not fit in with. His novels are boring even to the extent of being used by people suffering from insomnia (*Ind,* 2 Oct. 1994).

Underlying the view of Scott as unreadable is a concept of unpopularity being a sign of low quality. Journalists' neglect of his nineteenth-century success helps to maintain this concept. Evading references to Scott's former success also means that the question of what about his novels may once have appealed can be ignored. That the public generally do not challenge newspapers' version of Scott indicates that they are not aware of, or do not care about, other options – with Austen, inaccuracies often lead to letters to the editor of the respective paper; with Scott, such reactions rarely occur.

Scott the man

While articles presuppose knowledge of none of the novels, they regard the man as more familiar to readers, and allude to events relating to his life, such as his bankruptcy and ensuing heroism or his supposed political convictions, without further explanation.

The quality that articles always presuppose as known is his Scottishness and his being somehow culturally significant for Scotland and its history. Articles regard him as typical of Scotland to the extent of being a symbol of it. In the debate about a European currency, there is the wish for Scottish banknotes to bear 'some Scottish effigy – the thistle, Edinburgh Castle or Sir Walter Scott, perhaps' (*Ind*, 2 Dec. 1991). Even the known events of his life are seen as typically Scottish:

> one of the charms of the Scottish character is that ... almost anything they attempt as a concerted national effort runs into trouble through lack of management and lack of money. ... [The writer] sometimes think[s] that Sir Walter Scott can stand as an emblem for the whole nation, with his huge international success followed by his business collapse and gruesome final financial ordeal. (*Ind*, 29 Jan. 1996)

Scotland is 'Scott-land' (*T*, 29 Nov. 2000) and Scott is connected to a number of issues that constitute Scottish identity. Most frequently recurring is his role in creating Scottish tourism, especially through Scottish tartans, which articles describe as having been 'specially designed by that arch-Romantic Sir Walter Scott' (*Ind*, 3 Sept. 1992) when Scott had been master of ceremonies for George IV's visit to Scotland in 1822. As in articles on the novels, romantic takes on a negative quality because it is opposed to reality. Just as some journalists see his novels as portraying 'a horribly romantic caricature of Scottishness, and one that has infected the world's view of Scotland ever since' (*Ind*, 4 Jan. 1994), some blame him for having invented 'tartanalia' for the King's benefit, and for 'encouraging a caricature of Scotland now found on postcards and shortbread tins' (*T*, 25 July 1992). Though the historical accuracy of both these ways of holding Scott responsible for a romantic image of Scotland either through novels or his role in the 1822 festivities is at least questionable, newspaper articles take them as given facts. No distinctions are made between Highland and Lowland customs though Scott clearly differentiates them in his novels, nor are any details given about Scott's inventions of tartans. While articles all share the view of Scott as having created a vision of Scotland, not all blame him for it, some seeing his cultural significance in having 'kept Scottishness alive, even imperfectly, at a time when it was in decline and might have died entirely' (*T*, 25 July 1992).

In addition to being regarded as having turned Scotland into a tourist attraction, Scott himself is also described as appealing to tourists: in an article on Tennyson, Philip Oakes in the *Independent* states that in contrast to Tennyson, of whom no souvenirs are made, 'we already have a surfeit of Sir Walter Scott shortcake, and Shakespearean sundries' (*Ind*, 15 Apr. 1990). Scott's works are by no means as well known as Shakespeare's, yet he and Shakespeare are used as a contrast to Tennyson. Since Scott's literary popularity is not nearly high enough to justify the souvenirs, or the journalist's awareness of them on the same level as Shakespeare's, they testify to Scott's high cultural status. Oakes' statement also shows Scott's being bound up with Scotland: the souvenir example is shortbread, itself already a Scottish souvenir, so that Scott souvenirs are not only representing him but also Scotland – independent of his literary reputation.

As in articles on his novels there are some journalists who regard him as having contributed to British politics, usually through seeing him as having recognized the necessity of the Union, but they still view him as romantic and therefore unrealistic: James Cusick in the *Independent* states that

> if Mr Forsyth now imagines himself as Sir Walter Scott reincarnated and is intent on continually reinforcing the symbolic power of 300 years of union with England as the foundation of his election campaign, Mr Robertson is equally a touch romantic when he speaks of, perhaps predictably, 'new Scotland, new Union'. (*Ind*, 3 Dec. 1996)

While Scott here gains significance for British as well as for Scottish politics, he yet remains a romantic visionary of a romantic country.

Film adaptations of Scott's novels[3]

Ivanhoe is the only adaptation of a Scott novel between 1990 and 2003 and it was shown in six parts on BBC1 early in 1997. (There are numerous previous adaptations of Scott's novels, including *Ivanhoe*.) It had been intended as their 'flagship production for the coming year' (*Ind*, 12 Sept. 1996), in the hope that it would 'rival the success of [the 1995] production of Jane Austen's *Pride and Prejudice*' (*T*, 23 Oct. 1996), and, as with Austen's novel, Penguin produced a TV tie-in edition with actors from the film on the cover. In the event, the film was described as a disappointment, though it drew an audience of about eight million, falling to about five million, compared to *Pride and Prejudice*'s record audience of more than ten million for the final episode. These numbers already indicate films' independence from an author's works and reputation, since the gap in popularity between Austen's and Scott's novels is far greater than that between the appeal of the film adaptations of *Pride and Prejudice* and *Ivanhoe*.

The film does not appear to have had an impact on Scott's reputation, nor does it seem to have induced many people to read the novel. Only one new edition appears: the Penguin TV tie-in, and while there may have been reprints of this and previous editions, the fact that no new publishers print a novel which is out of copyright indicates the limits of public demand. Most articles concern themselves with the film only, mentioning Scott not at all or very briefly, and revealing no knowledge of the novel. Sweeping statements such as 'as for Walter Scott, I'm sure he did a lot of very thorough research, but he does romanticise the era a bit' (*Ind*, 19 Jan. 1997) show this unfamiliarity with the novel. Where the film is criticized as too romantic and out of date Scott is brought in: 'Walter Scott – slapping his cards on the table – called *Ivanhoe* a romance. It touches reality at no known point. But romance has been out and realism in for a long time now' (*G*, 13 Jan. 1997). The film is uninteresting, 'inarticulate and humourless (all of which is Sir Walter Scott's fault)' (*Ind*, 19 Jan. 1997).

The 1995 film version of *Rob Roy* is not an adaptation of Scott's novel. Journalists tend to ignore the novel just as they do *Ivanhoe*, but where they do mention it in their reviews of the film they are usually unaware that what connects the novel and film is primarily the title.

* * *

From journalists' position of not reading or knowing the novels, two attitudes become apparent: the novels are either dismissed as adventure stories that are obscured by Scott's heavy style, or they are held in awe and respected from a distance, as something abstract and archaic yet somehow important. Where Scott is referred to as a writer it is without any discussion of the novels, which shows the novels' insignificance in today's society. While numbers of both single and collected editions go up in the 1990s, this rise is not yet discernable in Scott's general reputation with the public as testified to in newspaper articles. Scott's undisputed cultural status stands unconnected to his literary reputation, but his literary reputation is influenced by his high cultural status since the man's being important makes the works appear yet more overwhelming.

Scottish journalist Alan Hamilton's assessment in *The Times* is typical of the prevailing view of Scott (except for his realization that Scott is concerned with Scottish and British history):

> Today's schoolchildren are generally spared the ordeal of being dragged by the hair through the dense, lengthy prose of Sir Walter Scott, who ladled a rich sauce of romance over the dry bones of Scottish and English history. But he remains an important historical figure in his own right, if only because he was the public relations genius behind Scotland's return to favour when King George IV forgave the country for the Jacobite uprising of 1745. (*T*, 7 Aug. 1995)

While Scott's works are reduced to trivial romantic stories, the man is regarded as culturally significant for Scotland. Scott's cultural reputation overshadows his literary reputation: Scott the Tory partisan is remembered and this image is projected onto Scott the writer, while the novels' contents and past readings of them are ignored. Scott the author, being proudly Unionist, writing about not only Britain but Europe, cannot be used as a source of national pride in the Scottish nationalist sense: his works do not lend themselves to construct pre-union Scotland as a lost paradise, and post-union Scotland as subservient to England.

Paradoxically, Scott's being the 'arch-romantic' (*Ind*, 3 Sept. 1992) can be forgiven culturally but not literarily, so that the cultural status of the man can be high in spite of the low literary reputation of his works. Because his works are seen as unrealistically romantic, and confined to Scottish history, they are denied any significance for British readers today, whereas culturally, Scottishness is precisely what makes him significant. Articles mention Scott in connection with issues regarding Scotland and history, tartans and law, and, in contrast to his works, his cultural importance is taken for granted and it is assumed the public will know his name and connect it with Scotland. His public popularity in the late twentieth century thus manifests itself in his cultural, narrowly nationalist, not in his literary significance.

Jane Austen

Though there are not many newspaper articles focusing entirely on Walter Scott's novels, some at least exist, whereas for Jane Austen's works I could find none. Between 1990 and 1994, there is no article that focuses exclusively on Austen as a writer or on her novels and every article after 1995 is somehow informed by the films and so cannot be seen as solely concerned with Austen's works. The majority of articles focusing entirely on Scott's works appear in connection with the launch of the EEWN, of which there is no equivalent for Austen in the 1990s.

Up to 1995, Austen therefore only ever features peripherally. The main function of her and her works is to serve as an example for issues connected to literature. 'Great art' is defined as 'lifelong works, to which, like the novels of Jane Austen or Shakespeare, you can repeatedly return' (*Ind*, 22 June 1994). This statement is typical of articles' attitudes as it shows Austen to be primarily seen as a writer, so that for Austen, there is no such split between literary reputation and cultural status as there is for Scott. The statement also indicates the connection between her and high literary culture, which is stressed by putting her on the same level as Shakespeare.

Articles testify to Austen's works, like Shakespeare's, never really being part of the debate about which texts are classics or what should be on schools' syllabi, as both these authors' significance is regarded as being beyond dispute: 'apart from Shakespeare and Jane Austen, all [participants] chose different writers and titles' (*Ind*, 10 Sept. 1992) when asked to nominate literary classics.

In contrast to Scott, the greatness of Austen's literary achievement is never doubted, even where critical voices make themselves heard. At the same time, again in contrast to Scott, her novels are written about as read and as readable. Retaining a high-culture image makes reading them reflect positively on the reader. John Major lets it be known that he is 'a great Jane Austen fan [who] rereads her regularly' (*T*, 11 Feb. 1991), as does Iain Duncan Smith. (In the light of how reading Scott or Austen reflects on the reader, Tony Blair's decision to announce *Ivanhoe* as his favourite novel is all the more unusual. The novel has, however, safe and inclusive connotations, being by a Scottish author, about English history and several peoples, and compromise not antagonism as a solution.)

However, although articles assume readers to be familiar with the novels' titles, they make little reference to the works' contents. As regards Austen's characters or plots, articles are almost as abstract as they are with Scott's, which hints at a limited acquaintance with the novels. Two surveys reported about in newspapers illustrate the extent of public familiarity with Austen's novels as well as her literary status further: according to a 1991 survey of what teachers read (teachers generally, not just of English), 'Hardy and Jane Austen topped the list of teachers' favourite authors' (*Ind*, 1 July 1991). Teachers are not representative of the public at large, being found 'to read more and own more books than average', so that this does not indicate general familiarity with Austen's works but their definitely being among the books read by those who read a good deal anyway. A survey about the knowledge of 17-year-olds shows that 'only half identified the Jane Austen novel about the Bennet family' (*Ind*, 20 Sept. 1993), which is even less impressive than it may appear as they were given four novels to choose from – *Madame Bovary*, *The Heart of Mid-Lothian*, *Clarissa* and *Pride and Prejudice* – so that they only had to make the connection between *Pride and Prejudice* and Jane Austen rather than knowing anything about the plot. Austen is thus used as a measure of education and high culture. With the general public, though her name is familiar as a writer of high literature, the content of her novels is not necessarily known, so that authors of articles refrain from referring to it.

There are articles arguing over the right way of reading Austen, indicating that she is actually being read. Austen's novels are read in more varied ways than Scott's, mainly because she is being read at all, whereas opinions on Scott largely consist of stereotypes. Rather than blaming the author for weaknesses, as Scott is blamed for romanticizing and writing in 'dense, lengthy prose' (*T*, 7 Aug. 1995), Austen's readers blame one another for wrong readings. *Independent*-reader James Essinger complains in a letter to the paper that

> too many modern fans of Jane Austen admire her because they enjoy indulging in fantasies of living in large country houses rather than because Jane Austen's best work ... is no less alive today than when it was written (*Ind*, 17 Feb. 1994),

revealing the attitude so often expressed by Austen readers throughout the centuries of his reading being the right one.[4]

Articles emphasize Austen's gender as well as her concern with women's lives. They refer to her as 'Jane Austen', whereas other writers tend to be referred to by their surnames only. Listings appear as 'Brontës, Jane Austen and Tennyson' (*ST*, 3 May 1992), 'Shakespeare, Bach, Jane Austen and Nietzsche' (*G*, 6 Jan. 1995), or 'Shakespeare, Shaw, Jane Austen, Freud' (*G*, 8 Aug. 1995), stressing her femininity as well as evoking a sense of familiarity. Two apparently contradictory concepts of femininity are applied together: one connects Austen's femininity to emancipation, the other to gentleness and history. In neither case is the distinction between Austen and her works clearly drawn, corresponding to the vague nature of references to the novels in the articles generally. As with Scott, the image of Austen given is extended beyond the facts. Journalists present her as having 'turned down two marriage proposals in order to write, perhaps for the money or for the sake of her art' (*T*, 20 Sept. 1993) so that concepts of the 1990s, of choices between career versus wife and mother, are projected onto Austen, who emerges as progressive and topical. On the other hand, her femininity is connected to her presentation of the domestic interior of English village life in 'gentler times' (*T*, 20 Sept. 1993) and therefore defined by restrictedness. She is 'the most English of novelists' (*T*, 11 Feb. 1994) which not only further limits her in scope, but makes her all the more comforting through that, since she is also 'the greatest portrayor of village life' (*G*, 13 Nov. 1993). The Englishness she stands for is always a historical Englishness, which makes it easier to see reading her as 'a tremendous escape from a high-pressure job' (*T*, 20 Sept. 1993). While Scott represents historic romantic Scotland, Austen represents historic England, domestic Regency England of the higher classes, and a feminine Regency England in its restrictedness, politeness and gentleness. However, while Scott is denied realism because of his romantic backward-oriented vision that is the opposite of topical, Austen's realism and truth are part of her appeal: what she describes is regarded not as a wishful imagined version of a past that never existed, but an Englishness that was real and is now past, and which can be easily reimagined by visiting Chawton, Bath, or Lyme Regis. Yet her realistic depictions give readers the option to idealize her period and society, which adds to her appeal by opening her novels as a 'tremendous escape'.

References to Austen occur in a literary context. Journalists see her as high culture, but as readable high culture, and stress femininity and historical Englishness, usually without clearly distinguishing novel and author. The cultural significance she has gained comes through her novels, so that before 1995, her cultural status is dependent on her literary reputation, which is based on the novels.

Film adaptations of Austen's novels

From 1995 onwards, articles testify to Austen's reputation being inextricably bound up with the film adaptations of her novels. This is the year that Andrew Davies's adaptation of *Pride and Prejudice* came out, and though not the first TV adaptation of an Austen novel, none had been nearly as popular. The connotations of her name stay the same, however, since she is still regarded as high culture. This image is projected onto the films, hence TV channels and cinemas are fond of Austen: films based on her works fetch 'a large upmarket audience' (*G*, 13 Oct. 1995) who come 'out of hiding and hopefully they will re-establish a cinema-going habit' (*Ind*, 22 June 1996). She remains high culture while at the same time being regarded as 'the Quentin Tarantino of the middle classes' (*G*, 13 Oct. 1995). The films bring people to the novels' plots who do not read them, and the novels and their image bring people who do not usually watch films to the adaptations. Austen is therefore seen as a mediator between 'high and low culture' (*Ind*, 9 Feb. 1996), uniting 'the literati and the lads' (*T*, 15 Oct. 1995).

In addition to bringing new viewers to film, the adaptations are generally assumed to bring new readers to the books. With *Ivanhoe*, this only happens to a very limited degree: only one edition appears in the year the film is broadcast, and articles in newspapers continue not to refer to the contents of the novel. With *Pride and Prejudice*, the film's impact on numbers of editions is greater: six new editions appear, by as many different publishers. They all want a share in the *Pride and Prejudice* market, which indicates higher demand for this novel than for *Ivanhoe* in the years of the respective films.

However, 1995 is not the only year in which six editions come out. Figure 7.3 shows editions of *Pride and Prejudice* published in Britain between 1983 and 2003.

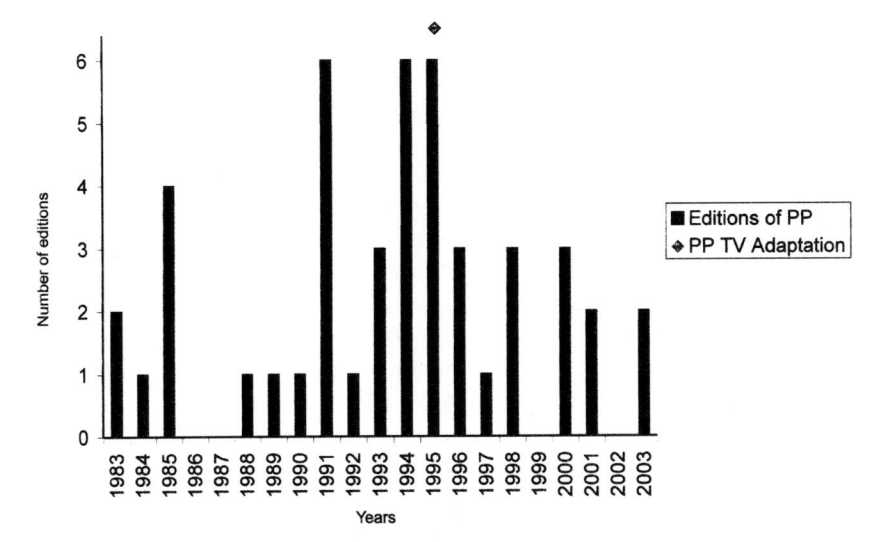

Figure 7.3 Editions of *Pride and Prejudice* published in Britain between 1983 and 2003. The graph of editions of *Pride and Prejudice* includes single editions as well as publications of *PP* that appeared as part of collected editions of Austen's works.

Six is the highest number of editions in any year between 1983 and 2003. Yet this number comes out in 1991, 1994 and 1995. The film is therefore one factor that triggers new editions of a novel. While the film of *Pride and Prejudice* ensures this high level of new editions, it does not cause an influx of them. Moreover, its influence on editions is not long lived, since before and after 1995, the average number of *Pride and Prejudice* editions per year stays constant at slightly more than two a year.

In combination with sales numbers and library borrowing records, editions are one factor that indicates the effect of film on a novel's popularity. All three measurements show a short period of increased interest in the novel that quickly goes down again. The Penguin tie-in edition with Jennifer Ehle and Colin Firth on the cover sold 148,000 copies from August 1995 to January 1996 (*Ind*, 23 Jan. 1996), and sales numbers of several *Pride and Prejudice* editions in October 1995 (when the serial was still being broadcast) amounted to 12,000 a week, which was 'right up there with the new Catherine Cookson and John Grisham' (*G*, 13 Oct. 1995). These sales records, combined with the evidence of editions, intimate a short intensive period of people buying the book, and interest going down again just as suddenly as it flared up. The film therefore had a brief effect on the sales of the novel, but rather than being sold in its own right, the novel seems to have been sold as an adjunct to the film: Penguin's *The Making of Pride and Prejudice* by Sue Birtwistle and Susie Conklin sold equally well, with 112,000 copies bought between September 1995 and January 1996 (*Ind*, 23 Jan. 1996). In Dillons' Bestseller list, published in *The Times* in December 1995, the paperbacks chart includes three books connected to the film, along with works by writers such as Colin Dexter, Patricia Cornwell, Danielle Steel. Apart from *Pride and Prejudice*, no other nineteenth-century work features. *The Making of Pride and Prejudice* (Penguin) ranks at number 3, at 12 *Pemberley* by Emma Tennant (Sceptre), and at 15 *Pride and Prejudice* (the TV tie-in edition, Penguin). This ranking order testifies to the film's dominance over the novel. Rather than causing interest in the novel as a work of fiction in its own right, the film caused a longing for more of itself.

Library lending records indicate a similarly short period of increased interest. Table 7.1 shows the limited long-term impact films have on the popularity of Austen's novels. It also shows the traceable short-term effects: Austen goes up to position three in the second half of 1995 and remains there until June 1997. The year 1995 saw four film adaptations of her novels and 1996 two. The next film based on an Austen text did not come out until 1999 (Patricia Rozema's *Mansfield Park*), when Austen again attains a slightly higher position. While each film appears to have a short impact on borrowing statistics of the novels, films do not result in the novels' generally being more frequently borrowed: Austen remains among the top ten, on no permanently higher position than prior to the films.

Most newspaper articles do not convey any sense of differentiation between novel and film. Characters are referred to without specifying which version of them is meant and 'Jane Austen' is used indiscriminately, without stipulating whether the person, her novels or the film adaptations of those novels are referred to. Without making it explicit or even necessarily being aware of it, the majority of articles refer to film versions of the novels and their characters. Especially where references occur in a non-literary context they demonstrate that characters denote an image that is the films', not the novels'. Men 'look like Mr Darcy' (*G*, 14 Feb. 1998), or a new boyfriend 'seems like Mr Darcy – must be irresistible to go "lalalala look, have got boyfriend with pounds 15m who adores me"' (*Ind*, 13 Aug. 1997). In an article on viewers of Sky Sports, rich young men are referred to as 'these young Mr Darcys' (*Ind*, 7 April 1997),

	July 1991–92	1992–93	1993–94	1994–95	1995–96	1996–97	1997–98	1998–99	1999–2000	2000–01	2001–02	2002–03	
1	Hardy	Du Maurier	Potter	Potter	Potter	Potter	Potter	Hemingway	Milne	Milne	Tolkien	Tolkien	1
2	Tolkien	Potter	Du Maurier	Du Maurier	Du Maurier	Du Maurier	Du Maurier	Potter	Potter	Tolkien	Heyer	Heyer	2
3	Dickens	Hardy	Hardy	Milne	Milne	Milne	Milne	Milne	Du Maurier	Potter	Milne	Milne	3
4	Milne	Tolkien	Milne	Trollope	Hardy	Shakespeare	Austen	Du Maurier	Tolkien	Du Maurier	Potter	Potter	4
5	Austen	Dickens	Trollope	Dickens	Dickens	Hardy	Shakespeare	Shakespeare	Dickens	Dickens	Tranter	Austen	5
6	Lawrence	Trollope	Dickens	Hardy	Trollope	Dickens	Dickens	Dickens	Austen	Shakespeare	Dickens	Dickens	6
7	Trollope	Austen	Tolkien	Austen	Tolkien	Tolkien	Tolkien	Austen	Shakespeare	Austen	Shakespeare	Shakespeare	7
8	Kipling	Milne	Austen	Shakespeare	Trollope	Trollope	Hardy	Hardy	Hardy	Hardy	Du Maurier	Tranter	8
9	Orwell	Shakespeare	Shakespeare	Tolkien	Tolkien	Kipling	Trollope	Trollope	Orwell	Orwell	Austen	Du Maurier	9
10	Doyle	Lawrence	Kipling	Kipling	Kipling	Forster	Forster	Trollope	Trollope	Hemingway	Hardy	Orwell	10

Table 7.1 Most borrowed classic authors in public libraries in Britain, 1991–2003[5]

and the article ends with the question of whether 'even Mrs Bennet [would] have spent £743 million to get her hands on some rich young men'. Both Darcy and Mrs Bennet have come to stand for traits that do not have to be explained: the plot and the characters of the film version of *Pride and Prejudice* have become general knowledge and exist independently from either the novel or its author. After 1995, articles assume that readers are familiar with Austen's time and with characters that feature in 1990s film adaptations. No one refers to Catherine Morland or Henry Tilney because no 1990s film version exists, and references to Austen's other heroes and heroines come in predictably when the respective films come out, starting in 1995 with *Sense and Sensibility, Persuasion* and *Pride and Prejudice*, followed by two versions of *Emma* in 1996 and an adaptation of *Mansfield Park* in 1999.

That no articles after 1995 are independent of the films shows that Austen's novels are assimilated into the public vision of the films. The novels become assets to the films, rather than existing in their own right. That even journalists do not discriminate and therefore use the film versions shows the films' dominance. Before 1995, journalists do not always distinguish author and novel; after 1995, they do not distinguish between author, novel or film.

The films lead to an increase in visitor numbers both at Chawton Cottage, where Austen lived from 1809 until her death in 1817, and at Lyme Park, the Pemberley of the 1995 TV series. While prior to 1995 Chawton Cottage had an average of 25,000 admissions annually and Lyme Park 33,000, visitor numbers rise to 58,000 in 1996 for Chawton Cottage and to 91,500 for Lyme Park.[6] This development, too, shows the dominance of the films, that of the visual over the written, the screen characters over those in the novels and over their creator. Like numbers of editions, sales numbers and borrowing statistics, visitor numbers testify to interest going down again soon after it flared up. The exact records for Chawton Cottage are:

1994	1995	1996	1997	1998	1999	2000	2001	2002	2003
25,000	28,275	58,359	49,144	40,870	34,373	31,180	28,056	24,996	29,067

As the novelty of the *Pride and Prejudice* film wears off, visitor numbers decline.

Austen's image does not substantially change. Her high-culture reputation influences the film's image, but while the films add the connotation of period-drama and family viewing to Austen's name and intensify the identification of Austen with her period stronger through making period features such as costume, furniture and customs visual, they do not fundamentally change her reputation. Though she retains her high-culture image this is no longer solely informed by literary status of her writing but also by social rank and that of her characters as depicted in the films. Characters from her novels can now be alluded to without explanation, which they could not before 1995, but what is alluded to are the film not the novel-versions, showing that films reach a broader audience than the novels.

In spite of being connected mainly to film rather than literature in the articles, and thus to a medium that has a popular connotation, Austen retains a high-culture status. There are contradictory concepts employed here: although Austen through the film versions reaches a broad audience, it is a cultural elite that she is being connected to, so that she herself is seen as belonging to, writing about, and being consumed by higher social classes. Under the influence of the films' depiction of Regency gentry life, Austen's own social class is usually made higher than it really was, which adds to the public view of her as addressing an elite audience. Her high-culture image adds to her public popularity, since it justifies reading and viewing her in a way not applicable to most best-sellers or films. She therefore embodies the contradictions there are about the concepts of high literature: a best-seller is not usually regarded as high culture because best-selling implies popularity with an unelite readership, yet being a best-seller is an attribute that attracts more buyers. As references to Scott's low popularity show, the appeal of best-sellerdom also applies the other way round, since not being read reflects negatively on the novels' quality.[7] While not only writing about and belonging herself to a social elite of the past, Austen's novels and the film versions open the way to feeling part of a cultural elite of today. At the same time, Scott is renounced as a narrow-minded, conservative writer, yet he includes the whole social spectrum in his novels.

A widening divergence

Austen's cultural status before and after 1995 hinges on her being a novelist. Though intimate acquaintance with the novels cannot be presupposed with general readers before 1995, her public literary reputation is nevertheless based on her novels, whereas after 1995, it is based on the film versions of them. Paradoxically therefore, though still known primarily as an author, her public literary reputation is not chiefly based on the novels themselves. Scott's cultural status is independent of his literary reputation throughout the period of 1990–2003, and it is not founded on any knowledge of the novels. Both authors' cultural status thus remains the same throughout the 1990s: Austen is known as a writer of high-culture yet readable novels; Scott as a Scotsman, whose writerly activities are not dwelt on because his novels are regarded as unreadable. Both authors' literary reputations, too, remain the same, but once the films come out Austen's is no longer based on the novels. After 1995 therefore, both Austen's and Scott's cultural status is independent of their novels.

Films of Austen make a version of her novels widely known, but do not change her reputation. Films of Scott's novels do not have any effect on his reputation. He hardly features in reviews of film adaptations of his novels, whereas Austen adaptations are not even differentiated from her own works: to view an 'Austen'-film is a high-culture activity because of her novels' high literary reputation. The evidence of editions, sales numbers and borrowing statistics shows that film adaptations of Austen's novels lead to a short period of increased interest in the respective work. For both authors, newspaper articles indicate that acquaintance with the novels themselves is not substantially higher after the films than it was before.

Articles show the extent to which preconceived ideas influence readers' judgements of an author. Scott's literary reputation does not depend on knowledge of his novels at all, instead the reputation of his works prevents them from being read. Similarly, articles show that Austen's high literary reputation with the public does not depend on individual readings of her novels but on preconceived ideas about her quality. Both authors' works are therefore judged before they are read, so that readers' cultural context and their view of a writer's literary qualities determine readers' expectations and interpretations. Writers' literary reputation can therefore be independent of the extent to which their novels are read, as well as of the authors' cultural status, but not of readers' cultural context.

Chapter 9

Critical Reception, 1960–2003

From the 1960s, simple reprints of classic novels were for the most part replaced by reprints that included critical introductions. This was partly an effect of the passing of time. As late as 1914–39, the main rhythms of life were not too dissimilar from the early nineteenth century: agriculture, static life in villages, horses, few cars, largely unchallenged social and gender hierarchies. By 1960, the world of the texts was no longer familiar but had to be historically imagined.

Austen as well as Scott had become a classic, a status that required intermediaries to interpret. She had ceased to be just a good read. In addition, she became an author needing to be taught. Many of the editions aim not only at the general reader but also specifically at university students, a result of the massive expansion in tertiary education in the 1960s. As with other classics, editing a text is an activity that can create a reputation for an academic, so that editions become a site of contestation for competing theories and ideologies.

Relating introductions throughout the second half of the twentieth century to one another therefore allows for the tracing of developments: what was thought important to communicate to a reader in 1960 or 2003? Do introductions reflect, influence, or both, developments in an author's public reputation? Of all scholarly essays on a novel, introductions are most likely to reach general readers. The kind of readership introductions address reveals critics' perceptions of the relation between public and critical readers, as well as the extent to which they construct rather than just reflect expected readership, and whether they see themselves as cultural mediators. I have chosen to look at introductions in Oxford University Press (OUP) and Penguin editions as representative of academic opinions. OUP and Penguin are also the editions most often recommended and read.

Jane Austen

Below is a list of all critical introductions to Austen's novels that appeared in OUP and Penguin editions.

Sense and Sensibility

Tony Tanner (Penguin 1969), pp. 355–83 (printed as Appendix to 2003 Penguin edition).
Claire Lamont (OUP 1970), pp. vii–xxi.
Margaret Anne Doody (OUP 1990), pp. vii–xxxix.
Ros Ballaster (Penguin 1995), pp. xi–xxxi (quoted from 2003 edition).

Pride and Prejudice

Frank Bradbrook (OUP 1970), pp. vii–xvi.
Tony Tanner (Penguin 1972), pp. 368–408 (printed as Appendix to 2003 Penguin edition).
Isobel Armstrong (OUP 1990), pp. vii–xxvi.
Vivien Jones (Penguin 1996; 2003), pp. xi–xxxvi.

Mansfield Park

Tony Tanner (Penguin 1966), pp. 440–64 (printed as Appendix to 2003 Penguin edition).
John Lucas (OUP 1970), pp. viii–xviii.
Marilyn Butler (OUP 1990), pp. vii–xxix.
Kathryn Sutherland (Penguin 1996), pp. xi–xl.
Jane Stabler (OUP 2003), pp. vii–xxxvi.

Emma

Ronald Blythe (Penguin 1966), pp. 7–32.
David Lodge (OUP 1971), pp. vii–xvi.
Terry Castle (OUP 1995), pp. viii–xxviii.
Fiona Stafford (Penguin 1996), pp. vii–xxii.
Adela Pinch (OUP 2003), pp. vii–xxix.

Northanger Abbey

John Davie (OUP 1971), pp. vii–xix (includes intro. to *Persuasion*).
Anne Henry Ehrenpreis (Penguin 1972), pp. 7–24.
Terry Castle (OUP 1990), pp. vii–xxxii.
Marilyn Butler (Penguin 1995), pp. xi–l (quoted from 2003 edition).
Claudia Johnson (OUP 2003), pp. vii–xxxiv.

Persuasion

D. W. Harding (Penguin 1965), pp. 7–26.
John Davie (OUP 1971), pp. vii–xix (includes introduction to *Northanger Abbey*).
Claude Rawson (OUP 1990), pp. vii–xxxvii.
Gillian Beer (Penguin 1998), pp. xi–xxxiv (quoted from 2003 edition).

Introductions to Austen's novels can be divided into two groups: those that were written in the 1960s and 1970s, and those that were written in the 1990s and 2000s. No new introductions appear in either Penguin or OUP in the 1980s, and I could not discern a general difference in introduction-writing between the two publishing houses, especially since sometimes the same people are involved in editions of both publishers, and the majority of writers are university based. In making the selection, the aim is not to give a summary of each introduction, but to pick out common and comparative features. The two periods are divided sharply by the arrival of new theories of literature, which swept away older assumptions that the job of the critic is to point out and savour the felicities, and led to changes in critical approach.

Feminism and femininity

The biggest change is the rise of feminism, both as a political movement and as an approach to literature. Earlier introductions tend not to address gender at all, whereas later ones deal with it in depth and connect most other issues to this theme. Introductions also differ as regards gender distribution of authors: of the 12 introductions written in the 1960s and 1970s, 10 are written by men and 12 by women; of the 15 introductions that have been written since 1990, 14 are written by women and 1 by a man.

Earlier introduction writers typically see the heroine as being educated by the wiser hero. John Lucas in his 1970 introduction to *Mansfield Park* sees Edmund as 'correct[ing] and strengthen[ing] Fanny's judgement', and presents him as the one who 'alone knows what is wrong with Maria and Julia, just as he suspects that Mary Crawford's mind may have been tainted by her upbringing' (xi). By contrast, Marilyn Butler, in her 1990 introduction that replaces Lucas's, sees Fanny's narrative commentary as 'silently correct[ing] Edmund's' (MB, *MP* xx). While it is Edmund's view that we get 'out loud' (MB, *MP* xix), it is unconvincing as his 'external reading of the situation [is] one that shows no subtlety or specificity whatsoever in respect of his own sisters, and not the smallest insight into his own emotions about Mary Crawford' (MB, *MP* xix). Butler sees Fanny as 'strikingly intelligent' (xviii), whereas Lucas contends that she is 'not particularly intelligent' (xv–xvi): his Fanny is to be educated and has to develop. Lucas's is a content-based reading that does not discuss narrative, and thereby misses the main point upon which Butler rests her argument, of Fanny's being empowered through narrative since we necessarily share her point of view.

Similar to Lucas, John Davie in his 1971 introduction to *Northanger Abbey* sees Henry unequivocally as 'the mentor-hero' (xiii), who teaches Catherine 'a far greater knowledge of the world ... [and] leads her to a greater understanding of herself' (xiii). By contrast, Terry Castle in her 1990 introduction does not see Henry as patronizing, but regards hero and heroine as moving towards a relationship of equality, so that 'Henry does not so much tell Catherine *what* to think as show her that she *can* think' (TC, *NA* xii). Castle regards *Northanger Abbey* as making a larger political statement about women's intellectual abilities. With the novel, Austen is participating in the contemporary debate about women's education by 'dramatiz[ing] Wollstonecraft's thesis' (xix), as expressed in *A Vindication of the Rights of Woman* (1792). According to Castle,

> Catherine Morland's failure to think [is connected] to the fact that she has never been *taught* to think. The problem is not individual incapacity but lack of education: Catherine has been made stupid – by a society which fails to honour the intelligence of its female members. (xix)

Castle goes beyond the immediate text. Incorporating Austen's cultural context leads her to view Catherine's and Henry's relation in a political light and shapes her interpretation of the individual characters: 'Austen's hero, one suspects, has read his Wollstonecraft too' (xiii), so that Henry becomes not personally motivated in his talks with Catherine, but politically.

Earlier critics use 'he' to mean both male and female readers. Later ones specify, and tend to view Austen's readers, then and now, as female. Castle argues that by defending the novel as displaying 'the greatest powers of mind', Austen sets a novelist 'like herself ... [up] as a beacon to her female readers' (xxv) and Margaret Doody addresses the problems that 'many female readers' (MD, *SS* xvii) may have encountered in their readings of *Sense and Sensibility*. Vivien Jones in her 2003 introduction finds that 'Elizabeth Bennet seems to connect most directly with the active, visible, independent identity of modern femininity' (EJ, *PP* xiii), whereas Tony Tanner in his 1972 essay describes Elizabeth's 'immense charm' (TT, *PP* 369) as consisting of her 'combination of energy and intelligence, her gay resilience in a society tending always towards dull conformity' – attributes that are not intrinsically feminine, so that it is the person, rather than the woman, that appeals to Tanner and his implied reader. Both writers describe similar traits, but in different terms. Where earlier introductions see Austen's novels as appealing particularly to women today, it is not because of their 'modern femininity' but the opposite: D. W. Harding states in his 1965 introduction that *Persuasion* 'was begun in 1815, and 150 years later the problem [of the rights and wrongs of Lady Russell's persuasion and of Anne's yielding], in spite of an easier economic situation, is not unknown to girls of nineteen and their mothers' (DWH, *P* 12). The difference between women's situation in 1815 and 1965 is not a social but an economic one. Harding sees Austen's novels as appealing to readers who have the same social predicaments as Austen's characters and consequently he does not see political implications in the novel.

Neither Claire Lamont in her introduction to *Sense and Sensibility* (1970) nor Anne Ehrenpreis in her essay on *Northanger Abbey* (1972), the only two women writing introductions before the 1990s, concern themselves with gender issues, making this a difference resulting from introduction writers' cultural context, rather than gender. What most interests critics in the post-1990 introductions is what the novels imply for women, including the advancement of women writers into literary canons, cultural constructions of femininity as revealed in literary texts, women as authors, and women as readers.

Literary, cultural and historical context

Earlier introductions are not much concerned with the literary, cultural and historical context of Austen and her novels. If context features, it is usually to place Austen in a general historical setting or her novels in a rough chronological position, rather than to trace the influence of her immediate context on her texts. For the majority of introductions written in the 1960s and 1970s, Austen was 'brought up on eighteenth-century thought and was fundamentally loyal to the respect for limits, definition, and clear ideas which it inculcated' (TT, *PP* 405), and would never question 'the great "acceptance" doctrine of subordination which Dr Johnson extolled' (RB, *E* 25). Her literary indebtedness is seen as being to mid-eighteenth-century authors such as Fielding, Richardson and Sterne. Where her contemporary literary context comes up, critics use it to emphasize Austen's originality in being different from or going against contemporary trends in fiction. John Davie sees her as 'mischievously but characteristically ... mak[ing] fun not only of the Gothic or the sentimental novel, but also of the overtly moral narrative' (JD, *NA&P* x), without denying the moral integrity of Austen's novels, however. David Lodge asserts that contemporary fiction only features in Austen to be mocked, since the 'ironic invocation of literary stereotypes is one of the ways by which Jane Austen reinforces the realism of her own fiction' (DL, *E* xiii). Realism is not seen as fixing the novels in a certain time and place but as conditioning the works' eternal validity. The issues they deal with are seen as timeless, often connected to issues of morality, such as 'the fallibility of human understanding' (DL, *E* ix) or 'the ongoingness of social life' (TT, *PP* 369), the debate between 'prudence and ... love' (DWH, *P* 12), or the lesson that 'in life as in literature, imagination must be ruled by judgment' (AHE, *NA* 24).

Other proofs of her timelessness are links to Shakespeare as well as classic authors. Tanner contends that like *King Lear* and *Oedipus Rex*, *Pride and Prejudice* is a '[drama] of recognition' (TT, *PP* 369) that deals with the unfolding of 'the "real character" of both the good and the bad' (381). Elizabeth's error is 'of the same kind' as Lear's (377), since she, like Othello and Lear, 'ask[s] for the wrong kind of evidence' (381) to assess a character. Not only is Austen the author aligned with timeless male authors, her characters are linked to male characters too. Frank Bradbrook in his introduction to *Pride and Prejudice* maintains that Austen, though aligned 'with the age of Pope' also looks beyond that to 'the world of Shakespearian comedy, as well as forwards to the age of romanticism' (xv). He emphasizes 'Shakespearian undertones' (xvi) as well as drawing parallels between individual characters: 'Mr Collins is the ghost of Malvolio in his tone and accents, though the character of the steward has been transferred to Whickham's father, who is a good man.' Bradbrook here draws a connection between Austen and Romanticism, but Romanticism happens in the future, not contemporary with Austen, and her more obvious links are to Shakespeare. Ronald Blythe asserts that Austen 'was to advance the eighteenth-century novel along the road which led to Henry James and Proust' (RB, *E* 14). Rather than being part of a particular context, Austen's novels pave the way for the nineteenth- and twentieth-century novel. Though discussing novels that were begun at different periods, *Pride and Prejudice* and *Emma* respectively, Bradbrook's and Blythe's arguments illustrate that Austen's works are not being placed in the Romantic period regardless of when the respective novel was written and published.

Earlier introductions' general unconcern with literary and historical context is connected to their not seeing Austen as including historical circumstances in her novels. Though she may have been aware of changes around her, her novels remain concerned with 'a small section of society locked in an almost timeless present in which very little will or can change' (TT, *PP* 369). Therefore,

> the ability to enter her social world and its outlook – counts for less than ... the ability to notice the people and the institutions of our own time on which her eye would have rested and her judgement been passed. (DWH, *P* 18)

The novels' greatness is their capacity to apply to any society.

For post-1990 introductions Austen's historical and literary context is relevant to an interpretation of her novels because they are seen as engaging with it. Her being a female author writing about women mostly causes this preoccupation with context: what other female authors wrote what kind of novels at the time, and what contemporary debates about women's role in society existed are questions repeatedly addressed. The approach is the other way round from that which previous introductions apply. Rather than discussing the text only, perhaps looking at a wider context where it seems essential, critics consider the immediate historical and literary context and then place the novels into that, stressing their intertextuality.

The parallels are drawn not between Austen and Shakespeare, but between Austen and near-contemporary women writers such as Burney, Radcliffe and Wollstonecraft. Their techniques and topics are seen as being taken up by Austen. Even where she parodies the Gothic, she at the same time 'acknowledge[s] her powerful precursor [Radcliffe]' (TC, *NA* xi). Rather than breaking with fictional traditions, critics regard her as appropriating them.

Introduction authors of the later period often draw connections not only between Austen and near-contemporary female novelists, but also between Austen and specifically Romantic writers. Kathryn Sutherland places *Mansfield Park* in the immediate literary context of 1814 by comparing it to two major works that appeared in the same year, Wordsworth's *The Excursion*, and Scott's

Waverley. By showing up thematic links between these three works she positions Austen in an immediately contemporary context. For Sutherland,

> Fanny is a Romantic heroine, and only surprisingly so because we tend to think of Romanticism as a peculiarly masculine and poetic phenomenon, and one with which Austen had little to do. In [her] ... subjectivity, ... solitude, ... diet of poetry, ... contemplation of nature, ... Fanny is formed as a contemporary of Wordsworth and Coleridge. (xvii)

Sutherland sees Austen as engaging with male and female exact contemporaries.

Another characteristically 1990s and 2000s feature is to identify contemporary meanings and connotations of a term when interpreting Austen's novels. Isobel Armstrong draws attention to eighteenth-century definitions of the title words of *Pride and Prejudice*, especially Hume's and Johnson's which would have been applied by Austen, to show that in its contemporary meanings, 'the negative meanings [of Pride] predominate over positive signification ... [and] *prejudice*, that which pre-judges, must be an inherent attribute of Pride ... [so that] moral and ideological blindness are virtually inevitable' (IA, *PP* xii). This redefining of terms contributes to Armstrong's aim of showing the complexities behind the novel's 'superficially glittering surface' (IA, *PP* viii) and again means that the novel's context determines interpretation.

Later introductions' historical approach fundamentally changes critics' interpretations, especially regarding Austen's heroines. As a woman, Austen is seen as having necessarily engaged in contemporary feminist debates. Terry Castle is the only critic to admit that there is 'no direct evidence that Austen had read Mary Wollstonecraft's *Vindication of the Rights of Woman*' (TC, *NA* xviii), yet she and other introduction writers of the later period take the evidence in Austen's novels as a strong enough proof of the accuracy of Claire Tomalin's statement that 'nobody could live through the 1790s without being aware of Mary Wollstonecraft's *Vindication of the Rights of Woman*'.[1] (William St Clair has since shown that, given the small numbers of copies produced, in fact very few women readers would have had direct access to Wollstonecraft's *Vindication*.[2]) Awareness of context means that any author's text, whether fiction or not, participates in contemporary debates. Instead of Tanner's 1960s textual interpretation of Marianne as losing her true self in a society that does not tolerate sensibility, whether male or female, Marianne is, in Doody's 1990s interpretation, an expression of Austen's feminist attitudes, her marriage to Colonel Brandon asserting a woman's right to a second choice. Tanner's society is taken from within the novels, whereas for Doody, the novel's society is Austen's own.

Austen's femininity means that her text is seen in the context of the productions of contemporary women writers. The feminist interpretation of each individual novel as an expression of Austen's political opinions means writers tend to need to see a consistency between the novels. Though Elizabeth with her spirit and independence most obviously appeals to modern femininity, other Austen heroines embody the same type and therefore have to be seen as meeting similar fates to convey similar political messages, so that Marianne becomes a victor against society's restrictions.

Earlier introductions focus mainly on the texts themselves and mostly disregard their context. They align Austen with Fielding, Richardson and Sterne, while contemporary literary conventions are only taken up to be mocked by her. Her literary links are with timeless great authors such as Sophocles, Malory, Chaucer, Shakespeare, and twentieth-century ones such as Joyce or James. Her writing timelessly great novels independent of her context conditions her significance.

Post-1990 introductions not only establish her historical context, but show that Austen engaged with it literarily, socially and politically. The more Austen can be proven to be concerned with contemporary debates, the greater her novels become. Armstrong's defence of *Pride and Prejudice* against charges of it being too light by arguing that the novel '*is* only too strongly marked by history, however indirectly' (IA, *PP* ix) is representative of the prevailing post-1990 attitude. Writing by a woman is thus necessarily marked by the position of women in society. Because a late-twentieth-century viewpoint regards this situation as difficult, Austen must have had an opinion specifically about this issue, which must be expressed in her novels. Her heroines therefore fulfil political functions, rather than narrower ones within the text.

In the later period, greatness necessarily includes engagement with contemporary literary and social debates: it is the paradox of timeful timelessness that renders her topical. Critics appropriate her to fit her in with their own image, so that regardless of whether Austen's novels are actually about twentieth-century concerns, such as femininity, she is made topical through them.

Biographical issues

Since Austen's biographical record is fragmentary, her life attracts attempts to fill in the gaps, both factual and psychological, so that the established facts can be endlessly rearranged to give drastically different biographical narratives.

The earlier introductions' text-based approach means the life is only referred to occasionally and in general terms. They bring in biographical information as a result of discussing aspects of the novel, rather than discussing the novel from a biographical point of view. By contrast, later ones often look at context and biography and then discuss how this is reflected in the novel. Earlier ones focus on the novels, and resort to biographical matters if they offer an explanation for aspects of a novel. The perceived difference in tone between *Pride and Prejudice* (1813) and its immediate successor *Mansfield Park* (1814) leads to references to Austen's life. John Lucas asserts that

Jane Austen seems to be writing from a position of evangelical earnestness which we [1970s readers] may be ready to find oppressively humourless and morally priggish, and feel to be deeply at odds with the position she had adopted in her previous novel, *Pride and Prejudice*. (JL, *MP* vii)

To explain 'so sudden and radical a change of view' (JL, *MP* vii), both John Lucas and Tony Tanner in their essays on *Mansfield Park* resort to biography: Austen was no longer

> twenty-three ... and still living happily at her birthplace [but thirty-six]. In the meantime her father had died, ... she had had an unhappy love affair, ... she was resigned to spinsterhood and was, inevitably, of a more serious cast of mind. ... By the time of *Mansfield Park*, much of the lightness and brightness has gone out of the world and, although Jane Austen's incomparable comic sense is as alive as ever, she now seems more aware of the real evils and real sufferings inextricably involved in life in society.' (TT, *MP* 461–2)

The death of Austen's father ranks on the same level as her resignation to spinsterhood, which reveals assumptions about what would have fulfilled a female author and made her continue to write in the lighter tone of *Pride and Prejudice*. Both Lucas and Tanner neglect that since Austen revised *Pride and Prejudice* before it was published in 1813, the compositional gap between it and *Mansfield Park* only existed to an extent.

Butler in her 1990 introduction to *Mansfield Park* also perceives a change in tone. Like Lucas and Tanner, she argues that Austen considered herself 'too old for marriage' (viii) by the time she wrote *Mansfield Park*, but instead of presenting this as a reason for Austen's more subdued tone, Butler argues that Austen 'found compensations' (vii). Her maturity contributes to the achievement of *Mansfield Park* – whereas Lucas especially does not see *Mansfield Park* as Austen's best work. Also, rather than regarding Austen's 'shift of theme, from courtship to topics of wider concern' as a result of her immediate biographical circumstances, Butler contends that 'it may be more relevant ... that the same shift of theme ... occurs in other reputable novels after 1800' (viii).

Where later introductions bring in biographical circumstances they go into more detail than the earlier ones. Rather than attempting to explain puzzling aspects of a novel with vague references to Austen's life, they see specific episodes from Austen's life mirrored in her works. Gillian Beer in her 1998 introduction to *Persuasion* draws parallels between the novel and Austen's life: Austen's niece Fanny asked advice about entering a long engagement. Austen 'was appalled both by having responsibility for the engagement shifted onto her and by the prospects for the relationship over an engagement of six or seven years' (xi), which for Beer underlines that persuasion and dissuasion are terms ambiguous and combative from the outset. Although they differ widely in their underlying attitude and assumptions, both Victorian and post-1990 interpretations of the works are thus directly influenced by their understanding of Austen's life as an unmarried woman.

Defence and critique

Earlier introductions tend to cover a greater number of aspects, take less reader knowledge for granted, and explain more. Claire Lamont in her 1970 introduction to *Sense and Sensibility* explains the eighteenth-century 'cult of sensibility', as well as citing passages from Radcliffe's *Udolpho* to illustrate a heroine of sensibility, that she then contrasts with Marianne. Similarly, Anne Ehrenpreis in her 1972 introduction to *Northanger Abbey* illustrates the meaning of 'gothic novel' by giving textual examples. Not only is the target audience of earlier introductions thus wider as regards gender, but also as regards reader-specialization. They are writing for the general reader.

Earlier introductions are concerned with the place of the novel they introduce within the Austen canon. They criticize and praise more and in stronger terms than later ones, giving the reader a more defined guideline, whereas later ones are not concerned with evaluation. *Emma* is 'the climax of Jane Austen's genius and the Parthenon of fiction' (RB, *E* 7), it 'most perfectly represents her genius' (DL, *E* vii), *Pride and Prejudice* is 'a masterpiece' (FB, *PP* vii). On the other hand, 'the introduction of Mrs. Smith is *Persuasion*'s only serious flaw' (JD, *P* xvii), 'the structural relationship between the Bath episodes and the Northanger experience is not comfortable' (AHE, *NA* 13); in *Sense and Sensibility*, 'the whole machinery of the two Elizas is clumsy' (CL, *SS* xviii), *Mansfield Park*'s 'central problem is, however, the novel's heroine' (JL, *MP SS* viii), and 'very real limitations to the novel [*MP*] begin to emerge' (JL, *MP* xvii).

Placing a novel within the Austen canon also involves statements about a novel's popularity in relation to other Austen ones. The first sentence of Lucas's introduction is that '*Mansfield Park* is perhaps the least popular of all Jane Austen's novels' (vii). Although he obviously agrees with this public verdict since he criticizes *Mansfield Park* severely, he yet has to defend the novel as 'a great achievement' (xviii). This statement redeems the author as well as the novel. Later introduction writers direct their essays at a more specialized readership and even distance themselves from general readers. Butler sees *Mansfield Park*'s unpopularity as testifying to its depth, since 'almost anyone can enjoy Jane Austen's shallows' (MB, *MP* vii), which is an argumentation reminiscent of Austen-Leigh's 'Cheney-test'.[3] Public opinion thus appears not to influence later introductions, while earlier ones give it some credit. These attitudes indicate who the writers of each period believe to be writing for.

Defence and praise of Austen's novels leads some writers no longer to distinguish between writer and novels. For Blythe, admiration for the works is always bound up with an admiration for their author, just as it was for Victorian reviewers. His praises recall those of Austen-Leigh's *Memoir*.

the brilliant surface and the endlessly satisfying depths of her novels are not the chance things of casual genius, but the results of an uncommonly sane mind, a gay heart and a most dedicated and meticulous workmanship. ... There is a moral tone which defies the dreariness of that expression – Jane Austen can in fact get more drama out of morality than most other writers can get from shipwreck, battle, murder or mayhem – there is a balance, there is a serenity which leaves a contentment at the core of the heart similar to that perfect *rightness* which one experiences when listening to Mozart. (RB, *E* 8–9)

Connected to this protection of the woman appears writers' use of 'Jane Austen' or 'Austen'. With few exceptions, the introductions written pre-1970s feminism refer to her as 'Jane Austen' throughout, whereas the later ones write about 'Austen'. The use of 'Jane' in the earlier introductions emphasizes the fact that she is a woman, and contributes to a sense of some earlier introductions' defence of her being almost a chivalric duty – a reverence for the woman rather than purely an appreciation of the writer's work. D. W. Harding in his introduction to *Persuasion* first criticizes the novel and then excuses its author: 'How far and in what ways *Persuasion* falls short of the novel Jane Austen would have written if she had been in full health can only be guessed at' – and speculates on what Austen would have changed and added. He does not appear to realize that his attempted defence in this form presents his most damning criticism. Again, this defence of the woman is similar to that found in Victorian reviews.

Social and political issues; narrative technique

Earlier and later introductions differ in the role they impute to society in the novels. The former discuss the individual in society. They are concerned with Austen's 'theme of reconciling private and public behaviour' (JL, *MP* ix). Later ones specifically look at women in a particular society. Both Margaret Doody and Ros Ballaster in their respective 1990 and 1995 introductions to *Sense and Sensibility* discuss sensibility in its relation to society – as do Tony Tanner and Claire Lamont in their 1969 and 1970 introductions. The difference, is however, that Doody and Ballaster consider sensibility in its connection with femininity, whereas Tanner's and Lamont's concepts of sensibility can apply to both 'the hero or heroine of sensibility' (CL, *SS* vii). Ballaster addresses the relationship between society and specifically 'the bourgeois heroine' (RB, *SS* xviii), finding that in works by Austen, Wollstonecraft and Edgeworth, 'sensibility is presented as a problematic form of selfhood for women' (xx). Doody argues that sensibility 'poses particular dangers for women' (MD, *SS* xiii) because they live in 'a social and financial system which is so systematically heartless in its treatment of women' (xi). She cites passages from *A Vindication of the Rights of Woman* to then link Austen to its criticism of women's predicaments in society: 'Austen and Wollstonecraft both see that delicate feminine sensibility as a mark of upper-class pretension may only mask serious economic disability, and can impede or even damage the female who cultivates it.' (MD, SS xiv). Tanner sees social codes as forcing compliance to rules. The individual's 'natural sensibility' is at odds with society's values, and Marianne is the embodiment of this conflict. Her 'muffled scream' presents a critique of society's rational ways, but this critique is general, not specific to society's treatment of women. Sensibility 'had to be subordinated' (TT, SS, 378). Marianne is 'irreconcilably at odds with society because of her passional intensities' (380), which are not defined by her femininity. Along with her sensibility, 'Marianne does, in effect die. Whatever the name of the automaton which submits to the plans of its relations and joins in the social game it is not the real Marianne' (380). By contrast, Doody regards Marianne's marriage to Colonel Brandon as Austen joining those contemporary female writers such as Wollstonecraft or Mary Hays, who supported

> woman's right to find a second love. Austen does not go so far as to argue for the right of the woman already seduced or violated or sexually experienced to find a second love, but she is looking in that direction, and, in making Marianne bid farewell to a fantastic constancy, she is definitely joining in an argument about female sexuality. (MD, SS xv)

Doody sees the novel as emphasizing women's second loves generally and does not mention once that Elinor in fact marries her first love. Both Tanner and Doody see Marianne's sensibility as preventing her from accessing her sense, and also see sensibility in Marianne as being conquered by the end of the novel, but while Doody sees this as a victory for women's rights and Marianne as a survivor, Tanner sees it as a loss of true self. Doody therefore views Austen as making a political statement in the context of debates about gender; Tanner sees Austen as commenting on society's ways and values generally. Again, analysing the text on its own or in its cultural context leads to different readings.

Other introduction writers are similar in their view of society in relation to either the individual or specifically the female individual. To Isobel Armstrong, 'all women in the novel [*PP*] are caught by the despotism of convention, ... they are likely to be victims of oppression or misunderstanding' (IA, *PP* xxii). D. W. Harding in his 1965 essay sees Austen as concerned with society's pressures on the individual.

> The functioning of individuals while they are hemmed in by others, all mutually controlled by the system of social forces, was one of her general preoccupations. The small country neighbourhood, with little travel, and no escape from the family by going to work in a large organization, precluded the individual from having the degree of anonymity we take for granted. He

was, as Henry Tilney remarks in *Northanger Abbey*, 'surrounded by a neighbourhood of voluntary spies'. (DWH, *P* 14)

Harding's example is Henry, not one of Austen's heroines, and his argument is general, not specifically applicable to women. One might even question how many women in the 1960s went to work 'in a large organization', and whether his standpoint is not a particularly masculine one that almost excludes women. In Tanner's essay on *Mansfield Park*, he sees the novel in a tradition 'of many great novels [that] concern themselves with characters whose place in society is not fixed or assured' (440). His examples include Tom Jones, Becky Sharp and Jude Fawley – both male and female protagonists. He thus sees social insecurity generally as a literary theme, not specifically women's position in society. His contention that 'many of the characters in Jane Austen's later fictional world remind one of Sartre's notion – "hell is other people"' (TT, *MP* 462) indicates that his is a timeless society, rather than one defined by a specific historical context.

Earlier introduction writers do not see Austen's novels as making political statements, certainly not as challenging the status quo. Through the later introductions' preoccupation with women's role in society, the political dimension emerges. The concern with Austen's political position in post-1990 introductions replaces the earlier introductions' concern with timeless morality. She is variously seen as conservative, progressive, or, by Jones, Armstrong, and the majority of introduction writers, as having 'assimilated both positions and moved on' (VJ, *PP* xxviii) to a post-revolutionary, rather than anti-revolutionary position. An exception is Butler's view of a conservative Austen, but in contrast to Tanner's eighteenth-century Toryism, she sees Austen's as 'modified by early nineteenth-century patriotism, efficiency, and purposefulness' (MB, *MP* xiii). Armstrong notes: 'if [*PP*] is implicitly about averting revolution, it is just as strongly concerned with challenging repression, and the double programme creates complexities' (IA, *PP* viii). Political, social and gender issues are intermingled, since 'political issues are explored through sexual signals' (viii)

Both earlier and later introductions discuss Austen's narrative technique. Earlier introductions are again more likely to criticize the narrative as 'less successful' (JD, *NA&P* xiii), but also more likely to describe it as the manifestation of her genius, whereas later ones analyse the shifting between 'the third person narrative [which] is persistently broken by free indirect style, dialogue, quotations and letters' (FS, *E* xvi). Later introductions go into greater detail in their discussion of Austen's narrative techniques and viewpoints used and connect this to what they see as Austen's occupation with gender-issues: even a heroine like Fanny, who 'never becomes outwardly articulate, never encroaches on male discourse' (MB, *MP* xix), makes her power felt through narrative. While writers of both groups recognize that the reader's perspective is intertwined with the heroine's, only later ones view this as connected to a statement by Austen about women's situation in society.

In the 1960s and 1970s, the gender and nationality of critics cited correspond exactly to those of the introduction writers. Almost all critics referred to are British, and apart from Q. D. Leavis, they are all male ('Mrs Leavis', 'Lionel Trilling', 'Arnold Kettle', 'Dr R.W. Chapman', (RB, *E* 30–1)). After 1990, critics cited include international ones, and some of the introductions are written by scholars at US universities (such as Terry Castle at Stanford or Claude Rawson at Yale). About half of the critics mentioned are women, such Mary Lascelles, Margaret Oliphant and Julia Kavanagh.

Fourteen out of fifteen post-1990 introductions are written by women, yet half the critics cited in these are male. This may point to publishers deliberately choosing women to introduce Austen to post-1990 readers, which in turn may hint at an expected readership of mainly women. Not only the introductions themselves but also blurbs back this up. The blurb to OUP's 1990 edition of *Northanger Abbey* starts off by drawing attention to the specifically feminine significance of the novel. '*Northanger Abbey* is the earliest of Jane Austen's great comedies of female enlightenment', and the novel deals with 'the painful difficulties (especially for women) involved in growing up'. By contrast, blurbs to earlier editions are either more generally about people, men and women, or more specifically about the heroine as an individual. The blurb to OUP's 1970 edition of *Mansfield Park* states that 'Jane Austen uses Fanny's emotional involvement with the members of these families to explore the social and moral values by which she and the others try to order their lives'. The blurb to Penguin's 1966 edition of *Emma* asserts that the heroine's 'progress through the mismanagement of other people's affairs to the crisis and resolution of her own, is a whole comedy of self-deceit and self-discovery'.

Some of the writers are mentioned in both earlier and later introductions, including Richardson, Fielding, Johnson, Burney and Radcliffe. All of these are cited more often by later introductions than earlier ones. Some writers, however, only occur in the later ones, including Wordsworth, Wollstonecraft and Burke, and their being mentioned again testifies to the trend of placing Austen's novels in their historical, literary and intellectual context.

* * *

Earlier introductions adopt New Criticism's attitude of looking at the texts on their own terms, separated from both the biographical and the social context of the texts' origin. In contrast to Victorian reviewers' concern with Austen's morality, and to a Jamesian occupation with whether she could have consciously composed her art, introduction writers of the 1960s and 1970s are not concerned with Austen's personal character traits, views and aims.

In the context of the general post-structuralist reaction against this text-based approach, and especially New Historicism's emphasis on an author's unique historical, political and social context, critics' approach to Austen and her novels changes. Like the late nineteenth century, the late twentieth century focuses on Austen the woman and looks at the texts via her. What is revolutionary is that Austen is no longer a kindly aunt with an exclusively domestic horizon, but a politically aware participant in early nineteenth-century debates. All introductions of the later period assume that she cannot have lived unaware of her political and social context. While introductions vary as to the specific political view assigned to Austen, all approach the novels via the author's context, so that the works of an author whose political and social context had in no previous period been seen as having had an impact on her novels are now seen as necessarily reflecting her political opinions, especially as regards women's situation.

Rather than being seen as concerned with timeless character traits of a section of society, she is now regarded as commenting on the whole socio-political scene and its effects on people at a particular time – the exact opposite of nineteenth-century reviewers' notion of her as dealing with a limited spectrum. Ironically therefore, what gains her critical appreciation in the late twentieth century is the view of her as contributing to society's debates, while it is the perceived lack of any contribution to society that keeps her from achieving true greatness in the eyes of Victorian reviewers. Just as ironic is the similarity between the late-twentieth-century insistence on Austen's political awareness and late-nineteenth-century affirmation of her moral integrity: in both cases the person has to fulfil certain requirements that are necessarily reflected in the novels and make them topical.

While her gender contributes to Victorian critics' view of her as never having the option of becoming great if she is to retain female virtues, it is her gender that renders her yet greater in the late twentieth century. Writing itself becomes a liberating act and a political statement, in spite of most novel-writers in the 1810s having been female. Austen's writing is thus seen as conscious on two levels, both of which are politicized: writing itself, as a woman in the early nineteenth century, and writing about women in contemporary society, through a female consciousness.

While introductions reflect critical trends of the period they are written in, the adherence to these trends is less strict in earlier introductions, because the concept of a critical introduction also changes. The major critical movements in the 1960s – New Criticism, Formalism, Structuralism – focus on the analysis of form, which is one aspect of earlier introductions but never the main focus. They write for an audience that is less familiar with the text than they are, explaining more and covering a variety of textual aspects, consequently quoting more from the text. Austen's greatness does not constitute itself in her dealings with her context but in the texts themselves, especially in their timeless moral appeal, rather than their specific social or political morality. For later introductions, the context of a text determines possible meaning more than the text itself. Though approach shifts from a text-based to a context-based one, both groups of introduction writers focus on content as much as on technique.

Later introductions go into greater detail about fewer aspects. Rather than introducing the novels to a possibly non-academic, first-time reader, later ones choose to discuss various points liable to interest or puzzle such a reader. They represent academic essays arguing a definite position, frequently presupposing a good deal of previous knowledge of recent and current theories and academic debates. By addressing their remarks, not to the actual general readers of all ages that are the majority of the market, but to a narrower constituency limited both by intended gender and by presumed sophistication, they assert that this exclusive group alone has the ability to read Austen correctly. This further stresses Austen's topicality through her femininity and feminine concerns, especially since most introduction writers explicitly address women readers. Through that, they imply that Austen, too, wrote for female readers, so that she is marketed as a woman writer addressing women readers.

The introduction that most stands out is Fiona Stafford's 1996 essay on *Emma*: she identifies two broad approaches that account for the division. One fixes the novel 'in a specific time and place' (FS, *E* vii). The other makes it 'independent of place, period and even author'. By offering her readers both approaches as part of her attempt to assist their understanding and appreciation, Stafford is untypical of her time.

Just as rise of feminism excludes more and more people as implied readers, it also increases the gap between male and female interpretations in introductions. The differences between Claude Rawson and the fourteen women in the later period are greater than between Claire Lamont, Anne Ehrenpreis and the ten male critics of the earlier period.

While in all periods, critics' approaches are largely determined by the assumptions of their age, introduction writers of the earlier period aim to give primacy to explaining the texts. By contrast, in the most recent introductions, texts are being quarried for confirmation of ideas and the theories brought from outside.

Walter Scott

The following is a list of all critical introductions that appeared in OUP and Penguin editions.

Waverley

Andrew Hook (Penguin 1972), pp. 9–27.
Claire Lamont (OUP 1981), pp. ix–xxii.

The Tale of Old Mortality[4]

Angus Calder (Penguin 1975), pp. 9–43.
Jane Stevenson and Peter Davidson (OUP 1993), pp. ix–xli.
Douglas Mack (Penguin 1999), pp. xii–xxix.

The Heart of Mid-Lothian

Claire Lamont (OUP 1982), pp. vii–xx.
Tony Inglis (Penguin 1994), pp. ix–l.

Ivanhoe

A. N. Wilson (Penguin 1984), pp. vii–xxix.
Ian Duncan (OUP 1996), pp. vii–xxvi.
Graham Tulloch (Penguin 2000), pp. xi–xxix.

Redgauntlet

Kathryn Sutherland (OUP 1985), pp. vii–xxiii.
David Hewitt (Penguin 2000), pp. xiii–xxxi.

The Bride of Lammermoor

Fiona Robertson (OUP 1991), pp. vii–xxix.
Kathryn Sutherland (Penguin 2000), pp. xiii–xxxv.

The Antiquary

David Punter (Penguin 1998), pp. xiii–xxx.
Nicola Watson (OUP 2002), pp. vii–xxvi.

Kenilworth*

J. H. Alexander (Penguin 1999), pp. xiii–xxxi.

Chronicles of the Canongate*

Claire Lamont (Penguin 2003), pp. xi–xxix.

Guy Mannering*

Jane Millgate (Penguin 2003), pp. xi–xxvii.

Rob Roy*

Ian Duncan (OUP 1998),[5] pp. vii–xxviii.

Quentin Durward*

Susan Manning (OUP 1992).

The Two Drovers and other Stories*

David Cecil (OUP 1987) (though this is not a novel).

* Since the last six titles are only published in one of the two publishing houses, I have not discussed these introductions.

Introductions to Scott's novels can, like Austen's, be usefully divided into two groups according to the period in which they were written. Six introductions appeared between 1972 and 1985, three written by men and three by women, compared to ten introductions appearing between 1991 and 2002, three by women, six by men, and one by a woman and a man together – plus the introductions I am not discussing, one in the earlier period and five in the later. The time gap between the two groups is not as long as with introductions to Austen's novels – six years (1985–91), compared to eighteen years (1972–90), but since differences in approach still emerge along these temporal lines it is a useful division.

Scott's political, social and biographical context

Introductions written in the earlier period are not concerned with Scott's historical context, so that only later introductions discuss connections between Scott's novels and his own time. Elements from the novels are connected to Scott's biography and to early nineteenth-century events and persons. Douglas Mack in his 1999 introduction to *The Tale of Old Mortality* (1816) insists that Tillietudlem is based on Craignethan castle that Scott visited in 1799. Mack further contends that not only did Scott attack the tenth Duke of Hamilton in an 1819 pamphlet in the aftermath of Peterloo, he also criticized him through *OM*: '[the novel's] Duke of Hamilton carries heavy responsibility ... [for failing] to bind society together' (DM, *TOM* xix) – failing because he 'vanishes from [the novel's] pages', so that Scott's critique of Hamilton manifests itself in the Duke's '[highly significant] absence and ineffectiveness' (xix). Mack's reference to a biographical detail to support a point about the text is typical of later introduction writers' approach. More directly biographical, Tony Inglis sees connections between the novel and Scott's attitude to his brother Daniel, 'the black sheep of *his* family' (TI, *HOM* xliv): 'It seems probable that ... ambivalent emotions [about Daniel] complicated by guilt, account also for the assembly of such disparate elements and attitudes in *The Heart of Mid-Lothian*' (xliv). Inglis's biographical knowledge therefore shapes his view of the novel.

Later introductions see Scott as commenting on his own time through the novels. They stress this as remarkable about the novels for a modern reader, who gets what Jane Stevenson and Peter Davidson in their 1993 introduction to *OM* call a 'double historical perspective' (xxxix): history filtered through 'the preoccupations and anxieties of the early nineteenth century' (D/S, *OM* xxxix), through the eyes of someone living in and 'participat[ing] fully in the social and economic currents of his age' (TI, *HOM* xii). To them, the novels have to be read within their early nineteenth-century context to arrive at valid interpretations. The majority of introduction writers seem to be unaware that they, too, are providing a perspective and apply a certain viewpoint, so that for a reader of the novel and their introduction, there is a triple perspective at work here, and yet another choice about taking a writer's context into account has to be made.

Graham Tulloch in his 2000 introduction to *Ivanhoe* similarly argues that 'in a year of social turmoil like 1819 the political symbolism of an English king and his subjects united in harmony cannot be ignored' (xvi), and Ian Duncan, in his 1996 introduction to the same novel, similarly points out its being based in 1819. He sees it as taking part, through its historical setting, in a political debate about the cultural formation of Britain, as well as participating in the post-Peterloo political climate. Duncan supports this view with references to Scott's anti-radical actions after Peterloo, rather than with references to the text itself. In fact, the novel's contribution 'is more relaxed and generous than the fierce prognostications to be found in Scott's correspondence' (ID, *I* xv), which leaves unclear what exactly the significance of this correspondence is for *Ivanhoe*, especially since Duncan realizes that *Ivanhoe* was composed 'largely anterior to the crisis' (xv). Again, he can only judge the novel in the political context of 1819, in spite of its having been written mostly before the main events that shape his interpretation, and despite Scott's not having revised the earlier parts after Peterloo.

For introductions of the later period, Scott's novels are thus necessarily interpreted through an early nineteenth-century context. By contrast, earlier introductions are not concerned with whether details from Scott's historical plots can be connected to the early nineteenth century or to events in his life. They focus on the text. If links to Scott's biography are made, they are general, and, as with Austen, often refer to disposition rather than to a particular situation, such as seeing Waverley's 'romanticizing impulse ... undoubtedly present in Scott' (AH, *W* 24). Not only are the novels not connected to Scott's biography, they are not seen as being at all concerned with his contemporary events. A. N. Wilson in his introduction to *Ivanhoe* asserts that the novel does not 'contain some gloss on early nineteenth-century history' (xxiv). When he then goes on to 'play the game, and imagine [this] for a moment' (xxiv), he sees general parallels between *Ivanhoe* and Scott's Scottish novels, and therefore applies *Ivanhoe* not to 1819, but generally to Scotland's, or any smaller nation's, situation: Scott

> saw, with terror, his nation being made to destroy its past; and he recognized (this is the great importance of *Ivanhoe*) that a nation without links with its

past is the victim of every lying dictatorship which could come along. (AW, *I* xxvii)

'Racial and ethnic heritages' should be preserved while 'recognizing our interdependence and our common good. Inevitably, this will mean that one racial or social group will have predominance'. Wilson's vocabulary is distinctly general; for him, *Ivanhoe*'s 'appeal to be *one nation*' goes beyond 1819: it applies to all nations and times, extends to the 'Victorians', and promotes 'our common good' today.

As with Austen's novels, earlier introductions give Scott's works timeless and general significance, and through that topicality for today. Claire Lamont in her 1982 introduction to *HOM* contends that Jeanie's 'predicament has not lost its power to disturb' (xvii), and that the novel as a whole 'touches our contemporary preoccupations' (xvii). Angus Calder in his 1975 introduction to *OM* sees Scott as a humanist who promotes in the novel the eternal truth that 'all men are ends in themselves' (36). Scott's conservatism is a modern, 'democratic' (37), one. Calder emphasizes Scott's focus on lower-class characters who, with their 'vitality ... [represent] the real victors' (40), rather than the 'neurotically self-repressed young genteel lovers' (40). The 'peasants' (41) represent the future.

Calder uses elements of the novels to render both Scott's works and personal attitudes topical: Scott is able to write about lower-class-characters because 'he always talked to all manner of people' (14), so that biography and novel are connected, but on a general, not a specific level. Calder thus uses the novel to prove a point about Scott's character, rather than judging the novel through its author's personal traits.

Davidson and Stevenson in their 1993 introduction to *OM* by contrast see Scott's outlook not as timeless, nor as progressively democratic, but as that of a stern early nineteenth-century Tory. His characters 'act as anachronistic spokesmen for the values of the Regency gentry' (D/S, *OM* xxiv). Rather than lower-class characters representing the future, 'it is clearly to Morton and Edith that Scott looks for the future of Scotland: a new, revitalized gentry' (xix). The introduction brings in knowledge outside the text to show where Scott's characters deviate from history and why, so that the novel becomes an expression of Scott's Regency Tory views. The structure of the two analyses is typical of their respective periods: Calder organizes his chronologically by plot, Stevenson and Davidson theirs by social class, already pointing to their focus of elements outside the text.

For earlier introductions, context is not relevant to a reading of the novel. They are not concerned with historical accuracy and do not see Scott as commenting on his own time through the novels. Instead, they focus on the timeless relevance of Scott's texts. Later introductions look at context and interpret the novels within it, seeing them as necessarily commenting on early nineteenth-century events and politics.

Scott's literary context

As with Austen, earlier introductions are not concerned with the literary context in which Scott wrote. They draw links to timeless greats rather than immediate contemporaries. Later introductions look at novel and author in context, drawing connections among Scott's novels in addition to relating them to general Romantic trends and individual Romantic works.

David Hewitt in his 2000 introduction to *Redgauntlet* sees Darsie as a Romantic autobiographer who has to escape from 'moral, social and intellectual narrowness' (xx) that encloses him in Edinburgh. This 'release from moral suffocation' (xx) is necessary to enable Darsie's 'Romantic creativity' (xxi). Hewitt finds himself, and any reader, 'inevitably reminded of the opening lines of Wordsworth's 1805 version of *The Prelude*' (xxi) (not published, as Hewitt himself points out, until 1850), and sees Scott and Wordsworth as sharing Romantic values that are incorporated in their works.

Kathryn Sutherland's 1985 introduction to *Redgauntlet* is the last of those in the earlier period to appear and therefore incorporates traits of both earlier and later introductions. However, where Hewitt sees Darsie as Romantic, Sutherland regards him as an 'irresponsible romantic' (ix) who develops from 'misconceiv[ing] reality' (xi), and being comparable to 'that self-deluding romancer [Don Quixote]' (xii) to facing reality through writing, as does Richardson's Pamela. Like earlier introductions to Austen's novels, Sutherland sees links with not-immediately contemporary works. Like later introductions, however, she supports her argument for an affinity between Darsie and Pamela by pointing out that in 1824, the year of *Redgauntlet*'s publication, Scott's biography of Richardson came out, thereby linking text and biography.

In Sutherland's reading, Darsie cannot continue a dreamer but has to accept modern society which places 'social conformity over personal autonomy' (xxii). Hewitt regards Darsie as 'articulating a profound cultural shift in which the individual became more important than society' (xxix), and therefore the novel as 'a paradigm of Romanticism' (xxix). His introduction is entirely centred around one character, that of Darsie, which mirrors Hewitt's occupation with Romantic ideas about the individual, whereas Sutherland is at least as much concerned with Alan as with Darsie. Hewitt applies a late-twentieth-century discourse to the novel by seeing Darsie as homosexual. While Hewitt here stays within the novel in his interpretation rather than using outside sources, it is yet a reading consciously informed by 'the late twentieth century, not ... 1824' (xxviii). This reading of Darsie as homosexual supports Hewitt's view of Darsie not as a figure of the eighteenth but of the early nineteenth century since it contributes to making him the Romantic 'other' (xxx). Darsie becomes 'a Romantic artist ... [who] frees himself from inherited discourses' (xxix). Just as later introductions to Austen's novels see her as engaging with gender issues and feminism in a modern sense and regard this as contributing to her literary significance and topicality, Hewitt's reading of *Redgauntlet* as engaging with homosexuality as a form of otherness similarly renders Scott topical for modern readers.

By 1985, Scott's context already features, but it is not the main focus of the introduction, whereas 15 years later, the interpretation hinges entirely on Scott's Romantic context. Also, where earlier introductions emphasize timeless relevance, later introductions see Scott as engaging with issues especially topical to a modern readership.

Later introductions necessarily discuss Scott's literary context, sometimes in cases where they themselves invalidate it in their ensuing discussions. Sutherland in her 2000 introduction to *The Bride of Lammermoor* links the novel, which Scott wrote during a severe illness in 1819, to Coleridge's 'opium experiments in poetry, notable among them "Kubla Khan"' (1816): 'Coleridge's explanatory preface and the anecdotes surrounding Scott's composition of *The Bride of Lammermoor* share an anxiety about creation and a concern with the mechanism of the imagination.' Yet her elaboration ends in refuting the idea of Scott's having written the novel in a dream-like state as this version of its composition is 'not borne out by the facts' (xv). She uses detailed (extra-textual) knowledge of the manuscript as proof of Scott's having written four-fifths himself (rather than dictated major parts), as well as having inserted 'pre-publication corrections' (rather than not being able to remember anything about the novel when it was presented to him after publication). In her introduction to *The Bride of Lammermoor*, written 15 years after her introduction to *Redgauntlet*, the urge to bring in Scott's Romantic context has increased: for *Redgauntlet*, she can still show Scott as engaging with Romantic values but not wholly embracing them (Darsie goes back into society), whereas in *BOL*, she brings it in even though she herself sees the link as inappropriate because the circumstances of *BOL*'s writing history were not what myths would have them.

The majority of earlier introductions do not bring in Romanticism at all. Where they do, it is in general terms, not showing up links between a novel or its composition and a specific Romantic work. The differentiation between Romantic and romantic is not usually made, so that rather than stressing similarities, the emphasis tends to be on distancing Scott from the movement. Andrew Hook in his 1972 introduction to *Waverley* sees one of the reasons for the decline of Scott's status in his having been read throughout the nineteenth century in a way that was 'ignoring the unromantic dimension of [Scott's] work' (15), and to redeem Scott, he points out that Scott 'is at best a reluctant romantic ... [since] the Waverley Novels ... are far from being expressions of an uninhibited romanticism' (13). Like earlier introductions to Austen's novels, Hook discusses contemporary authors only to show how Scott differs, thereby emphasizing Scott's originality. Contemporary authors such as Maria Edgeworth and Jane Porter 'cannot be said to have directly inspired [Waverley]' (17), partly because, as Hook argues, the novel had been begun in 1805.[6] His account of the writing history of *Waverley* is the one given by Scott in his General Preface to the Magnum Edition (the edition Hook uses), including a mathematical mistake that has been published in the Penguin introduction since its first appearance in 1972 and is still included in their most recent reprint of 2004: Hook defines 1814 as 'sixty years since 1745' (26). While such a mistake is not representative of earlier introductions, it still shows their less scientific approach to the subject, and their limited concern with exact details of context. It also testifies to the carelessness of the publishers since then, and hints at Scott's limited popularity: not only has the same introduction been used for more than thirty years, it has also never been corrected.

Lamont in her 1981 introduction to *Waverley* argues that Scott's 'predecessors here were not the novelists but the ... eighteenth-century Scottish "philosophical" historians who had theorized on the development of societies' (xvii), thereby giving the novel significance beyond fiction and linking it with trends beyond those of Scott's immediate context. *Waverley* can therefore be regarded as "the first historical novel ... [and as] the first political novel" (xvii), which enhances its originality. Earlier introductions' reluctance to consider links between Scott and his contemporaries is connected to their generally presenting him in more admiring terms.

Earlier and later introductions differ in their approach to context: in the earlier ones, Scott as an author features only in general terms and the focus is on detail of the text. Later essays, by contrast, are concerned with Scott's biography in connection with the novels, as well as with detail of early nineteenth-century society and how the novels reflect and address that. The development from New Criticism to New Historicism leads to a new view of Scott's novels. Instead of taking Scott's interpretation of history as the only one that matters for an interpretation of the text, later introductions focus on discrepancies between Scott's version and the official one, drawing conclusions from that about Scott's and his novel's attitude to the time of its composition. The historical novel thus acquires a new definition, because it is no longer primarily about the period and characters depicted but about the period it was written in. Earlier introductions' moral realism along the lines of Lukács's argument that the 'historical faithfulness in Scott is the authenticity of the historical psychology of his characters, the genuine *hic et nunc* (here and now) of their inner motives and behaviour'[7] no longer applies. The points are not proven from the text only but with reference to outside facts.

Realism

Perceptions of realism differ in earlier and later introductions and again testify to extrinsic and intrinsic readings of Scott's texts. To earlier ones, it implies a moral realism, materializing in realistic and consistent character descriptions. To later ones, it also denotes historical accuracy.

Wilson, writing in the earlier period, dispenses with realism as historical accuracy because *Ivanhoe* displays 'a sort of realism. It is moral, not historical, realism' (AW, *I* xi). To criticize the novel for its lack of historical precision would be like 'attacking opera because people sing instead of speak' (ix). Calder similarly asserts that Scott depicts 'human truth' (AC, *OM* 22). Lamont states that the portrayal of the Porteous Riot is 'for the most part accurate, although Scott altered some details for effect' (CL, *HOM* viii), but she does not elaborate on these alterations. Scott's changes are not relevant to her reading because she sees the tale as 'a historical novel, but ... of the Porteous affair, not a tale of Whig and Tory' (xix). Her introduction centres on the text itself. She mostly discusses issues concerning plot and character consistency, refuting charges against Jeanie's going to London and obtaining a pardon for her sister 'as a lucky, but evasive solution' (xiii) to the moral dilemma: 'that quality which makes her adhere to truth in the first part, makes her capable of obtaining mercy in the second' (xiii). Lamont is not concerned with historical accuracy, context of the novel's composition or Scott's biographical circumstances.

By contrast, Inglis in his 1994 introduction to *HOM* is not content with an account 'for the most part accurate' but investigates the inaccuracies. Again, he sees Scott's 'known political attitudes' as motivator for the changes made: 'Not wishing to provide a revolutionist's handbook, he omits ... adapts ... smooths down' (xxx). Inglis accounts for alterations with a political aim and thereby renders them conscious. In contrast to Lamont's account of history, his does not include quotations from the novel, showing a less immediate focus on the text.

Extratextual historical knowledge can also be used to justify accounts given or modes used by Scott. Hewitt argues that though a journal-form novel was unfashionable in 1824, when *Redgauntlet* was published, Scott was justified in using the journal because of the novel's setting in 1765 roughly coinciding with James Boswell's journal. 'Through his friendship with the Boswell family Scott would certainly have known of Boswell's journal although none of it was published until the twentieth century' (DH, *R* xvi). The mode of narration as well as contents thus has to be historically accurate in later introductions.

Scott's language is another of difference. While earlier ones are generally laudatory about Scott's use of language, later ones are again more critical because they refer to actual facts. Calder states he is 'convinced that, granted Scott's objectives, Macbriar and Mucklewrath are as they should be; and it is worth pausing here to praise the ventriloquist's gifts which enable Scott to move [from one idiom to another]' (AC, *OM* 34). Scott's objectives are to make Scots convincing for the reader, which is the only criterion that matters to Calder's approach. By contrast, Stevenson and Davidson entitle a whole section of their introduction 'The Problem of Scott's Language' (S/D, *OM* xxviii), arguing that because Scots was perceived as 'rustic, comic, and awkward' (xxix) Scott's heroes necessarily speak 'the purest standard literary English .... Realistically, the educational opportunities open to such children of provincial gentry would have been very limited' (xxx). They are concerned with what would be accurate and again see imprecisions as politically motivated.

Even when referring to the text rather than outside sources to support their arguments, the later introductions show a more evidence-dependent approach. To support his argument that Darsie is in love with Alan, Hewitt counts how often they use the terms 'dear' and 'dearest' of each other ('"dear" on some twenty-five occasions ... "dearest" on five', DH, *R* xxvii). Similarly, to prove the statement that inheritance is one of *Ivanhoe*'s themes, emphasized by the novel's being 'full of wandering and deracinated people' (GT, *I* xxiv), Tulloch gives an exact account of how often and to whom the words 'wandering' and 'errant' occur. As with introductions to Austen's novels, later ones are more argumentative, focusing on fewer aspects in greater detail than earlier ones. The points made from the text, as well as the ones supported with references to extratextual material, depend on factual evidence. While later introduction writers use expressions such as 'historical sins' (ID, *I* xiv), 'notorious invention' (ID, *I* xv), 'anachronistic' (S/D, *OM* xvii), earlier ones accept Scott's versions of historical events as 'probabilities' (AC, *OM* 23). Scott 'goes beyond the "factual", yet he is "real"' (AC, *OM* 22).

As with Austen, earlier introductions are more likely to include overall evaluations of a novel. They also have a more emotional approach and praise in more absolute and general terms: Scott is a 'great novelist [even] by today's austere standards of criticism' (AW, I vii). Later introductions' praise and defence occurs with precise reasons. Hewitt argues that *Redgauntlet* 'offers no solutions, and comes to no conclusions; this openness is the ultimate mark of its greatness' (xxx). Duncan appeals to late-twentieth-century readers, 'the generation that has forgotten *Ivanhoe*, [as] well placed to rediscover [it]' (ID, *I* x), since the novel should be recognized as 'an ancestor of the archival comedy of Umberto Eco' (x). Linking Scott to Eco gives Scott postmodern qualities and significance, which fits into the general trend of later introductions' focus on elements outside the plot. Thus later introduction writers grant greatness if Scott's works can be seen as meeting late-twentieth-century criteria of great fiction, and not, as earlier writers do, on timeless and absolute terms.

Scott's artistic consciousness

Earlier introductions are not concerned with the novel's use of literary allusions. Where other works feature in the essays it is to draw general comparisons and underline Scott's originality and greatness. The inclusion of literary allusions is seen as an unconscious act: they 'poured out of him in a fluent torrent, and [had] not been "looked up", ... evident from the frequent inaccuracy with which he quotes' (AW, *I* xvii). Instead of giving examples and condemning them as imprecise, Wilson emphasizes the 'naturalness [of] this habit of composition and of mind which Scott himself believed distinguished him from his many imitators' (xvii). Where Scott's mode of composition features in earlier introductions, it thus adds to his greatness through naturalness, which is similar to Lukács's and the Victorian reviewers' view of Scott as more artistic than he was conscious of.

By contrast, later introductions emphasize that Scott's use of quotations and allusions 'cannot have been casual' (DH, *R* xxvi). The novels' intertextuality stresses Scott's consciousness of their fused nature, and draws attention to their limited authority. Inglis observes that 'the point is not that the reader should contextualize or even recognize every source ... but that the composite texture of the writing ... should be felt and acknowledged.' (TI, *HOM* xxv–xxvi). While both earlier and later introductions see the novels as art, the concept of art changes between the two periods: for the earlier ones, just as for Victorian reviewers, genius can create art without artistic consciousness. Awareness could even potentially impede the work's naturalness. For the later ones, the author has to be conscious of the act of creating.

Not only emphasis on Scott's literary allusions but also explorations of the novels' narrative modes in later introductions serve to show Scott's conscious construction of his novels. Tulloch organizes his introduction around *Ivanhoe*'s genre, arguing that the novel is neither history nor romance, but that 'in the subject matter of chivalry the two genres of history and romance converge' (GT, *I* xxi), which adds to the novel's complexity. However, he looks at the concept of chivalry, romance and history less from the text than with reference to *Ivanhoe*'s 'Dedicatory Epistle' as well as to Scott's 'Essay on Chivalry' and 'Essay on Romance'. Rather than just concerning himself with genre, Tulloch shows Scott's awareness of it. Scott's ideas about genre are necessarily informed by nineteenth-century concepts, so that apart from showing his conscious construction of the novel, Tulloch uses the discussion of genre as yet another device to place the novel in the context of its genesis. The year of the novel's composition directly influences its genre: having uncovered Scott's deviations from the historical King Richard, especially in his 'interest in English or England' (xvi) which Tulloch shows the historical Richard not to have had, Tulloch concludes that 'by departing from history in the direction of romance Scott has been able to make a plea for the social harmony he feared was disappearing in radical revolt' (xvi). *Ivanhoe*'s mixture of history and romance is therefore deliberate, and motivated by a political aim.

Earlier introductions do not discuss genre, but give brief statements about what genre they see the respective work as belonging to, usually to emphasize the novels' originality, and often concerned with the contrast between realism and romance. Lamont states that if *HOM* were a romance, its 'happy outcome ... [could be] simply the result of chance' (CL, *HOM* xiii), but since it is a 'realistic novel' there have to be reasons, which Lamont sees in the power and consistency of the heroine. A discussion of the appropriateness of the term 'realistic novel', or of the question of whether the novel incorporates other narrative modes does not arise, since the focus is on plot and character consistency. Andrew Hook sees *Waverley* as consisting simultaneously of romance and novel rather than unifying the two, the genre mirroring the plot's promotion of compromise. In contrast to later introduction writers, Hook sees genres as explored through the hero, so that 'the conflict between romance and realism is not so much a struggle between competing literary modes as an essentially *moral* issue' (AH, *W* 23), reflected in Edward Waverley's lack of a 'truer sense of reality' (22). Hook's discussion is therefore not a means of exploring Scott's artistic consciousness. For him, genre is an issue intimately connected with and therefore emphasizing the central moral debate of the novel's main plot and character. Earlier introductions establish the genre from the text rather than referring to outside sources.

Scott's introductory chapters are of no specific importance to earlier introductions. Calder even recommends, especially to first-time readers of *Old Mortality*, to 'ignore ... the rather tedious Cleishbotham and perhaps even the interesting Pattieson, and begin at once with Chapter 2' (AC, *OM* 9). Later introduction writers disagree. To show Scott's artistic awareness, they include considerations of Scott's introductory chapters in their discussions, sometimes devoting more space to these first chapters than to the rest of the novel. Robertson, in her introduction to *BOL*, discusses at length the novel's two frame narratives, the one concerning Peter Pattieson and Dick Tinto, and Scott's own, written for the Magnum Edition more than a decade after *BOL*'s first appearance in 1819. They not only serve to deflect 'authority for the tales away from Scott, or indeed from any answerable source ... [but also remind] readers that story-tellers may be unreliable, prejudiced, and obtuse' (FR, *BOL* xii). As with intertextuality and narrative technique, regarding the first chapters as setting the texts up as self-reflective raises the novels as works of art. The frame narratives serve 'a vital function in preparing the reader for the novel's provisional, arbitrary, and morally ambiguous presentation of history' (FR, *BOL* xiii). Sutherland, in her 2000 introduction to *BOL*, similarly argues for the significance of the frame narrative as being concerned with methods of 'presenting a tale, ... [thereby] offer[ing] a carefully judged interpretative statement about what follows' (KS, *BOL* xix–xx), though she also observes that 'from the evidence of the manuscript, the opening chapter ... appears to have been an afterthought'.[8] Both Robertson and Sutherland thus knowingly emphasize an 'afterthought': Robertson the introduction to the Magnum Edition, Sutherland the frame narrative, which, while it may inform readers' interpretation of the novel and may illustrate Scott's later thoughts about the novel as well as about his writing in general, is limited in its relevance to the novel's composition and implied reader. The importance Robertson and Sutherland give Scott's own introduction to the work and the frame narrative in their interpretations of the novel again testifies to later introductions' aim of showing Scott as 'highly self-conscious' (FR, *BOL* xv) in constructing his work. Just as they consciously read the novel through its framework, and are aware of the act of reading, they emphasize the novel's construction more than its story or possible moral message, since both story and moral message can only ever be ambiguous. Their discussions also again illustrate their technique of referring to sources outside the immediate story to support their arguments.

Earlier introductions' concern with the novels themselves, their stories and with moral messages is replaced in later introductions with a postmodern emphasis on Scott as conscious of the arbitrary and composite nature of his texts. The novels convey the relativity of stories and history and indicate that there can be no absolute truth or morality. Instead of praising or criticizing the plot itself, later introductions praise Scott for imposing restrictions on the 'independent development of plot' (FR, *BOL* xx) through the literary allusions and the frame narratives. In their concern with genre, metafictionality and conscious creation of art, they testify to every text's being shaped by its time of composition: in the context of post-structuralism, an analysis of just a novel's text is not possible; instead a work of fiction is necessarily discussed with reference to its own context. If an analysis of a text is to be justified, that text has to show self-reflexivity and ambiguity. The majority of later introductions are not aware of their own interpretations being a version shaped by context, and therefore do not address the paradox of insisting on historical accuracy on the one hand while stressing the arbitrariness of historical stories on the other.

Gender

As with Austen, only later introductions discuss Scott's gender attitudes. Both Duncan and Tulloch in their introductions to *Ivanhoe* see Scott as depicting women as victims of an oppressive society. Tulloch describes Rebecca as 'the symbol of all that women can suffer from men' (GT, *I* xxvi), and Duncan argues that through Rebecca's exclusion Scott shows that 'Jews and women inhabit a different history from the official, imperial one of expansion and synthesis' (ID, *I* xx). He again stresses Scott's awareness of the unreliability of any version of history, exploring this issue through narrative as well as plot.

Wilson stays in the text in his interpretation, stating that it is due to Rebecca's exhibiting 'a classic type of rigidity which Scott finds so attractive in his heroines [that] she must be an exile' (AW, *I* xii) and does not see any larger social implications in this. Duncan, by contrast, regards Rebecca as representing 'the categories – sexuality and race – that will mark the limits of "culture", the fluid space of national identity formation, in nineteenth-century discourse' (ID, *I* xxv). Typical of later introductions, his focus is not on the individual character but on what the character reveals about society. Duncan cites the novel's reception history – again a source outside the text – to support his view that Scott deliberately makes readers regret Rebecca's exclusion, an effect 'carefully crafted rather than inadvertent' (ID, *I* xxv–xxvi), giving the novel significance through seeing it as consciously exploring culture's excluded groups.

In his discussion of Madge Wildfire, Inglis shows a similar occupation with a character in specifically feminine terms. Seeing her in a Romantic and feminine discourse of madness, she points 'towards Bertha Mason, Gwendolen Harleth and Tess Durbeyfield' (TI, *HOM* xlii). In contrast to the exclusively feminine parallels that Inglis draws, Lamont links Madge to Blanche in *The Lady of the Lake,* and to Davie Gellatly in *Waverley* and classes her as 'someone on the edge of sanity who expresses insights and warning by means of song' (CL, *HOM*, xviii), in not specifically feminine terms.

Both Robertson and Sutherland in their introductions to *BOL* see Scott's depiction of women in the novel as showing female power to be dangerous and unnatural, women as irrational, and female narrative and history as incapable of progress, and thus distinct from male rationality and ability to compromise. Sutherland supports her view of the novel's attitude to gender by relating the story of the death of Scott's great-aunt who was 'hacked to death by a crazed woman servant' (KS, *BOL* xxxi), so that the story's 'every connection was for Scott feminine and steeped in violence' (xxxi). Male rationality is rendered irrelevant by the non-progressive female narration of an inescapable and violent past.

While it is only later introductions that are concerned with gender, it appears that this is an issue where the gender of the introduction writers influences interpretation. Where Duncan and Tulloch see Scott as sympathetically depicting women as oppressed by and excluded from society, Robertson and Sutherland read his depiction as not granting women rationality, let alone allowing them to hold positions other than traditional ones in society, as Lady Ashton does. Inglis does not argue in any particular direction as regards Scott's attitude to gender, but his analysis shows the typical later introduction writers' awareness of gender issues. Nicola Watson and David Punter in their introductions to *The Antiquary* show similar attitudes: while Watson sees Scott as hostile towards women, Punter is aware of differences between the characterization of men and women but does not see this as a hostile depiction. As with issues of context, genre and intertextuality, later introductions' concern with gender places them into their own critical context and shows that they see Scott, like Austen, as engaging with gender issues. The difference between male and female introduction writers' views of Scott's attitude to gender issues is therefore a point where writers' period is not the only determining factor. In the light of this, the prefaces to Austen's novels written by women giving gender more importance than the only one written by a man may not be coincidental.

Comparison

The importance given to the authors' context is the main difference between introductions of different periods: just as categorically as New Criticism excludes context, New Historicism insists on including it. The EEWN, appearing from 1993, is in itself evidence of the increased emphasis on context and the connection between biography and text: 'it is the first return to what Scott actually wrote in his manuscripts and proofs'.[9] By going back to Scott's original texts, rather than that of the Magnum edition that had hitherto been used,[10] the editors emphasize the circumstances of the novel's composition. The EEWN is also evidence of the later period's reading of Scott as an artistically conscious composer of his texts and of his generally increased critical status. It is on the EEWN that Penguin bases its new editions of Scott's novels, and often the EEWN editors who provide the Penguin introductions. Not only the EEWN, but also the increase in Penguin and OUP editions of Scott's novels that carry critical introductions (six compared to fifteen), indicates the rise in Scott's status.

Earlier introductions focus on the text, emphasizing plot, story and characters as Scott's main features, as well as defending his novels as pieces of art, without going into detail or seeing Scott as consciously artistic. They are not concerned with authorial intention. As with earlier introductions to Austen's novels, formal aspects feature little since introductions focus on a variety of aspects. This broader focus shows introduction writers to be addressing a general readership. In Scott's case, the lack of focus on formal aspects in spite of prevalent critical trends also appears due to writers not interpreting his texts as fulfilling these criteria. Hook sees Scott's art in opposition to Austen's since 'where Jane Austen is strong, Scott is weak' (AH, W 12), especially as regards form, language and irony. Not reading Scott as fulfilling some of the prevalent criteria explains critics' insisting on his greatness in more defensive tones than is the case in later introductions, while presenting him as great against Austen shows her status to have become high but not yet superlative. At the same time, the focus of the prevalent critical trends being on text rather than author facilitates introductions' presenting Scott's texts as great because writers can ignore the debate about the existence of Scott's artistic consciousness. The texts are high quality and worthy of notice regardless of the author's intentions. New Criticism therefore paradoxically shapes Scott interpretation in the earlier introductions in the direction of plot, so that period, introduction writers' target audience, and the text determine the introductions' content.

For later introductions, artistic consciousness and technical skill are conditional to an author's greatness. They align Scott with Austen to emphasize that he is an artistically conscious writer, seeing his novels as strong in the majority of the points Hook finds them weak in: narrative form is deliberately varied, and while his outlook is not ironic, it is self-reflective so that he is a self-conscious artist engaging with literary forms and social concerns – the opposite of the unconscious genius Victorian critics so much admired. Alignment with Austen testifies to introduction writers' wanting to elevate Scott and indicates Austen's immensely high status. References to Austen also demonstrate the belief that a detailed acquaintance with her novels can be presupposed, since her novels, and characters from them, are mentioned without any explanation or naming of the author. The situation in the 1990s and 2000s is thus the exact reverse of the early nineteenth century, when comparing Austen to Scott was the highest praise a reviewer could bestow on her.

While in both periods his texts are appropriated to fit prevailing criteria, the difference between his status in the earlier and later period shows that the more he is made to fit into prevalent values, the higher his critical status becomes. In the 1990s and 2000s, Austen and Scott are shown to possess what has in no previous period been seen as theirs – Austen political awareness and

Scott artistic awareness – since in the critical context of the later period, greatness manifests itself in the authors' conscious participation in their political, social, cultural and literary context. The technique with which this is established differs, however: while for both Austen and Scott twentieth-century sources are used to determine the historical context, as well as especially Romantic works referred to to ascertain the literary context, it is primarily for Austen that non-fictional texts by her contemporaries are cited. For Scott, it is his own non-fiction that is mainly referred to. These different techniques of showing the authors' contextual awareness indicate introduction writers' need to see both authors as politically and artistically aware. Though every text is necessarily part of the context of its production, it becomes greater the more conscious its author can be shown to be, which is paradoxical given that most introduction writers show no awareness of their own texts' dependence on context.

That introductions to both authors' novels show up the same approaches indicates that introduction writers are more influenced by general critical trends than by individual studies on Austen or Scott. Academic studies of Austen and Scott tend to feature the same trends as critical introductions, though often with a gap of a few years.[11] Introductions as well as critical studies are therefore participating in the general critical trends of their period, rather than introductions appropriating academic studies specifically on the author they are concerned with. What is striking though is that there are a number of critical approaches that do not commonly feature in the introductions, e.g. psychoanalysis and Marxism.

In later introductions, Austen's and Scott's texts are of particular relevance to a modern audience, which makes previous interpretations invalid and feeds into later introductions creating a more exclusive audience. They define their audience not only by period but also by degree of specialist knowledge and, in the case of Austen, gender. By contrast, earlier introductions' reading of a text's timelessness as rendering it topical leaves an option for previous readings being valid still. They address a more general audience, and emphasize Scott's art as much as his entertainment.

In contrast to later introductions to Austen's novels, those to Scott's do not specifically address a male or female readership. In the later period he is, however, like her, presented to a more specialized audience by both introduction writers and publishers. Instead of the abridged and children's versions of his novels published in mid-century decades, the majority of editions now are scholarly, carrying introductions and notes. While his critical status has increased, newspaper articles show that he has not as yet become a writer in the public mind, which indicates the gap between critics and general readers.

Austen's implied audience in the later period is also specialized. That introduction writers of both authors address a limited audience suggests that this is not due to an elitist attitude and critics' wishing to retain Austen as high culture, protecting her against public readings by excluding these readers, but due to a general shift in the concept of a critical introduction.

The implied readership of introductions to Austen's novels is also limited largely to female readers. The ratio of male and female introduction writers to Scott's novels is much less extreme than with Austen and it develops in the contrary direction from Austen introductions, since there are more male than female introduction writers in the later period. Publishers therefore deliberately choose female introduction writers for Austen's novels in the later period and market her towards a female readership. While cultural and critical context generally shapes reading more than any other factor, gender is the only point where introductions writers' sex discernibly influences their reading of both authors. In the earlier period, no such gender-influenced reading becomes apparent. While overall approach is defined by period, the difference between female and male introduction writers within a period becomes greater through the influence of feminist awareness and criticism.

In the late twentieth century, as in all periods, critical notice of an author is to some degree mirrored in an increase in public attention. However, the public's ways of reading are not generally determined by critical approaches, so that similarities in choice of text and ways of reading are due to the influence of overall cultural movements. The rise of feminism leads to Austen's femininity playing a much bigger role in readings after the 1970s than before. Critical introductions as well as newspaper articles voice their opinion about Austen's concern with gender issues. Numbers and kinds of editions, too, hint at the public's emphasis on Austen's dealings with gender. The popularity of individual novels shifts between periods. While in the 1960s, *Emma* is more popular than *Pride and Prejudice*, this order reverses itself: between 1960 and 1969 there are 9 editions of *Emma* and 8 of *Pride and Prejudice*, between 1970 and 1979 there are 7 of each, and between 1980 and 1989 there are 9 relaunches of *Emma* but 15 of *Pride and Prejudice*. These shifts occur before any of the hugely popular film adaptations come out. That *Pride and Prejudice* should rise in popularity, with arguably the most spirited heroine who can most easily be interpreted as corresponding with modern ideas of femininity, shows the impact of general cultural trends on readers, both critical and public. This development again testifies to both context and text determining interpretation: in spite of readings being largely independent of the actual text, some texts lend themselves more to appropriations into a certain direction. Yet Austen's other heroines, too, are made to fit a prevalent concern with gender and feminism, so that even Fanny, arguably the most passive and vulnerable of Austen's heroines, acquires power in a late-twentieth-century reading. Correspondingly, while similar issues are read into Austen's and Scott's texts, Austen is yet more highly regarded than Scott because her works fit prevalent images more easily.

Of the main constituents of identity that have fascinated critics since the 1980s – gender, ethnicity and social class – attention has been overwhelmingly focused on the first in the case of Austen, and on the other two in the case of Scott. Despite the attempts to break away from earlier assumptions, Austen is still presented essentially as a woman writer concerned with women's matters, Scott as a male writer operating in the wider masculine public sphere.

Retrospect

The patterns that emerge from the study are clear. Scott's novels become immensely successful as soon as they appear. Austen's works, too, are more popular than those of the average novelist of her day. For both authors, there is a steadily rising admiration and increasing readership throughout the nineteenth century, until at least 1914. However, although starting from a far lower base Austen gradually gains on Scott over the decades and at some point in the early twentieth century overtakes him. Scott then turns sharply down, while Austen continues to rise so that by today we have an exact reversal of the initial situation.

This pattern of development, with its crossover, is of much the same shape whichever indicators we use: publishers' relaunches, sales numbers, library catalogues and lending figures, recorded critical opinions, private comments in diaries and letters, newspaper articles, popularizations.

Changes occur both in the curve and in the discourse. Hence, although this longitudinal study has been arranged into calendar periods, they do not always give an adequate picture of the trends. Though the curve is for the most part fairly smooth with substantial consensus, we can detect occasional quite sharp changes, such as the coming out of copyright of Scott's and Austen's novels, the academization of Austen, the advent of literary theory and feminism.

What explanations offer themselves? The fact that a longitudinal study shows such a strong and consistent pattern suggests that we should be looking for deep and long-run trends, rather than using the circular argument of simply attributing these developments to changes in taste without looking into the causes. Explanations can only be found by looking outside the texts to the interactions of readers with these texts.

Did general social trends in the nineteenth century, especially the emergence of a large leisured class, cause the developments outlined above? But Austen's novels are as long as the Waverley novels, and by the end of the nineteenth century both authors were widely read outside the leisured classes. Did readers' gender have an impact? Readerships of both authors could have been gendered, with Scott being read by boys and men, and Austen by girls and women. However, although Scott is in some sense a masculinist author, his portrayals of women were also much admired and commended, and Austen does not write only about women. The evidence shows that both authors were read by both sexes, from the moment the novels first appeared, and that readers' gender did not on the whole determine interpretation. From the later twentieth century onwards Austen has been marketed as a female author writing about and for women, but that still does not exclude men as her readers, as evidence such as that of newspaper articles indicates.

Knowledge of the authors' lives does not appear to have influenced reading patterns either. When biographical information became available – first through the breaking of the anonymity in 1818 for Austen and in 1826 for Scott, then through the publications of the Austen-Leigh *Memoir* (1870) and Lockhart's *Life* (1837) – this made little difference to the shape of the trajectories. Indeed, the biographies were not only triggered by the novels' popularity but to an extent were also shaped by what readers saw as the works' contents: Lockhart presented Scott as an archetypal Tory gentleman, and Austen's comparative obscurity and seclusion was, if anything, exaggerated. In all but purely formalist approaches, there is a tendency to make the lives and works of the authors correspond.

The authors' gender, however, seems to have to a degree influenced reading, all the more so since this is a factor that cannot be changed through interpretation. Throughout the nineteenth century, Scott's novels are seen as the fitting products of a gentleman, masculine in their scope and content and noble in their moral message. Conversely, Austen's being a woman limits the possibilities that nineteenth-century readers see in her novels, whereas today, it is precisely that politicized femininity which adds to her relevance.

Intrinsic qualities of the text also influence reception patterns, since some texts lend themselves more than others to being appropriated to suit the preferences of a certain period. The style of Scott's novels was much admired throughout the nineteenth century, whereas it seems long-winded to many readers of today's fast-moving societies. Texts in combination with cultural context can create criteria: the overwhelming literary status of the Waverley novels in the early nineteenth century influenced readers' attitudes to novels generally. While Scott's works contributed to the rise in the status of the novel, they also had an impact on the criteria applied to the evaluation of fiction. Though imagination had not before been wanted, it now became essential, so that reviewers criticize Austen for the lack of imagination in her novels. Through the influence of Scott's works, a hierarchy was established in the 1810s that valued works which combined an imaginative with a realistic quality above purely realistic works, causing lack of imagination to remain a major point of criticism of Austen's works throughout the nineteenth century.

It is striking that Scott rises to a peak and then goes sharply down at a specific historical conjuncture, the 1920s. Scott had many imitators in the long historical novel, such as Harrison Ainsworth and Edward Bulwer-Lytton, whose readerships and reputation also fell away suddenly. It is fair therefore to look for specific events. The disaster of the First World War can be linked with the states of mind that resulted from the immersion of the reading nation in the Waverley novels.[1] This shattering of confidence in progress coincided with the advent of modernism and its distrust of grand unifying narratives. In material terms the stereotype plates that had supplied extremely cheap copies had been melted for munitions and a positive decision had been taken not just to relaunch but to incur the capital costs of printing new editions.

In this new mid-twentieth-century situation, Austen's world became more manageable. Her novels' small social, geographical and historical scope, that had been criticized in the previous century, now became attractive. Her irony, which had earlier been overlooked, began to be perceived as intrinsic to her style. This multiplicity of meaning chimed in with modern understandings of the complexities of language and literature. And although the plates of Austen editions had also been melted, new markets were being created by the post-First World War nostalgia for a rural, largely pre-mechanical, polite and gentrified society.

The theme of interpersonal relations in Austen's novels appeared easier to deal with than Scott's historical conflicts on national and international levels. Once he ceased to be seen as a great moral teacher, his works became historical classics, written long ago and with apparently diminishing universal relevance. While his characters had stuck in readers' minds at least as much as Austen's had throughout the nineteenth century, their historical fixity, with their predicaments arising out of a specific historical situation, appeared to render them less relevant to contemporary society. Though Austen's characters also belong to a definite society, their problems are less dependent on history, and can be more easily appropriated across time and place. Her texts now seem richer the more they are studied. Who would have guessed that, by reading silences, Austen could turn out to be a prime text for topics such as slavery, the slave trade and attitudes to the wars? Scott, by contrast, whose theme of how to preserve national identity within a larger unit at least could make him very topical to a twenty-first-century postcolonial world, or a Scotland with a regained parliament, is regarded as historical, and no longer relevant.

There is at present little sign that the long-run trends are about to change, let alone go into reverse. Scott's novels clutter second-hand bookshops and are sold at extremely low prices. Every major publisher, from university presses to the cheapest paperback reprinter, relaunches Austen frequently.

Of two points we can be sure. After 200 years, both authors are set to endure, secure in the national literary pantheon. Readers will, however, continue to bring the concerns of their own times to their interactions with the texts, receiving them in new ways, creating new interpretations and deriving new meanings.

Notes

Introduction

[1] Jane Austen to Anna Austen, 28 September 1814, in *Jane Austen's Letters*, ed. and coll. Deidre Le Faye (Oxford: Oxford University Press, 1995), p. 277.

[2] Walter Scott, journal entry of 14 March 1826, in *The Journal of Sir Walter Scott*, ed. W. E. K. Anderson (Oxford: Oxford University Press, 1972), p. 112.

[3] *The Critical Review*, March 1813, p. 323.

[4] Margaret Anne Doody, Introduction to *Sense and Sensibility* (Oxford: Oxford University Press, 1990), pp. vii–xxxix (p. xv).

[5] Leslie Stephen, 'Some Words about Sir Walter Scott', *Cornhill Magazine*, 24 (September 1871), xxiv, 278–93. Reprinted in John O. Hayden, ed., *Scott: The Critical Heritage* (London: Routledge & Kegan Paul, 1970), pp. 439–58 (p. 458).

[6] Ian Duncan, Introduction to *Ivanhoe* (Oxford: Oxford University Press 1996), pp. vii–xxvi (p. xx).

[7] Wolfgang Iser, *The Implied Reader: Patterns of Communication in Prose Fiction form Bunyan to Beckett.* (Baltimore, MD: Johns Hopkins University Press, 1974).

[8] Hans Robert Jauss, *Toward an Aesthetic of Reception*, translation from German by Timothy Bahti, introduction by Paul de Man (Brighton: Harvester Press, 1982), p. 21.

[9] Stanley Fish, 'Interpreting the *Variorum*', in *Reader-Response Criticism: From Formalism to Post-Structuralism*, ed. Jane Tompkins (Baltimore, MD/London: Johns Hopkins University Press, 1980), pp. 164–84 (p. 184).

[10] An exception is Deidre Lynch's 'Introduction: Sharing with Our Neighbors', in *Janeites: Austen's Disciples and Devotees*, ed. Deidre Lynch (Princeton, NJ: Princeton University Press, 2000), pp. 3–24.

[11] Joseph Cady and Ian Watt, 'Jane Austen's Critics', in *Jane Austen: Critical Assessments*, ed. Ian Littlewood (Mountfield: Helm Information, 1998), pp. 231–45; Kurt Gamerschlag, *Sir Walter Scott und die Waverley Novels* (Darmstadt: Wissenschaftliche Buchgesellschaft, 1978); Fiona Robertson, 'Walter Scott', in *Literature of the Romantic Period: A Bibliographical Guide*, ed. Michael O'Neill (Oxford: Clarendon Press, 1998), pp. 221–45; Fiona Stafford, 'Jane Austen', in *Literature of the Romantic Period*, ed. Michael O'Neill; *Jane Austen: The Critical Heritage*, ed. Brian Southam (2 vols, London: Routledge & Kegan Paul, 1968 and 1987); *Scott: The Critical Heritage*, ed. John O. Hayden; Claudia L. Johnson, 'Austen Cults and Cultures', in *The Cambridge Companion to Jane Austen*, ed. Edward Copeland and Juliet McMaster (Cambridge: Cambridge University Press, 1997), pp. 211–26; Nicola Trott, 'Critical Responses, 1830–1970', in *Jane Austen in Context*, ed. Janet Todd

(Cambridge: Cambridge University Press, 2005), pp. 92–100'; *A Companion to Jane Austen Studies*, ed. Laura Cooner Lambdin and Robert Thomas Lambdin (Westport, CT: Greenwood Press, 2000); Reimer Jehmlich, *Jane Austen* (Darmstadt: Wissenschaftliche Buchgesellschaft, 1995).

The three book-length studies were written more than three decades ago: James T. Hillhouse, *The Waverley Novels and Their Critics*, 2nd edn (New York: Octagon Books, 1968; first published 1936); Horst Tippkötter, *Walter Scott, Geschichte als Unterhaltung* (Frankfurt am Main: Vittorio Klostermann, 1971); Joseph Duffy, 'Jane Austen and the Nineteenth-century Critics of Fiction 1812–1913' (unpublished doctoral thesis, University of Chicago, 1954).

Chapter 1: Reviewing in the Romantic Period

[1] Walter Scott, 'On the Present State of Periodical Criticism', in *Sir Walter Scott's Edinburgh Annual Register*, ed. Kenneth Curry (Knoxville, TN: University of Tennessee Press, 1977), pp. 132–70 (p. 170).

[2] William Hazlitt, 'The Periodical Press', *ER*, 38 (1823), reprinted in *The Complete Works of William Hazlitt*, ed. P. Howe (21 vols, London: J. M. Dent and Sons, 1930–34), vol. XVI, pp. 211—39 (p. 213).

[3] John D. Hayden, *The Romantic Reviewers, 1802–1824* (London: Routledge & Kegan Paul, 1969), p. 39.

[4] Peter Garside, 'The English Novel in the Romantic Era', in *The English Novel 1770–1829: A Bibliographical Survey of Prose Fiction Published in the British Isles*, ed. Peter Garside, James Raven and Rainer Schöwerling (2 vols, Oxford: Oxford University Press, 2000), vol. II, pp. 15–103 (p. 16).

[5] Walter Bagehot, 'The First Edinburgh Reviewers', in *Literary Studies by the Late Walter Bagehot*, ed. Richard Holt Hutton (London: Longmans, Green and Co., 1891), pp. 1–40 (p. 1).

[6] Scott, 'Periodical Criticism', p. 146.

[7] Scott, 'Periodical Criticism', p. 142.

[8] Lord Byron, 'English Bards and Scotch Reviewers. A Satire', in *Lord Byron: Selected Poems*, ed. S. J. Wolfson and P. J. Manning (London: Penguin, 1996), pp. 6–48 (p. 23).

[9] John Gross, *The Rise and Fall of the Man of Letters: Aspects of English Literacy Life since 1800* (London: Weidenfeld and Nicolson, 1969), p. 2.

[10] William St Clair, *The Reading Nation in the Romantic Period* (Cambridge: Cambridge University Press, 2004), p. 573; Richard Altick, *The English Common Reader: A Social History of the Mass Reading Public 1800–1900* (Chicago, IL: University of Chicago Press, 1957), p. 392.

[11] Kathryn Sutherland, 'Events ... have made us a world of readers': Reader Relations 1780–1830', in *The Romantic Period*, ed. David B. Pirie (London: Penguin, 1994), pp. 1–48 (p. 28).

[12] Gross, p. 2.

[13] St Clair, p. 574.

[14] Lord Byron, 'Journal', entry for 17 November 1813, in *Byron's Letters and*

Journals, ed. Leslie A. Marchand, 13 vols (London: Murray, 1973–94), vol. III, p. 209.

15 Gross, p. 2.

16 Peter F. Morgan, *Jeffrey's Criticism* (Edinburgh: Scottish Academic Press, 1983), p. 10.

17 I shall therefore refer to individual reviewers as 'he' throughout; read 'he or she' each time.

18 In a Ferris, *The Achievement of Literary Authority: Gender, History and the Waverley Novels* (Ithaca, NY/London: Cornell University Press, 1991), p. 30.

19 Marilyn Butler, 'Culture's Medium: the Role of the Review', in *The Cambridge Companion to British Romanticism*, ed. Stuart Curran (Cambridge: Cambridge University Press, 1993), pp. 120–47 (p. 125).

20 Garside, pp. 16, 38.

21 *BC*, Jan. 1812, p. 39.

22 Garside, pp. 16–17.

23 Scott, 'Periodical Criticism', p. 166.

24 Hazlitt, p. 235.

25 *BC*, April 1815, pp.442–3.

26 Garside, p. 74.

27 1833 edition of *SS*, p. viii.

28 *QR*, Oct. 1815, p. 188. (The article did not in fact appear until March 1816.)

29 Sutherland, 'Reader Relations', p. 9.

30 From 9s to £1.11.6; St Clair, pp. 202–3.

31 Austen, letter to Fanny Knight, November 1814, in Le Faye, p. 287.

32 Sutherland, 'Reader Relations', p. 12.

33 St Clair, p. 244.

34 Fiona Robertson, 'Novels', in *An Oxford Companion to the Romantic Age: British Culture 1776–1832*, gen. ed. Iain McCalman (Oxford: Oxford University Press, 1999), pp.286–95 (p. 287).

35 William B. Todd and Ann Bowden, *Sir Walter Scott: A Bibliographical History 1796–1832* (New Castle, DE: Oak Knoll Press, 1998), p. 537.

36 Garside, p. 45.

37 William Godwin, 'Essay of History and Romance', in *Political and Philosophical Writings of William Godwin*, ed. Mark Philip (7 vols, London: Pickering, 1993), vol. V, pp. 291–301 (p. 297).

Chapter 2: Austen and Scott Reviewed, 1812–1818

1 Reviews have been located using David Gilson's *A Bibliography of Jane Austen*, (New Castle, DE: Oak Press, 1997) William Ward's *Literary Reviews in British Periodicals, 1798–1820: A Bibliography* (New York: Garland, 1972), William Todd and Ann Bowden's *Sir Walter Scott: A Bibliographical History* and the databases *Periodicals Contents Index* and *Nineteenth Century Masterfile*.

2 St Clair, p. 245.

[3] Gilson, p. 8. All estimations for sizes of first editions of Austen's novels are taken from Gilson.
[4] Garside, p. 39; St Clair, p. 564.
[5] See St Clair, p. 244.
[6] Emma Parker's *Elfrida, Heiress of Belgrove* in *The Critical Review*; Amelia Opie's *Temper, or Domestic Scenes: a Tale* in *The British Critic*.
[7] *BC*, May 1812, p. 527.
[8] Garside, p. 66.
[9] Garside, p. 66.
[10] E.g. in a letter from Jane Austen to Francis Austen, September 1813, in Le Faye, p. 231.
[11] I refer to her as Austen throughout, though reviewers did not know her name.
[12] Gilson, p. 36.
[13] Gilson, p. 49.
[14] Gilson, pp. 67–9.
[15] Le Faye, p. 313.
[16] Gilson, p. 84.
[17] Henry Austen, Biographical Notice, in James Edward Austen-Leigh, *A Memoir of Jane Austen and Other Family Recollections*, ed. Kathryn Sutherland (Oxford: Oxford University Press, 2002), pp. 135–43 (p. 140).
[18] Biographical Notice, p. 139.
[19] See also Gilson, p. 209 onwards.
[20] Todd and Bowden, pp. 309–16.
[21] J. G. Lockhart, *Memoirs of the Life of Sir Walter Scott, Bart.* (7 Vols, Edinburgh: Robert Cadell; London: John Murray and Whittaker, 1837), vol III, p. 296.
[22] See bibliography for a complete list.
[23] Ferris, p. 3.
[24] Tippkötter, p. 46.
[25] Reviewers refer to him as the 'Author of Waverley'. I refer to him as Scott throughout.
[26] Walter Scott, *Waverley*, ed. Claire Lamont, p. 344. (The third edition came out in October 1814.)
[27] *Waverley*, p. 340.
[28] Claire Lamont, 'Waverley and the Battle of Culloden', *Essays and Studies*, 44 (1991), 14–26 (p. 24).
[29] Todd and Bowden, p. 439.
[30] Robertson, 'Novels', p. 287.
[31] Ein 'vorzüglicher, fesselnder Unterhaltungsroman, der mit dem nachprüfbaren Anspruch auftrat, Wahres zu berichten. ... der realistische Kern des Romans verschaffte [Zeitgenossen] ein überzeugendes Alibi für die Befriedigung ihres Unterhaltungsbedürfnisses, das sonst aus moralischen Gründen nur schwer zu rechtfertigen gewesen wäre.' (Tippkötter, p. 37, trans. mine).
[32] 'Geschichte als Unterhaltung', Tippkötter, p. 5, trans. mine.
[33] '*Waverley* war also für einen großen Teil der Zeitgenossen Scotts vor allem interessant erzählte Kultur- und Sozialgeschichte', Gamerschlag, p. 87, trans. mine.
[34] Southam, *CH* Vol. I, p. 1.

[35] Hayden, *CH*, p. 3.
[36] Ferris, p. 10.

Chapter 3: Private Readers' Responses in Letters and Diaries, 1811–1818

[1] Many of the comments used in this study have been taken from the collections of comments in David Gilson's *A Bibliography of Jane Austen* and in the Database of *British Fiction 1800–1829*.

[2] Le Faye, p. 508.

[3] Gilson, p. 469.

[4] Duffy, p. 28.

[5] Gilson, p. 469.

[6] Gilson, p. 26.

[7] Gilson, p. 25.

[8] Le Faye, p. 231.

[9] Le Faye, p. 277.

[10] *Romilly-Edgeworth letters 1813–1818*, ed. Samuel Henry Romilly (London: John Murray, 1936) p. 92.

[11] Ibid, p. 102.

[12] Romilly, p. 161.

[13] Joanna Baillie reporting Maria Edgeworth to have written it to her; *DBF* under *Guy Mannering*. (Their source: *The Collected Letters of Joanna Baillie*, ed. Judith Bailey Slagle (2 vols, Madison, NJ: Fairleigh Dickinson University Press, 1999), vol. I, p. 354.)

[14] Letter from Frances Waddington to Professor Monk, 1814; in *The Journals and Letters of Fanny Burney*, ed. Joyce Hemlow, Warren Derry et al. (12 vols, Oxford: Clarendon Press, 1972–84), vol. IX, p. 57.

[15] *DBF* under *Waverley*. (Source: *The Life and Letters of Maria Edgeworth*, ed. Augustus J. C. Hare (2 vols, London: Edward Arnold, 1894), vol. I, p. 226.)

[16] *DBF* under *Waverley*. (Source: *The Life of Mary Russell Mitford*, ed. A. G. L'Estrange (3 vols, London: Bentley, 1870), vol. I, pp. 292–3.)

[17] Crabbe to Scott, June 1815; *DBF* under *Waverley*. (Source: *Selected Letters and Journals of George Crabbe*, ed. Thomas C. Faulkner and Rhonda L. Blair (Oxford: Oxford University Press, 1985), p. 183.)

[18] Quoted in Lockhart, p. 301.

[19] Henry Cockburn, *Memorials of his Time* (Edinburgh: Adam and Charles Black, 1846), p. 281.

[20] *BC*, August 1814, p. 189.

[21] *The Croker Papers*, ed. Louis Jennings (3 vols, London; John Murray, 1884), vol. I, p. 112.

[22] Todd and Bowden, p. 321.

[23] E. T. A. Hoffmann, *Die Serapions-Brüder*, (Darmstadt: Wissenschaftliche Buchgesellschaft, 1979) pp. 924-5.

[24] G. H. Needler, *Goethe and Scott*, (Oxford: Oxford University Press, 1950) p. 81.

[25] J. G. Lockhart, *Letter to the Right Hon. Lord Byron* (1821), in *John Bull's Letter to Lord Byron*, ed. Alan Lang Strout (Norman, OK: University of Oklahoma Press, 1947), pp. 80–1.

[26] Charles Beecher Hogan, 'Jane Austen and her Early Public', *The Review of English Studies*, n.s. I (1950), 39—54 (p. 51).

[27] Gilson, p. 471.

[28] Gilson, p. 472.

[29] *The Life and Letters of Anne Isabella, Lady Noel Byron*, ed. E. C. Mayne (London: Constable, 1929), p. 55.

[30] *Memoir and Correspondence of Susan Ferrier, 1782–1854*, ed. John A. Doyle (London: John Murray, 1898), p. 117.

[31] *Romilly*, p. 92.

[32] Lady Kerr on *MP*, Southam, vol. I, p. 50.

[33] Gilson, pp.85–6.

[34] Gilson, p. 85.

[35] Claire Lamont, 'Meg the Gipsy in Scott and Keats', *English*, 36 (1987), 137–45.

[36] Lamont, 'Meg the Gipsy', p. 140.

[37] Marchand, vol. VII, pp. 70–1.

[38] *Ibid.*, p. 70.

[39] Le Faye, p. 323.

[40] *The Private Letter Books of Sir Walter Scott*, ed. Wilfred Partington (London: Hodder and Stoughton, 1930), p. 111.

[41] Coleridge to Thomas Allsop, March 1820; S. T. Coleridge, *Biographia Epistolaris*, ed. A. Turnbull. (2 vols, London: G. Bell and Sons Ltd, 1911), vol. II, p. 206.

[42] *DBF* under *Waverley*. (Source: Hare, vol. I, p. 225.)

[43] Hayden, *CH*, p. 173.

[44] Croker to an unknown correspondent, May 1817; Jennings, vol. I, p. 112.

[45] Ferrier to Clavering, 1816 (?); *DBF* under *Tales of My Landlord* (first series). (Source: Doyle, p. 132.)

[46] Constable to Cadell (?), August 1818; *DBF* under *Tales of My Landlord* (Second series). (Source: Thomas Constable, *Archibald Constable and his Literary Correspondents: A Memorial* (3 vols, Edinburgh: Edmonston & Douglas, 1873), vol. II, p. 97.)

[47] *DBF* under *Pride and Prejudice*. (Source: *The Scotswoman at Home and Abroad*, ed. Dorothy McMillan (Glasgow: Association for Scottish Literary Studies, 2000), p. 126.)

[48] Gifford to Murray, 1815 (?); Gilson, p. 27.

[49] Lady Gordon on *MP*; Southam, vol. I, p. 51.

[50] Princess Charlotte to Miss Mercer Elphinstone; *DBF* under *Sense and Sensibility*. (Source: *The Letters of Princess Charlotte 1811–1818*, ed. Arthur Aspinall (London: Home and Van Thal, 1949), p. 26.)

[51] Edgeworth to Ruxton, February 1818; *DBF* under *Northanger Abbey* and *Persuasion*. (Source: Hare, vol. I, pp. 246–7.)

[52] Mrs Cage on *Emma*; Southam, vol. I, p. 57.

[53] A. I. Millbanke to Mrs Millbanke, May 1813; Gilson, p. 25.

[54] *EdM*, May 1818, p. 454.

[55] Unknown correspondent to Lady Bury, March 1820; *DBF* under *Emma*.

(Source: Charlotte Bury, *The Diary of a Lady-In-Waiting*, ed. A. F. Steuart (2 vols, London: John Lane, 1908), vol. II, p. 261).

56 Gilson, p. 472.
57 Cady and Watt, p. 234.
58 Southam, vol. I, p. 56.
59 Lady Davy to Sarah Ponsonby, May 1813; Gilson, p. 26.
60 Doyle, p. 117.
61 Southam, vol. I, p. 86.
62 Southam, vol. I p. 51.
63 Southam, vol. I p. 85.
64 Anderson, p. 112.
65 Edgeworth to Sophy Ruxton, October 1814; *DBF* under *Waverley*. (Source: Hare, vol. I, p.225.)
66 Romilly to Edgeworth, November 1814; *Romilly*, p. 92.
67 *Ibid.*, p. 102.
68 *DBF* under *Waverley*. (Source: *The Letters of William and Dorothy Wordsworth: The Middle Years*, ed. Ernest De Selincourt, 2nd edn, rev. Mary Moorman and Alan G. Hill (Oxford: Clarendon Press, 1979), vol.II, part 2, p.203.)
69 Wordsworth to R. Gillies, April 1815; Hayden, p. 86.
70 Lord John Cam Hobhouse Broughton, *Recollections of a Long Life*, ed. Lady Dorchester (2 vols, London: John Murray, 1909), vol. II, pp. 12–13.
71 Edgeworth to 'the author of *Waverley*', October 1814; Hayden, *CH*, p. 76.
72 Partington, p. 115.
73 *DBF* under *Tales of My Landlord* (second series). (Source: Slagle, vol. I, p. 453.)
74 Edgeworth to 'the author of *Waverley*', October 1814; Hayden, *CH*, p. 78.
75 *Ibid.*, p. 77.
76 *DBF* under *Tales of My Landlord* (first series). (Source: *Henry Crabbe Robinson on Books and their Writers*, ed. Edith J. Morley (3 vols, London: J. M. Dent, 1938) vol. I, p.204.)
77 *DBF* under *Tales of My Landlord* (first series). (Source: Morley, vol. I, p.265.)
78 Elizabeth Hamilton to Miss J[oanna?] B[aillie?], July 1814; *DBF* under *Waverley*. (Source: *Memoirs of the Late Mrs Elizabeth Hamilton*, ed. Elizabeth Benger (2 vols, London: Longman, 1818), vol. II, p. 181.)
79 Helen Darcy Stewart to Constable, March 1815; *DBF* under *Guy Mannering*. (Source: Constable, vol. II, p. 40.)
80 Byron to Murray, July 1814; Marchand, vol. IV, p. 146.
81 Hayden, *CH*, p. 195.
82 Jeffrey in *ER*, Nov. 1814, p. 208.
83 Cockburn, pp. 280–1.
84 Ann Jones, *Ideas and Innovations: Best Sellers of Jane Austen's Age* (New York: AMS Press, 1986), p. 14.
85 Russell Mitford to Elford, December 1814; *DBF* under *Pride and Prejudice*. (Source: L'Estrange, vol. I, p. 300.)
86 Earl of Dudley to Mrs Helen Stewart, August 1814; Gilson, p. 50.
87 Gilson, p. 472.
88 Scott, Journal entry March 1826; Anderson, p. 114.

⁸⁹ Edgeworth to Ruxton, December 1814; *DBF* under *Mansfield Park*. (Source: Hare, vol. I, p. 231.)

⁹⁰ Russell Mitford to Elford, July 1816; *DBF* under *Emma*. (Source: L'Estrange, vol. I, p. 331.)

⁹¹ *Ibid.*

⁹² Gifford to Murray, 1815 (?); Gilson, p. 27.

⁹³ R. W. Chapman, *Jane Austen: A Critical Bibliography*, (Oxford: Oxford University Press, 1953), p. 20.

⁹⁴ Gilson, p. 71.

⁹⁵ Southam, vol. I, p. 49.

⁹⁶ Romilly to Edgeworth, November 1814; Romilly, p. 92.

⁹⁷ *Sense and Sensibility* (London: Richard Bentley, 1833), p. xv.

⁹⁸ Ferris, p. 35.

⁹⁹ Le Faye, p. 203.

¹⁰⁰ *Romilly*, p. 92.

¹⁰¹ Smith to Lord Grey, August 1818; *DBF* under *Tales of My Landlord* (second series). (Source: *The Letters of Sydney Smith*, ed. Nowell C. Smith (2 vols, Oxford: Clarendon Press), vol. I, pp. 297–8.)

¹⁰² *BC*, April 1815, p. 442.

¹⁰³ *DBF* under *Emma*. (Source: Doyle, p. 128.)

¹⁰⁴ Miss Bigg on *Emma*; Southam, vol. I, p. 55.

¹⁰⁵ Hemlow, Derry *et al.*, vol. IX, p. 453.

¹⁰⁶ Baillie to Scott, July 1816; *DBF* under *Guy Mannering*. (Source: Slagle, vol. I, p. 354.)

¹⁰⁷ Gilson, p. 472.

¹⁰⁸ Sarah Burney to Charlotte Barrett, March 1816; *DBF* under *Waverley*. (Source: *The Letters of Sarah Harriet Burney*, ed. Lorna J. Clark (Athens, GA/London: University of Georgia Press, 1997), p. 201.)

¹⁰⁹ Gilson, p. 85.

¹¹⁰ The hill is Maranscourt hill. 'As it climbs from 300 feet to 695, Southey had plenty of time'; Chapman, p. 20.

¹¹¹ Robert Southey to Samuel Egerton Brydges; Duffy, p. 54.

¹¹² This is 'presumably' Henry Stephen Fox; Chapman, p. 21. Letter: British Library manuscript.

¹¹³ Gilson, p. 469.

¹¹⁴ Lady Louisa Stuart to Scott, January 1817; *DBF* under *Tales of My Landlord* (First series). (Source: *The Letters of Lady Louisa Stuart*, ed. R. Brimley Johnson (London: John Lane, 1926), p. 151.)

¹¹⁵ Byron to Murray, October 1816; Marchand, vol. V, p.112.

¹¹⁶ William Godwin to Constable, May 1816; *DBF* under *Waverley*. (Source: Constable, vol. II, p.75.)

¹¹⁷ Helen Darcy Stewart to Constable, [mid-1816]; *DBF* under *The Antiquary*. (Source: Constable, vol. II, p.41.)

¹¹⁸ Broughton, vol. II, p. 13.

¹¹⁹ J. B. S. Morritt to Scott, July 1814; *DBF* under *Waverley*. (Source: Partington, p. 111.)

[120] Morritt to Scott, July 1814; *DBF* under *Waverley*.
[121] Morritt to Scott, July 1814; *DBF* under *Waverley*.
[122] Ferris, p. 79.
[123] Southam, vol. I, p. 2.
[124] *QR*, Oct. 1815, p. 188.

Chapter 4: Editions, 1832–1912

[1] See Todd and Bowden, pp. 319–20.

[2] *The Waverley Novels*: Copyright Edition (Edinburgh: Adam & Charles Black, 1867); *The Waverley Novels* (Edinburgh: Adam & Charles Black, 1877).

[3] The British Library Catalogue: http://catalogue.bl.uk ([last accessed April 2006); The National Library of Scotland Catalogue: http://www.nls.uk/catalogues/online/index.html (last accessed April 2006); *British Museum General Catalogue of Printed Books*, vols 8 and 217 (London: Trustees of the British Museum, 1964); Peter Garside and Anthony Mandal, 'Jane Austen', in *The Cambridge Bibliography of English Literture 1800–1900*, ed. Joanne Shattock, 3rd edn (Cambridge: Cambridge University Press, 1999), vol. XIV, cols 870–83; J. H. Alexander, 'Sir Walter Scott', in *Cambridge Bibliography of English Literture*, ed. Joanne Shattock, vol. XIV, cols 992–1063; Michael A. O'Malley Gregson, 'Victorian Criticism of the Waverley Novels of Sir Walter Scott' (unpublished doctoral thesis, The Open University, 1992); St Clair, *The Reading Nation in the Romantic Period*; *The London Catalogue of Books Published in London* (London: Robert Bent, 1831); *The London Catalogue of Books Published in Great Britain* (London: Thomas Hogdson, 1851); Robert Cadell, *Catalogue of the various editions now completed of the novels, poetry, prose writings, & life of Sir Walter Scott, Bart.* (Edinburgh: Cadell, 1847).

[4] The first edition to go back to the 1814 text was *Waverley*, ed. Claire Lamont (Oxford: Clarendon Press, 1981), followed by the Edinburgh Edition of the Waverley Novels, ed.-in-chief David Hewitt, (Edinburgh: Edinburgh University Press, 1993–).

[5] Copyrights: Scott: Archibald Constable up to 1829; Robert Cadell up to 1851; Adam and Charles Black up to 1871–74 (expired); Austen: That of *SS, MP, E* with Austen until 1817; that of *PP* with Thomas Egerton until 1832; that of *SS, MP, E, NA&P* with Cassandra and Henry Austen until 1832; that of *SS, PP, MP, E, NA&P* with Richard Bentley until expiry: *SS* 1839, *PP* 1841, *MP* 1842, *E* 1857, *NA&P* 1860.

[6] James Edward Austen-Leigh, *A Memoir of Jane Austen* (London: Bentley, 1870).

[7] Notably Southam in his introductions to *Jane Austen: The Critical Heritage*, vols I and II. Critics tend to follow his account uncritically, e.g. Robert Clark, in his introduction to *Sense and Sensibility and Pride and Prejudice: Contemporary Critical Essays*, ed. Robert Clark (London: MacMillian, 1994, pp. 1–25.

[8] Gilson points out that this publication is in fact a reprint of the 1833 Bentley edition (Gilson, p. 251). A new half-title and title page were added, however, to the Chapman & Hall edition, that draw attention to this volume being part of a series, which the equivalent pages of the 1833 Bentley edition had not done.

[9] Anon., *Adam and Charles Black, 1807–1957: Some Chapters in the History of a Publishing House* (London: Adam & Charles Black, 1957), p. 22.

[10] *Adam and Charles Black*, pp. 27–8.

[11] Lamont in *Waverley*, p. xxxiv

[12] *Waverley* (Edinburgh: Adam & Charles Black, 1870), p. 25.

[13] *Waverley* (Edinburgh: Adam & Charles Black, 1873), p. 5.

[14] Though, as Lamont notes, for the Dryburgh edition of 1892–94, "A. & C. Black had recourse again to the interleaved copy, correcting misprints and adding a note which is apparently Scott's'. (Lamont in *Waverley*, pp. xxxiv–v).

[15] Iain Gordon Brown, 'The Hand of the Master?', *Folio*, 9 (2004), 6–9 (p. 9).

[16] This is the only edition out of the ten appearing in this decade that neither the British Library nor the National Library of Scotland hold, which further emphasizes its physical ephemeralness.

[17] *Waverley*; lithographed in phonetic shorthand (London: F. Pitman; Glasgow: A. Steele & Co., 1868).

[18] *Adam and Charles Black*, p. 27.

[19] St Clair, p. 419.

[20] St Clair, p. 580.

Chapter 5: Library Catalogues, 1832–1912

[1] *The Library History Database:* www.r-alston.co.uk//contents.htm (last accessed February 2006).

[2] Robin Alston lists the names of libraries, but we do not have information on those that went out of business, amalgamated, changed their name, etc.

[3] For the period of 1800–29 library holdings are also assessed by the Database of *British Fiction*. However, they mainly take circulating libraries into account, which were the most likely of all kinds of libraries to include fiction, and therefore more likely to hold novels by Austen than libraries in general.

Chapter 6: Victorian Reviews and Criticism, 1865–1880

[1] Sources for the location of articles were Gilson's *Bibliography*, Southam's *critical Heritage* (Vols I and II), Hayden's *Critical Heritage*, and above all the databases *Nineteenth Century Masterfile* and *Periodicals Contents Index*.

[2] Untitled letter, *N & Q*, 4th s. I, 9 May 1868, p. 441.

[3] 'Sir Walter Scott's Works', *N&Q*, 4th s.V. 5 Feb 1870, p. 164.

[4] 'Sir Walter Scott's Misquotations'. *N&Q*, 4th s. VI, 2 July 1870, p. 13.

[5] 'A Letter of Sir Walter Scott', p. 284. *N&Q*, 5th s. XI, 12 April 1879.

[6] 'Sir Walter Scott', *N & Q*, 5th S. XII, 27 Sept 1879, p. 248.

[7] *N & Q*, 5th s. II, 4 July 1874, pp. 1–2.

[8] Letter from Sir William Stirling Maxwell to Lord Jerviswoode, 8 April 1871, quoted in *Catalogue of the Exhibition held at Edinburgh, in July and August 1871, on*

occasion of the commemoration of the centenary of the birth of Sir Walter Scott (Edinburgh: Edinburgh University Press, 1872), p. vii.

[9] Catalogue of the Exhibition held at Edinburgh, p. xi.
[10] Cady and Watt, p. 233.
[11] Austen-Leigh, pp. 9–10.
[12] *Ibid.*, p. 116.
[13] *Ibid.*, p. 90.
[14] *Ibid.*, p. 73.
[15] *Austen-Leigh*, p. 105.
[16] Because the copyright would have expired; see Chapter 4.

Chapter 7: Editions, 1913–2003

[1] For definition of edition, inclusion policies etc, see Chapter 4.
[2] See e.g. Hayden, Introduction to *The Critical Heritage*, p. 2; Hillhouse, pp. 231–328.
[3] The ones for which there is no edition in these 20 years are *The Black Dwarf, Peveril of the Peak, Count Robert of Paris* and *Castle Dangerous*.

Chapter 8: Media Reception and Cultural Status, 1990–2003

[1] Newspapers generally do not italicize titles; I have italicized titles throughout.
[2] *Rob Roy* in 1995, though this is not an adaptation of Scott's novel, and *Ivanhoe* in 1997.
[3] Feature film and TV series have not been distinguished.
[4] For a discussion of this issue, see e.g. Claudia L. Johnson, 'The Divine Miss Jane', in *Janeites*, ed. Deidre Lynch, pp. 25-44; Lynch, 'Introduction: Sharing with Our Neighbors', pp. 3–24.
[5] Throughout the period of 1990–2003, Austen ranks among the top ten most borrowed classic authors, whereas Scott does not feature at all. The data to compile this table was obtained from Public Lending Right, who monitor sample libraries. Most other libraries do not record borrowings, so that it is not possible to obtain lending records by individual library, by region, or even by novel.
[6] Sources: Letter from the Jane Austen Museum at Chawton, 15 Feb. 2004; for Lyme Park *The Times*, 20 Dec. 1996.
[7] For a discussion of concepts of high and popular culture and their reading audiences, see Jonathan Rose, 'Rereading the English Common Reader', in *The Book History Reader*, ed. David Finkelstein and Alistair McCleery (London: Routledge, 2002), pp. 324–39.

Chapter 9: Critical Reception, 1960–2003

[1] Claire Tomalin, *Jane Austen: Life* (London: Viking, 1997), pp. 138–9.
[2] St Clair, pp. 277-8.
[3] See Chapter 6.
[4] Douglas Mack's edition is entitled *The Tale of Old Mortality* since it is based on the first edition text. Other editions are based on the Magnum edition of 1829–33, which read *Old Mortality*.
[5] Penguin has two editions of *Rob Roy*, a Popular one and a Classics one, but neither includes an introduction or notes.
[6] Garside has since shown that the novel is more likely to have been begun in 1808–10.
[7] Georg Lukàcs, *The Historical Novel* (London: Merlin Press, 1989), p. 60.
[8] Sutherland only discusses one frame narrative because her introduction is to a text based on the first edition, and consequently without Scott's Magnum introduction.
[9] Hewitt, 'General Introduction' to the EEWN, in *The Black Dwarf*, p. xi.
[10] The single exception to using the Magnum text is Lamont's 1981 edition of *Waverley*.
[11] For accounts of developments in Austen and Scott criticism, see: Clark, 'Introduction', in *Sense and Sensibility and Pride and Prejudice*; Robertson, 'Walter Scott'; Stafford, 'Jane Austen'; Trott, 'Critical Responses' and Rajeswari Rajan, 'Critical Responses, Recent', in *Jane Austen in Context*, ed. Janet Todd, pp. 92–100, 101–10.

Retrospect

[1] See e.g. St Clair, *Reading Nation*; Paul Fussell, *The Great War and Modern Memory* (Oxford: Oxford University Press, 1975).

Bibliography

Contemporary reviews of Jane Austen

Sense and Sensibility

The British Critic (May 1812), p. 527.
The Critical Review (Feb. 1812), pp. 149–57.

Pride and Prejudice

The British Critic (Feb. 1813), pp. 189–90.
The Critical Review (Mar. 1813), pp. 318–24.
The New Review, or Monthly Analysis of General Literature (April 1813), pp. 393–6.

Emma

The Augustan Review (May 1816), pp. 484–6.
The British Critic (July 1816), pp. 96–8.
The British Lady's Magazine (Sept. 1816); reprinted in William S. Ward, 'Three Hitherto Unnoted Contemporary Reviews of Jane Austen', *Nineteenth-Century Fiction*, 26 (1971–72), pp. 476–7.
The Champion (Mar. 1816); reprinted in William S. Ward, 'Three Hitherto Unnoted Contemporary Reviews of Jane Austen', *Nineteenth-Century Fiction*, 26 (1971–72), pp. 469–74.
The Gentleman's Magazine (Sept. 1816), pp. 248–9.
The Literary Panorama (June 1817), cols 418–19.
The Monthly Review (July 1816), p. 320.
The Quarterly Review, (Scott) (Oct. 1815), pp. 188–201.

Northanger Abbey and *Persuasion*

The British Critic (Mar. 1818), pp. 293–301.
The Edinburgh Magazine and Literary Miscellany (May 1818), pp. 453–5.
The Gentleman's Magazine (July 1818), pp. 52–3.
The Quarterly Review (Whately) (Jan. 1821), pp. 352–76.

Contemporary reviews of Walter Scott

Waverley

The Antijabocin Review, 47 (Sept. 1814), pp. 217–47.
The British Critic, n.s. 2 (Aug. 1814), pp. 189–211.
The Caledonian Mercury (Sept. and Oct. 1814), pp. 101–2, 145–7.
The Champion (John Scott) (July 1814), pp. 238–9.
The Critical Review (Mar. 1815), pp. 288–97.
The Edinburgh Review (Jeffrey), (Nov. 1814), pp. 208–43.
The Monthly Museum (Sept. Oct. Nov. Dec. 1814), pp. 225–30, 294–8, 357–63, 411–16.
The Monthly Review (Merivale) (Nov. 1814), pp. 275–89.
New Annual Register for the Year 1814 (1815), p. 365.
The New Monthly Magazine (Sept 1814), p. 156.
The Quarterly Review (Croker) (July 1814), pp. 354–77.
The Scots Magazine (July 1814), pp. 524–33.
The Scourge (Oct. 1814), pp. 291–7.

Guy Mannering

The Antijacobin Review (June 1815), pp. 544–50.
The Augustan Review (July 1815), pp. 228–33.
The British Critic (April 1815), pp. 399–409.
The British Lady's Magazine (May 1815), pp. 355–8.
The Champion (April 1815), p. 118.
The Critical Review (June 1815), pp. 600–3.
The Edinburgh Review (Jeffrey) (Mar. 1817), pp. 193–259.
The Monthly Review (May 1815), pp. 85–94.
New Annual Register for the Year 1815 (1816), p. 432.
The New Monthly Magazine (April 1815), p. 256
The Quarterly Review (Croker) (Jan. 1815), pp. 501–9.
The Scots Magazine (Aug. 1815), pp. 608–14.

The Antiquary

The Antijacobin Review (July 1816), pp. 625–32.
The Augustan Review (Aug. 1816), pp. 155–77.
The British Critic (June 1816), pp. 633–57.
The British Lady's Magazine (Aug. 1816); reprinted in *Scott: The Critical Heritage*, ed. John O. Hayden (London: Routledge & Kegan Paul, 1970), pp. 104–5.
The Critical Review (May 1816), pp. 485–500.
The Edinburgh Review (Mar. 1817), pp. 193–259.
The European Magazine and London Review (Sept. 1816), pp. 238–50.
The Gentleman's Magazine (June 1816), pp. 521–3.

The Monthly Review (Jan. 1817), pp. 38–52.
The New Monthly Magazine (June 1816), p. 444.
The Quarterly Review (Croker) (April 1816), pp. 125–39.
The Scots Magazine (May 1816), pp. 365–73.

Rob Roy

The Antijacobin Review (Jan. 1818), pp. 417–31.
The Anti-Unionist, 53, (Jan.–Feb. 1818), pp. 7–10, 24–8.
The British Critic (May 1818), pp. 528–40.
The British Lady's Magazine (Mar. and June 1818), n.s. 2, pp. 119–23, 264–8.
The British Review, 11 (Feb. 1818), pp. 192–225.
The Edinburgh Advertiser (Jan. 1818), p. 94.
The Edinburgh Magazine (Morehead) (Jan.–Feb. 1818), pp. 41–50, 148–53.
The Edinburgh Observer (Mar. 1818), pp. 230–4.
The Edinburgh Review (Jeffrey) (Feb. 1818), pp. 403–32.
The European Magazine and London Review (Feb. 1818); reprinted in *Scott: The Critical Heritage*, ed. John O. Hayden (London: Routledge & Kegan Paul, 1970), pp. 146–7.
The Gentleman's Magazine (Mar. 1818), p. 243.
The Literary and Political Examiner, 2 (Feb. 1818), pp. 14–28.
The Literary and Statistical Magazine, 2 (Feb. 1818), pp. 45–60.
The London Literary Gazette (17 Jan. 1818) pp. 34–6.
The Monthly Review (Mar. 1818), pp. 261–75.
The Monthly Magazine, 45 (Feb. 1818), p. 63.
The Northern Star, 2, (Feb. 1818), pp. 126–35.
The Quarterly Review (Senior) (Oct. 1821), pp. 109–48.
The Scotsman (Jan. 1818), p. 7.
Theatrical Inquisitor, 12 (Jan. 1818), pp. 36–40.
The Visitor, or, Literary Miscellany, 1 (1817), pp. 177–83.

The Heart of Mid-Lothian

The Antijacobin Review (Nov. 1818), pp. 212–18.
Blackwood's Edinburgh Magazine (Aug. 1818), pp. 567–74.
The British Critic (Sept. 1818), pp. 246–60.
The British Lady's Magazine (Dec. 1818), pp. 268–73.
The British Review (Nov. 1818), pp. 396–406.
Clydesdale Magazine, 1 (July–Sept. 1818), pp. 25–7, 169–71, 218–19.
The Eclectic Review (Conder) (Nov. 1819), pp. 422–52.
The Edinburgh Advertiser (Aug. 1818), p. 100.
The Edinburgh Magazine and Literary Miscellany (Aug. 1818), pp. 107–17.
The Edinburgh Reflector (5–19 Aug. 1818), pp. 42–7, 53–6, 63.
The Edinburgh Review (Jeffrey) (Jan. 1820), pp. 1–54.

Fireside Magazine, 11 (Jan–Feb. 1819), pp. 32, 69–70.
The Gentleman's Magazine (Nov. 1818), pp. 426–9.
Green Man (Dec. 1818), pp. 68–9.
The Literary Journal (8 and 15 Aug. 1818), pp. 304–6, 324–7.
The Literary and Statistical Magazine (Aug. 1818), pp. 314–22.
The London Literary Gazette (8 Aug. 1818) pp. 497–500.
The Monthly Magazine (Sept. 1818), p. 158.
The Monthly Review (Dec. 1818), pp. 356–70.
The New Monthly Magazine (Oct. 1818), p. 250.
The New Times (Aug. 1818), p. 97.
The Quarterly Review (Senior) (Oct. 1821), pp. 109–48.
The Scotsman (Aug. 1818), p. 247.

Articles in periodicals 1865–80

Jane Austen

Anon., 'Miss Austen', *The Englishwoman's Domestic Magazine*, 2 (1866), 238–9, 278–82; reprinted in *Jane Austen: The Critical Heritage*, ed. Brian Southam, 2 vols (Routledge & Kegan Paul, 1968 and 1987), vol. I, pp. 200–14.

Anon., 'Jane Austen', *St Paul's Magazine*, 5 (1870), 631–43; reprinted in *Jane Austen: The Critical Heritage*, ed. Brian Southam, 2 vols (Routledge & Kegan Paul, 1968 and 1987), vol. I, pp. 226–40.

Anon., 'Life of Jane Austen', *Month*, 12 (1870), 371–2.

Anon., 'Jane Austen', *Month*, 15 (1871), 305–10.

Chorley, Henry F., 'A Memoir of Jane Austen and The Life of Mary Russell Mitford', *The Quarterly Review*, 128 (1870), 196–218.

Dallas, E. S., 'Felix Holt, the Radical', *The Times* (26 June 1866), 6; reprinted in *Jane Austen: The Critical Heritage*, ed. Brian Southam, 2 vols (Routledge & Kegan Paul, 1968 and 1987), vol. I, pp. 198–9.

Hutton, Richard H., 'The Memoir of Miss Austen', *The Spectator*, 25 (1869), 1533–5; reprinted in *Jane Austen: The Critical Heritage*, ed. Brian Southam, 2 vols (Routledge & Kegan Paul, 1968 and 1987), vol.II, pp. 160–4.

Hutton, Richard H., 'Miss Austen's Posthumous Pieces', *The Spectator*, 44 (1871), 891–2.

Kebbel, Thomas. E., 'Jane Austen', *Fortnightly Review*, 13 (1870), 187–93.

Oliphant, Margaret, 'Miss Austen and Miss Mitford', *Blackwood's Edinburgh Magazine*, 107 (1870), 290–313.

Payn, James, 'A Glimpse at a British Classic', *Chambers's Journal*, 47 (1870), 153–60.

Simcox, Edith, 'A Memoir of Jane Austen and Sense and Sensibility', *The Academy*, 1 (12 Feb. 1870), 118–19.

Simcox, Edith, 'A Memoir of Jane Austen, 2nd edition', *The Academy* (1, Aug. 1871), 367–8.

Simpson, Richard, 'A Memoir of Jane Austen', *North British Review* 52 (1870), 129–52; reprinted in *Jane Austen: The Critical Heritage*, ed. Brian Southam, 2 vols (Routledge & Kegan Paul, 1968 and 1987), vol.I, pp. 241–65.
Stephen, Leslie, 'Humour', *Cornhill Magazine*, 33 (1876), 318–26.
Thackeray, Anne Isabella, 'Jane Austen', *Cornhill Magazine*, 34 (1871), 158–74.

Walter Scott

Anon., 'Memoirs of the Life of Sir Walter Scott', *The Quarterly Review*, 124 (1868), 1–54.
Anon., 'Diana Vernon', *Macmillan's Magazine*, 22 (1870), 285–91.
Anon., 'How We Celebrated Scott', *London Society*, 20 (1871), 275–80.
Anon., 'Walter Scott: a Centenary Tribute', *London Quarterly Review*, 38 (1872), 35–59.
Anon., 'Genealogical Memoirs of the Family of Sir Walter Scott', *The Academy* (10 Aug. 1878), 136.
Anon., 'The Reflection of English Character in English Art', *The Quarterly Review*, 147 (1879), 81–112.
Coleridge, H. J., 'Lockhart's Life of Sir Walter Scott', *Month*, 15 (1871), 241–85.
Escott, T. H. S., 'Concerning the Centenary of Scott', *Belgravia*, 15 (1871), 382–8.
Oliphant, Margaret, 'A Century of Great Poems: Walter Scott', *Blackwood's Edinburgh Magazine* 110 (1871), 229–56.
Payn, James, 'Sham Admiration in Literature', *The Nineteenth Century*, 7 (1880), 422–33.
Pebody, Charles, 'The Scott Centenary', *The Gentleman's Magazine*, 231 (1871), 292–316.
Ruskin, John, 'Fiction – Fair and Foul', *The Nineteenth Century*, 7 (1880), 941–62.
Stephen, Leslie, 'Some Words about Sir Walter Scott', *Cornhill Magazine* 24 (Sept. 1871), 278–93; reprinted in *Scott: The Critical Heritage*, ed. John O. Hayden (London: Routledge & Kegan Paul, 1970), pp. 439–58.
Stevenson, Robert Louis, 'Victor Hugo's Romances', *Cornhill Magazine*, 30 (1874), 194–197; reprinted in *Scott: The Critical Heritage*, ed. John O. Hayden (London: Routledge & Kegan Paul, 1970), pp. 475–78.
Various, on Scott, *Notes and Queries*, between 11 (8 June 1867), p. 457 and 12 (27 Sept. 1879), p. 248.
Wedgwood, Julia, 'Sir Walter Scott and the Romantic Reaction', *Contemporary Review*, 33 (1878), 514–39; reprinted in *Scott: The Critical Heritage*, ed. John O. Hayden (London: Routledge & Kegan Paul, 1970), pp. 499–522.

Secondary sources

Alexander, J. H. and David Hewitt, eds, *Scott and His Influence* (Aberdeen: Association. for Scottish Literary. Studies, 1983).

Alexander, J. H., 'Sir Walter Scott', in *The Cambridge Bibliography of English Literature 1800–1900*, ed. Joanne Shattock, 3rd edn (Cambridge: Cambridge University Press, 1999), vol. XIV, cols 992–1063.

Allardyce, Alexander, ed., *Letters from and to Charles Kirkpatrick Sharpe, Esq.*, 2 vols (Edinburgh/London: William Blackwood, 1888).

Altick, Richard D., *The English Common Reader: A Social History of the Mass Reading Public 1800–1900* (Chicago, IL: University of Chicago Press, 1957).

Anderson, W. E. K., ed., *The Journal of Sir Walter Scott* (Oxford: Oxford University Press, 1972).

Anon., *Adam and Charles Black, 1807–1957: Some Chapters in the History of a Publishing House* (London: Adam & Charles Black, 1957).

Aspinall, Arthur, ed., *The Letters of Princess Charlotte, 1811–1818* (London: Home and Van Thal, 1949).

Austen, Henry, 'Biographical Notice', in James Edward Austen-Leigh, *A Memoir of Jane Austen and Other Family Recollections*, ed. Kathryn Sutherland (Oxford: Oxford University Press, 2002), pp. 135–43.

Austen-Leigh, James Edward, *A Memoir of Jane Austen and Other Family Recollections*, ed. Kathryn Sutherland (Oxford: Oxford University Press, 2002).

Bagehot, Walter, 'The First Edinburgh Reviewers', in *Literary Studies by the Late Walter Bagehot*, ed. Richard Holt Hutton (London: Longmans, Green and Co., 1891), pp. 1–40.

Benger, Elizabeth, ed., *Memoirs of the Late Mrs Elizabeth Hamilton*, 2 vols (London: Longman, 1818).

Birtwistle, Sue and Susie Conklin, *The Making of Pride and Prejudice* (London: Penguin, 1995).

British Museum General Catalogue of Printed Books, vols 8 and 217 (London: Trustees of the British Museum, 1964).

Broughton, Lord John Cam Hobhouse, *Recollections of a Long Life*, ed. Lady Dorchester, 2 vols (London: John Murray, 1909).

Brown, Iain Gordon, *Scott's Interleaved Copy of the Waverley Novels* (Aberdeen: Aberdeen University Press, 1987).

Brown, Iain Gordon, 'The Hand of the Master?', *Folio*, 9 (2004), 6–9.

Brown, Iain Gordon, ed., *Abbotsford and Sir Walter Scott: The Image and the Influence* (Edinburgh: Society of Antiquaries of Scotland, 2003).

Bury, Charlotte, *The Diary of a Lady-In-Waiting*, ed. A. F. Steuart, 2 vols (London: John Lane, 1908).

Butler, Marilyn, *Jane Austen and the War of Ideas* (Oxford: Clarendon Press, 1975).

Butler, Marilyn, 'Culture's Medium: the Role of the Review', in *The Cambridge Companion to British Romanticism*, ed. Stuart Curran (Cambridge: Cambridge University Press, 1993), pp. 120–47.

Byron, Lord George Gordon, 'English Bards and Scotch Reviewers. A Satire', in *Lord Byron: Selected Poems*, ed. S. J. Wolfson and P. J. Manning (London: Penguin, 1996), pp. 6–48.

Cadell, Robert, *Catalogue of the various editions now completed of the novels, poetry, prose writings, & life of Sir Walter Scott, Bart.* (Edinburgh: Cadell, 1847).

Cady, Joseph and Ian Watt, 'Jane Austen's Critics', in *Jane Austen: Critical Assessments*, ed. Ian Littlewood (Mountfield: Helm Information, 1998), pp. 231–45.

Catalogue of the Exhibition held at Edinburgh, in July and August 1871, on occasion of the commemoration of the centenary of the birth of Sir Walter Scott (Edinburgh: Edinburgh University Press, 1872).

Cavallo, Guglielmo and Roger Chartier, eds, *A History of Reading in the West*, trans. Lydia Cochrane (Cambridge: Polity Press, 1999).

Chapman, R. W., *Jane Austen: A Critical Bibliography* (Oxford: Oxford University Press, 1953).

Clark, Lorna J., ed., *The Letters of Sarah Harriet Burney* (Athens, GA/London: University of Georgia Press, 1997).

Clark, Robert, 'Introduction', in *Sense and Sensibility and Pride and Prejudice: Contemporary Critical Essays*, ed. Robert Clark (London: Macmillan, 1994), pp. 1–25.

Clive, John, *Scotch Reviewers: The Edinburgh Review, 1802–1815* (London: Faber and Faber, 1956).

Cockburn, Henry, *Memorials of his Time* (Edinburgh: Adam and Charles Black, 1846).

Coleridge, Samuel Taylor, *Biographia Epistolaris*, ed. A. Turnbull, 2 vols (London: G. Bell and Sons Ltd, 1911).

Constable, Thomas, *Archibald Constable and his Literary Correspondents: A Memorial*, 3 vols (Edinburgh: Edmonston & Douglas, 1873).

Corson, James C., *A Bibliography of Walter Scott* (Edinburgh/London: Oliver & Boyd, 1943).

Coleridge, Samuel Taylor, *Biographia Epistolaris*, ed. A. Turnbull, 2 vols (London: G. Bell and Sons Ltd, 1911).

De Selincourt, Ernest, ed., *The Letters of William and Dorothy Wordsworth: The Middle Years*, 2nd edn, rev. Mary Moorman and Alan G. Hill (Oxford: Clarendon Press, 1979), vol. III.

Doyle, John A., ed., *Memoir and Correspondence of Susan Ferrier, 1782–1854: Based on her Private Correspondence in the Possession of, and Collected by, her Grand-Nephew John Ferrier* (London: John Murray, 1898).

Draffan, Robert, 'Jane Austen and her Time', *History Today*, 20 (1970), 190–7.

Duffy, Joseph, 'Jane Austen and the Nineteenth-century Critics of Fiction 1812–1913' (unpublished doctoral thesis, University of Chicago, 1954).

Faulkner, Thomas C. and Rhonda L. Blair, eds, *Selected Letters and Journals of George Crabbe* (Oxford: Oxford University Press, 1985).

Ferris, Ina, *The Achievement of Literary Authority: Gender, History and the Waverley Novels* (Ithaca, NY/London: Cornell University Press, 1991).

Finkelstein, David and Alistair McCleery, eds, *The Book History Reader* (London: Routledge, 2002).

Fish, Stanley, 'Interpreting the *Variorum*', in *Reader-Response Criticism: From Formalism to Post-Structuralism*, ed. Jane Tompkins (Baltimore, MD/London: Johns Hopkins University Press, 1980), pp. 164–84.

Fussell, Paul, *The Great War and Modern Memory* (Oxford: Oxford University Press, 1975).

Gamerschlag, Kurt, *Sir Walter Scott und die Waverley Novels: Eine Übersicht über den Gang der Scottforschung von den Anfängen bis heute* (Darmstadt: Wissenschaftliche Buchgesellschaft, 1978).

Garside, Peter, James Raven and Rainer Schöwerling, *The English Novel 1770–1829: A Bibliographical Survey of Prose Fiction Published in the British Isles*, 2 vols (Oxford: Oxford University Press, 2000).

Garside, Peter, 'The English Novel in the Romantic Era: Consolidation and Dispersal', in *The English Novel 1770–1829: A Bibliographical Survey of Prose Fiction Published in the British Isles*, ed. Peter Garside, James Raven and Rainer Schöwerling, 2 vols (Oxford: Oxford University Press, 2000), vol. II, pp. 15–103.

Garside, Peter and Anthony Mandal, 'Jane Austen', in *The Cambridge Bibliography of English Literature 1800–1900*, ed. Joanne Shattock, 3rd edn (Cambridge: Cambridge University Press, 1999), vol. XIV, cols 870–83.

Gaskell, Philip, *A New Introduction to Bibliography* (Oxford: Clarendon Press, 1972).

Gilson, David, *A Bibliography of Jane Austen* (New Castle, DE: Oak Knoll Press, 1997).

Godwin, William, 'Essay of History and Romance', in *Political and Philosophical Writings of William Godwin*, ed. Mark Philip, 7 vols (London: Pickering, 1993), vol. V, pp. 291–301.

Gordon, Ian, *John Galt: The Life of a Writer* (Edinburgh: Oliver & Boyd, 1972).

Gower, the Hon. F. Leveson, ed., *Letters of Harriet Countess Granville, 1810–1845*, 2 vols (London: Longmans, Green and Co., 1894).

Gray, W. Forbes, *Scott in Sunshine and Shadow* (London: Methuen, 1931).

Gregson, Michael A. O'Malley, 'Victorian Criticism of the Waverley Novels of Sir Walter Scott, 1821 to 1900' (unpublished doctoral thesis, The Open University, 1992).

Gross, John, *The Rise and Fall of the Man of Letters: Aspects of English Literary Life since 1800* (London: Weidenfeld and Nicolson, 1969).

Hare, Augustus J. C., ed., *The Life and Letters of Maria Edgeworth*, 2 vols (London: Edward Arnold, 1894).

Halperin, John, ed., *Jane Austen: Bicentenary Essays* (Cambridge: Cambridge University Press, 1975).

Handley, Graham, *Jane Austen* (New York: St Martin's, 1992).

Harvie, Christopher, *Scotland and Nationalism* (London: Routledge, 1998).

Hayden, John O., *The Romantic Reviewers, 1802–1824* (London: Routledge & Kegan Paul, 1969).

Hayden, John O., ed., *Scott: The Critical Heritage* (London: Routledge & Kegan Paul, 1970).
Hazlitt, William, 'The Periodical Press', *The Edinburgh Review*, 38 (1823); reprinted in *The Complete Works of William Hazlitt*, ed. P. Howe, 21 vols (London: J. M. Dent and Sons, 1930–34), vol. XVI, pp. 211–39.
Hemlow, Joyce, Curtis D. Cecil, Althea Douglas, Patricia Boutilier, Edward A. Bloom, Lillian D. Bloom, Peter Hughes, Patricia Hawkins and Warren Derry, eds, *The Journals and Letters of Fanny Burney*, 12 vols (Oxford: Clarendon Press, 1972–84).
Hillhouse, James T., *The Waverley Novels and Their Critics*, 2nd edn (New York: Octagon Books, 1968), first published in 1936.
Hoffmann, E. T. A., *Die Serapions-Brüder* (Darmstadt: Wissenschaftliche. Buchgesellschaft, 1979)
Hogan, Charles Beecher, 'Jane Austen and her Early Public', *The Review of English Studies*, n. s. I (1950), 39–54.
Iser, Wolfgang, *The Implied Reader: Patterns of Communication in Prose Fiction from Bunyan to Beckett* (Baltimore, MD: Johns Hopkins University Press, 1974).
Jauss, Hans Robert, *Toward an Aesthetic of Reception*, trans. from German Timothy Bahti; intro. Paul de Man (Brighton: Harvester Press, 1982).
Jehmlich, Reimer, *Jane Austen* (Darmstadt: Wissenschaftliche Buchgesellschaft, 1995).
Jennings, Louis, ed., *The Croker Papers*, 3 vols (London: John Murray, 1884).
Johnson, Claudia L., 'Austen Cults and Cultures', in *The Cambridge Companion to Jane Austen*, ed. Edward Copeland and Juliet McMaster (Cambridge: Cambridge University Press, 1997), pp. 211–26.
Johnson, Claudia L., *Jane Austen: Women, Politics, and the Novel* (Chicago, IL: University of Chicago Press, 1988).
Johnson, Claudia L., 'The Divine Miss Jane', in *Janeites: Austen's Disciples and Devotees*, ed. Deidre Lynch (Princeton, NJ: Princeton University Press, 2000), pp. 25–44.
Johnson, Edgar, *Sir Walter Scott: The Great Unknown*, 2 vols (London: Hamish Hamilton, 1970).
Johnson, R. Brimley, ed., *The Letters of Lady Louisa Stuart* (London: John Lane, 1926).
Jones, Ann, *Ideas and Innovations: Best Sellers of Jane Austen's Age* (New York: AMS Press, 1986).
Joukovsky, Nicholas, 'Another Unnoted Contemporary Review of Jane Austen', *Nineteenth-Century Fiction*, 29 (1874–75), 336–8.
Kelly, Thomas, *Early Public Libraries: A History of Public Libraries in Great Britain before 1850* (London: The Library Association, 1966).
Lambdin, Laura Cooner and Robert Thomas Lambdin, eds, *A Companion to Jane Austen Studies* (Westport, CT: Greenwood Press, 2000).
Lamont, Claire, 'Meg the Gipsy in Scott and Keats', *English*, 36 (1987), 137–45.
Lamont, Claire, 'Waverley and the Battle of Culloden', *Essays and Studies*, 44 (1991), 14–26.

Le Faye, Deidre, ed. and coll., *Jane Austen's Letters* (Oxford: Oxford University Press, 1995).
L'Estrange, A. G., ed., *The Life of Mary Russell Mitford*, 3 vols (London: Bentley, 1870).
'Libraries', in *The Encyclopaedia Britannica*, 9th edn (Edinburgh: Adam & Charles Black, 1875), vol. XIV, pp. 542–5.
Littlewood, Ian, ed., *Jane Austen: Critical Assessments* (Mountfield: Helm Information, 1998).
Lockhart, J. G., *Letter to the Right Hon. Lord Byron* (1821), in *John Bull's Letter to Lord Byron*, ed. Alan Lang Strout (Norman, OK: University of Oklahoma Press, 1947), pp. 80–1.
Lockhart, J. G., *Memoirs of the Life of Sir Walter Scott, Bart.*, 7 vols (Edinburgh: Robert Cadell; London: John Murray and Whittaker, 1837).
The London Catalogue of Books Published in London (London: Robert Bent, 1831).
The London Catalogue of Books Published in Great Britain (London: Thomas Hogdson, 1851).
Lukács, Georg, *The Historical Novel* (London: Merlin Press, 1989).
Lynch, Deidre, 'Introduction: Sharing with Our Neighbors', in *Janeites: Austen's Disciples and Devotees*, ed. Deidre Lynch (Princeton, NJ: Princeton University Press, 2000), pp. 3–24.
Lynch, Deidre, ed., *Janeites: Austen's Disciples and Devotees* (Princeton, NJ: Princeton University Press, 2000).
Marchand, Leslie A., ed., *Byron's Letters and Journals*, 13 vols (London: John Murray, 1973–94).
Mayne, Ethel Colburn, ed., *The Life and Letters of Anne Isabella, Lady Noel Byron* (London: Constable, 1929).
McMillan, Dorothy, ed., *The Scotswoman at Home and Abroad* (Glasgow: Association for Scottish Literary Studies, 2000).
Millgate, Jane, *Scott's Last Edition: A Study in Publishing History* (Edinburgh: Edinburgh University Press, 1987).
Morgan, Peter F., *Jeffrey's Criticism* (Edinburgh: Scottish Academic Press, 1983).
Morley, Edith J., ed., *Henry Crabbe Robinson on Books and their Writers*, 3 vols (London: J. M. Dent, 1938).
Needler, G. H., *Goethe und Scott* (Oxford: Oxford University Press, 1950).
Partington, Wilfred, ed., *The Private Letter Books of Sir Walter Scott* (London: Hodder and Stoughton, 1930).
Rajan, Rajeswari, 'Critical Responses, Recent', in *Jane Austen in Context*, ed. Janet Todd (Cambridge: Cambridge University Press, 2005), pp. 101–10.
Reiman, Donald, ed., *The Romantics Reviewed* (London: Garland, 1972).
Richards, E. Grants, ed., *Letters Hitherto Unpublished, Written by Members of Sir Walter Scott's Family to their old Governess* (Oxford/London: n. pub., 1905).
Robertson, Fiona, 'Novels', in *An Oxford Companion to the Romantic Age: British Culture 1776–1832*, gen. ed. Iain McCalman (Oxford: Oxford University Press, 1999), pp. 286–95.
Robertson, Fiona, 'Walter Scott', in *Literature of the Romantic Period: A*

Bibliographical Guide, ed. Michael O'Neill (Oxford: Clarendon Press, 1998), pp. 221–45.

Romilly, Samuel Henry, ed., *Romilly-Edgeworth Letters, 1813–1818* (London: John Murray, 1936).

Rose, Jonathan, 'Rereading the English Common Reader', in *The Book History Reader*, ed. David Finkelstein and Alistair McCleery (London: Routledge, 2002), pp. 324–39.

Roper, Derek, *Reviewing before the Edinburgh 1788–1802* (London: Methuen & Co., 1978).

Rubenstein, Jill, *Sir Walter Scott: A Reference Guide* (Boston, MA: G. K. Hall & Co., 1978).

Sales, Roger, *Jane Austen and Representations of Regency England* (London: Routledge, 1994).

Scott, Walter, 'On the Present State of Periodical Criticism', in *Sir Walter Scott's Edinburgh Annual Register*, ed. Kenneth Curry (Knoxville, TN: University of Tennessee Press, 1977), pp. 132–70.

Shattock, Joanne, *Politics and Reviewers: The Edinburgh and the Quarterly in the Early Victorian Age* (London/Leicester: Leicester University Press, 1989).

Skelton-Foord, Christopher, 'Circulating Libraries in Britain between 1790 and 1830', in Rainer Schöwerling, Hartmut Steinecke and Günter Tiggesbäumker, eds, *Literatur und Erfahrungswandel 1789–1830* (München: Fink, 1996), pp. 31–45.

Slagle, Judith Bailey, ed., *The Collected Letters of Joanna Baillie*, 2 vols (Madison, NJ: Fairleigh Dickinson University Press, 1999).

Smith, Nowell C., ed., *The Letters of Sydney Smith*, 2 vols (Oxford: Clarendon Press, 1953).

Southam, Brian, ed., *Jane Austen: The Critical Heritage*, 2 vols (London: Routledge & Kegan Paul, 1968 and 1987).

Stafford, Fiona, 'Jane Austen', in *Literature of the Romantic Period: A Bibliographical Guide*, ed. Michael O'Neill (Oxford: Clarendon Press, 1998), pp. 246–68.

St Clair, William, *The Reading Nation in the Romantic Period* (Cambridge: Cambridge University Press, 2004).

Sullivan, Alvin, *British Literary Magazines: The Romantic Age, 1789–1836* (Westport, CT/London: Greenwood Press, 1983).

Sutherland, Kathryn, "Events ... have made us a world of readers': Reader Relations 1780–1830', in *The Romantic Period*, ed. David B. Pirie (London: Penguin, 1994), pp. 1–48.

Sutherland, Kathryn, *Jane Austen's Textual Lives* (Oxford: Oxford University Press 2005).

Tippkötter, Horst, *Walter Scott, Geschichte als Unterhaltung: Eine Rezeptionsanalyse der Waverley Novels* (Frankfurt am Main: Vittorio Klostermann, 1971).

Todd, Janet, ed., *Jane Austen in Context* (Cambridge: Cambridge University Press, 2005).

Todd, William B. and Ann Bowden, *Sir Walter Scott: A Bibliographical History 1796–1832* (New Castle, DE: Oak Knoll Press, 1998).
Tomalin, Claire, *Jane Austen: A Life* (London: Viking, 1997).
Tompkins, Jane P., ed., *Reader-Response Criticism: From Formalism to Post-Structuralism* (Baltimore, MD/London: John Hopkins University Press, 1980).
Trott, Nicola, 'Critical Responses, 1830–1970', in *Jane Austen in Context*, ed. Janet Todd (Cambridge: Cambridge University Press, 2005), pp. 92–100.
Ward, William S., 'Three Hitherto Unnoted Contemporary Reviews of Jane Austen', *Nineteenth-Century Fiction*, 26 (1971–72), 469–77.
Ward, William S., *Literary Reviews in British Periodicals, 1798–1820: A Bibliography* (New York: Garland, 1972).

Online resources and articles

The British Library Catalogue: http://catalogue.bl.uk (last accessed April 2006).
Garside, P., J. Belanger and S. Ragaz, *British Fiction, 1800–1829: A Database of Production, Circulation & Reception*, designer A. Mandal: www.britishfiction.cf.ac.uk (last accessed April 2006).
LexisNexis: http://web.lexis-nexis.com/xchange-international/ (last accessed March 2006).
The Library History Database: www.r-alston.co.uk/contents.htm> (last accessed February 2006)
The National Library of Scotland Catalogue: www.nls.uk/catalogues/online/index.html (last accessed April 2006).
Nineteenth Century Masterfile: www.paratext.com/19cm_intro.htm (last accessed November 2005).
Periodicals Contents Index: http://pci.chadwyck.co.uk (last accessed November 2005).
Public Lending Right *Most Borrowed Authors Archive Index*: www.plr.uk.com (last accessed February 2006).

Index

Abercorn, Lady Anne Jane (friend of Scott's) 50, 58, 71
Abercorn, Lord John James 50, 71
Academy 101, 106–7
Antijacobin Review 25, 28, 30, 33–5
Alexander, J. H. 151
Armstrong, Isobel 136, 141–2, 146–7
Augustan Review 32, 34–5
Austen, Cassandra
  Jane Austen's mother 51, 71
  Jane Austen's sister 76
Austen, Henry 11, 21–2, 51, 59, 71, 79, 81
Austen, Jane
  anonymity 53–4
  biography
    Henry Austen's biographical notice 21–2, 81
    twentieth century 142–4
    Victorian 101–4
  comments, Romantic period 47–74
  comparison with Scott: *see* comparison
  copyright to novels 15, 18–19, 40, 78–81, 167
  cultural status in twentieth century 126–34
  editions
    nineteenth century 78–91
    twentieth century 117–18
  feminism 137–9
  film adaptations 128–33
  imagination 21, 41–2, 62–3, 104, 139, 168
  realism 21, 40–1, 43, 60–4, 68, 73, 74, 104–5, 112, 139
  reviews
    Romantic 15–45
    Victorian 93–113
  sales of novels in Romantic period 15–23
  satire 22, 45, 73
  scope, limitations of 13, 17, 19, 20, 104–5, 107, 112–13, 138
Austen, Jane, works
  Emma 11, 19–20, 30, 40, 49, 62–3, 68, 70–1, 73, 79, 107, 132, 136, 140, 148, 150, 166
  Mansfield Park 18–20, 58, 68–9, 79–80, 130, 232, 136, 138, 141, 143–4, 147–8
  Northanger Abbey 20–3, 41, 43, 58, 63, 79–80, 136, 138, 144, 147–8
  Persuasion 10, 20–3, 41, 43, 58, 63, 79–80, 207, 132, 136, 138, 143, 144, 145
  Pride and Prejudice 1, 11, 17–18, 20, 53, 57–8, 61–3, 68–70, 79–80, 124, 127–32, 136, 139–44, 160
  Sense and Sensibility 7, 11–12, 15–17, 24, 53, 61, 68, 79–81, 132, 136, 138–9, 144, 145

Baillie, Joanna, 48, 64, 70
Ballaster, Ros 136, 145
Beer, Gillian 137, 143–4
Bentley, Richard 23, 68, 78–9, 80, 81
Bessborough, Henrietta, countess of 50
Black, A. & C. 78, 82–7
Blackwood's Edinburgh Magazine 94–7, 100, 102, 109–10, 113
Blythe, Ronald 136, 140, 145
Boringdon, Frances Parker, Viscountess 50, 53
Boringdon, Henry Villiers, Viscount 50
Boswell, Sir Alexander 50
Boswell, James 158
Bradbrook, Frank 136, 139–40
Bradbury, Agnew & Co 82, 86

Index

British Critic 7–45, 56
British Lady's Magazine 7, 19, 21
Broughton, Lord John Cam Hobhouse 50, 53, 59, 64, 72
Brown, Iain Gordon 84
Buccleuch, Charles, 4th Duke of 50
Burney, Fanny 48, 70, 107, 141, 148
Butler, Marilyn 9, 136–7, 143–4, 147
Byron, Lord George Gordon 8, 18, 48–9, 57–9, 64, 66, 71–2

Cadell, Robert (publisher) 48, 78, 81–2, 84
Cage, Mrs. Charles 51, 61
Calder, Angus 150, 154, 157–8, 161
Caledonian Mercury 25
Castle, Terry 136, 138, 141, 148
Cecil, David 152
Chambers's Journal 108–9, 111
Champion 19
Charleville, Lady 50
Charlotte, Princess of Wales (later Queen) 50, 61
circulating libraries: *see* libraries, circulating
Clarke, James Stanier (the Prince Regent's Librarian) 48
Cockburn, Henry 48, 55, 66, 72
Coleridge, Samuel Taylor 48–9, 59, 141, 156
comparison Austen and Scott
  comments, Romantic period 72–4
  editions
    nineteenth century 77–80, 88
    twentieth century 117–18
  library holdings 89–91
  reception, critical, twentieth century 163–9
  reviews
    Romantic 39–45
    Victorian 112–13
Constable, Archibald 9, 23–4, 48, 60
Contemporary Review 93, 95–6, 98
Cooke, Revd Samuel (Godfather to Jane Austen) 51, 68
Cooke, Mrs. Samuel 51
copyright 12, 40, 78–81; *see also* Austen, Jane, copyright; Scott, Walter, copyright

Cornhill Magazine 94–9, 101–6, 110–11
Crabbe, George 48–9, 55
Critical Review 7–45
Croker, John Wilson 26–7, 36, 48, 56, 60

Davidson, Peter 151, 153–4, 158
Davie, John 136–7, 139
Davy, Jane, Lady (wife of chemist Sir Humphrey Davy) 50, 62
Dicks, John 82, 86–7
Doody, Margaret Anne 138, 141, 145–6
Dudley, first Earl of 50, 68
Duncan, Ian 151, 153, 159, 162–3

Edgeworth, Maria 48, 53–4, 57, 59, 61, 64–5, 112, 145, 156
Edinburgh Edition of the Waverley Novels 120, 126, 163–4
Edinburgh Review 7–13, 26, 39, 66
Egerton, Thomas (publisher) 15, 18–19, 40, 48, 79
Ehrenpreis, Anne Henry 136–7, 144, 150
Englishwomen's Domestic Magazine 104–9
Erskine, William (later Lord Kinneder) 50, 55

feminism 137–9, 145, 149, 155, 166–7
Ferrier, Susan (novelist) 48, 58, 60, 70, 112
Ferris, Ina 9, 24, 45, 69, 72
Fielding, Henry 9, 71, 139, 142, 148
Fox, Henry Stephen (novelist) 48, 71

Gamerschlag, Kurt 40
Garside, Peter 7, 11
Gentleman's Magazine 7, 9, 21
George, Prince Regent (later King George IV) 19, 50
Gifford, William (editor of the *QR*) 8, 48, 60–1, 68
Godwin, William 13 23, 71
Goethe, Johann Wolfgang von 49, 56
Graham, Revd Patrick 51
Grant, Mrs 51
Granville, Harriet, Countess of 50
The Guardian 119–34

Harding, D. W. 137–8, 145–7
Haydon, Benjamin Robert (painter) 51, 65

Hazlitt, William 7, 10
Hewitt, David 151–2, 158, 160, 162–3
Hook, Andrew 150, 156, 160, 164
Hunt, Leigh 10

The Independent 119–34
Inglis, Tony 151–2, 158, 160, 162–3
Iser, Wolfgang 2, 74

Jauss, Hans Robert 2, 74
Jeffrey, Francis (editor of the *ER*) 8, 26, 29, 49, 55
Johnson, Claudia 136
Jones, Vivien 136, 138, 147

Kerr, Lady Robert 50, 58

Lamont, Claire 30, 58, 83, 126, 138, 144–5, 150–1, 154, 157–8, 160, 162
Landor, Walter Savage 49
Lane, William 12
Lewis, Matthew 49, 55
libraries
    catalogues 78, 80–1, 89–91, 98, 167
    circulating 12, 15, 25, 59, 89–91
    mechanics' institutes 89
Lochhead, T. & J. 82, 86–7
Lockhart, John Gibson 24, 49, 57, 168
Lodge, David 136, 139
London Quarterly Review 93, 95–7, 99, 100, 104, 112
Longman 9
Lucas, John 136–7, 143–4

Mack, Douglas 151–2
Mackenzie, Margaret (daughter of Henry Mackenzie) 51, 55
Macmillan's Magazine 97
Manning, Susan 152
Merivale, John 26
Millbanke, Anne Isabella (future Lady Byron) 50–1, 53, 58, 61
Millgate, Jane 151
Minerva library and novels 12–13, 15, 19, 24, 38
Mitford, Mary Russell (novelist) 19, 53–4, 57, 68, 98–9
Monthly Review 7, 15, 19, 26, 33–5
Moore, Thomas 49–58

Morritt, John Bacon Sawrey (Scott's friend) 51, 59, 72
Murray, John (publisher) 9, 19–20, 40, 49, 58, 71, 79

New Annual Register 33
New Monthly Magazine 25, 32
New Review 18
Nimmo, William 82, 87
Notes and Queries 99, 100, 111
novel in the Romantic period
    female authorship 10–12
    social exclusivity 12–13
    status 9

Pole, Mrs 51, 63
Pückler-Muskau, Prince Hermann L. H. von 50
Punter, David 151, 163

The Quarterly Review 7–13, 19, 21, 24, 26, 28, 31–3, 36–7, 39, 48–9, 56, 60, 95, 99, 102–3, 107, 110–11, 113

Rawson, Claude 137, 148, 150
reviews
    history of 7
    of novels by Austen and Scott: see Austen, Jane; Scott, Walter
    Romantic 7–13
        attitude to novels 9
        focus on morality 2, 16, 20, 22, 26–7, 37, 43, 45, 68–9, 73
        format 7–8
        influence on sales figures of novels 39–45
        political bias 9–10
        prices 8
        status 8–9
    Victorian 93–113
Richardson, Samuel 9, 139, 142, 148, 155
Robertson, Fiona 12, 151, 161, 163
Robinson, Henry Crabb (diarist) 49, 63, 65, 68, 70
Romilly, Anne, Lady 50, 54, 58, 64, 68–9
Routledge 80, 82, 86–8

St Clair, William 12, 88, 141
St Paul's Magazine 104–6, 108, 110, 112
Sandford, Henry 51, 71
Scots Magazine 25, 28–9, 31–2

Scott, Sophia 51
Scott, Walter
  anonymity 25–6, 53–6
  biography
    twentieth century 122–4, 152–4
    Victorian 93–6
  centenary exhibition 100
  comments, Romantic period 47–74
  comparison with Austen: see comparison
  copyright of novels 23–4, 40, 78–88, 93, 124, 167
  cultural status
    twentieth century 119–26, 133–4
    Victorian 93–100
  editions
    nineteenth century 78–91
    twentieth century 117–18
  film adaptations 124–6
  imagination 26, 40–2, 62, 72–3, 96, 156, 168
  masculinity 45, 72, 95
  realism 2, 13, 20, 30–2, 34–6, 41, 43, 64–7, 73, 96–8, 113, 125, 128, 157–9
  review of *Emma* 19–20
  reviews
    Romantic 15, 23–45
    Victorian 93–113
  sales of novels in Romantic period 23–4, 31, 33, 36, 37
  scope, social and geographical 2, 25, 42, 44, 73–4, 97, 107, 113, 168–9
  Scottishness 122–4, 126
    in novels 27–31, 36–7, 40, 65–7, 73, 121
  Victorian reverence for him 93–113
Scott, Walter, works
  The Antiquary 15, 19, 33–36, 39–40, 42, 59–60, 70–2, 151, 163
  The Black Dwarf 80, 120
  The Bride of Lammermoor 151, 156, 161–3
  Chronicles of the Canongate 151
  Guy Mannering 15, 31–3, 35, 40–2, 58, 64, 66, 71, 151
  The Heart of Mid-Lothian 15, 24, 36–7, 69–70, 80, 127, 151–2
  Ivanhoe 2, 120–1, 124–6, 129, 151, 153–4, 157, 159–60, 162
  Kenilworth 12, 56, 120, 151
  Quentin Durward 152
  Redgauntlet 151, 155–6, 158–9
  Rob Roy 37–9, 59, 120, 125, 151
  The Tale of Old Mortality 65, 70, 80, 120, 150, 152, 161
  The Two Drovers 152
  Waverley 1, 12, 15, 19, 23–33, 35–45, 54–6, 59–60, 64–6, 69, 71–2, 77–80, 82–7, 93, 99, 112–13, 118, 120, 122, 141, 150, 153, 156–7, 160, 162, 167–8
Shakespeare, William 18, 36, 95–7, 100, 102, 107–9, 118, 123, 126–7, 139–40, 142
Sharpe, Charles Kirkpatrick 49
Shelley, Lady Frances 50, 62
Shelley, Mary 49
Sheridan, Richard Brinsley (dramatist) 49, 68
Siddons, Mrs 64
Smith, Sydney 49, 60, 69
Somerville, Mary (scientist) 51, 60–1
Southey, Robert 49, 71
Stabler, Jane 136
Staël, Mme de 49
Stafford, Fiona 136, 150
stereotype (plates) 78, 83, 117, 169
Sterne, Laurence 9, 71, 139, 142
Stevenson, Jane 151, 153–4, 158
Stuart, Lady Louisa 50, 71
Sutherland, Kathryn 8, 136, 141, 151, 155–6, 161, 163

Tanner, Tony 136, 138–9, 141, 143, 145–7
The Times 119–34
Tippkötter, Horst 40, 42, 67
Tulloch, Graham 151, 153, 159–60, 162–3

Waddell, Revd P Hately 82, 86
Ward, Marcus 82, 86
Watson, Nicola 151, 163
Waverley novels 24, 31, 36, 38–40, 44–5, 54–6, 60, 72, 78, 82–4, 86–7, 93, 118, 120, 144, 156, 167–8,
  copyright 77–88
  novelty of 24–31
Wilson, A. N. 151, 153–4, 157, 159, 162
Wilson, D. 82, 86–7
Wordsworth, William 49, 62, 64, 141, 148, 155